Norm's work shows how the success or failure of crops depends on a minuscule number of plant genes. The bread of life and the thread of life are intimately entwined in the bonds of DNA.

Henry L. Shands, U. S. Department of Agriculture

If plant breeders are artists, Norm Borlaug is a Master. But he is a compassionate artist. He produced useful plants because he was driven by the global humanitarian imperative to eliminate hunger. Yet despite his accomplishments and global honors, he is still a humble and decent Iowa farm boy who is still working harder than most of us at age 85.

Alex McCalla, University of California, 1999

Norm was ever the student and ever the teacher. He lit a spark in the minds of young agricultural scientists in many parts of the world, in the conviction that this spark would develop into a flame that would motivate them to try and make life more tolerable for the less-fortunate.

Robert W. Herdt, The Rockefeller Foundation

Dr. Norman E. Borlaug and his many colleagues and team workers are the reason why the high yielding varieties of wheat developed in Mexico by he and his associates, are grown on 125 million acres in the lesser developed areas around the world.

Edwin J. Wellhausen, Former Director, CIMMYT.

Dr. Borlaug is a man committed to a cause. He was always constantly challenging as a teacher . . . A very important characteristic is his capacity to inspire people. Anytime I've gone down to visit him, I've found him out in the field, usually surrounded by young plant breeders from around the world. And then he starts to talk, and it becomes a walking, outdoor laboratory.

Sherwood O. Berg, Dean, Institute of Agriculture, University of Minnesota

Borlaug was equally effective with farmers in their fields, scientists in their experiment stations, and heads of government in their palaces.

Dana Dalrymple

We probably make more wheat crosses at Purdue than anywhere else in the United States, but for every cross we make Borlaug [in Mexico] makes at least a thousand.

Ralph Caldwell (one of America's top wheat breeders), 1971

In 1950 Mexico imported 400,000 tons of wheat. In 1956 she had become self-sufficient. The Mexicans say there are four reasons for the big change: seed, water, fertilizer and Borlaug.

The Illustrated Weekly of India, *March 14, 1971*

BOOKS BY NOEL VIETMEYER

For Bracing Books

Borlaug: Right off the Farm. 1914 – 1944*
Borlaug: Wheat Whisperer. 1944 – 1959*
Borlaug: Feeding the Millions. 1960 – 1970 [in preparation]
Liquid Life Savers: The Fluid-Food Revolution [in preparation]
Malaria and the DDT Dilemma

For National Academy of Sciences

NEW CROPS

Lost Crops of Africa: Volume 1 – Grains*
Lost Crops of Africa: Volume 2 – Vegetables*
Lost Crops of Africa: Volume 3 - Fruits*
Lost Crops of the Incas
Underexploited Tropical Plants
Tropical Legumes
The Winged Bean: A High-Protein Crop for the Humid Tropics
Amaranth: Modern Prospects for an Ancient Crop*
Jojoba: A New Crop for Arid Lands*
Quality-Protein Maize*
Triticale: A Promising Addition to the World's Cereal Grains*
Vetiver: A Thin Green Line Against Erosion*
Guayule: An Alternative Source of Natural Rubber
Neem: A Tree for Solving Global Problems
Leucaena: Promising Forage and Tree Crop for the Tropics
Mangium and Other Fast-Growing Acacias*
Calliandra: A Versatile Tree for the Humid Tropics*
Casuarinas: Nitrogen-Fixing Trees for Adverse Sites*
Firewood Crops: Shrub and Tree Species for Energy*

ANIMAL RESOURCES

Water Buffalo: New Prospects for an Underutilized Animal*
Butterfly Farming *
Crocodiles as a Resource for the Tropics*
Little-Known Asian Animals with Promising Economic Futures*
Microlivestock*

OTHER

Ferrocement: Applications in Developing Countries
Making Aquatic Weeds Useful
Mosquito Control: Perspectives for Developing Countries
More Water for Arid Lands
Sowing Forests from the Air*
Producer Gas: Another Fuel for Motor Transport*

* Available (while supplies last) from **BracingBooks.com**, see p300

BORLAUG

VOLUME 2

Wheat Whisperer, 1944 - 1959

NOEL VIETMEYER

BRACING BOOKS
LORTON, VIRGINIA

BORLAUG Volume 2, Wheat Whisperer. 1944 - 1959.
Copyright © 2004, 2009 by Noel Vietmeyer

Version 1.0: October 2009.

LIBRARY OF CONGRESS CATALOGUING-IN-PUBLICATION DATA

Vietmeyer, Noel Duncan, 1940-

ISBN 978-0-578-03856-8

Biography & Autobiography/Science & Technology

For more information on Norman Borlaug as well as updates on Volume 3 please visit **BracingBooks.com**. There also you can preview other books providing provocative, practical and perhaps priceless tools and methods helpful for reducing hunger and other planetary problems such as child malnutrition, deforestation, soil erosion, malaria, and atmospheric overheating.

Interested in using this inspirational biography for classroom use, promotions, academic awards, corporate goodwill gifts, a book club, or other purpose? We also sell it by the box (34 copies) at an exceptional discount. Purchases can be made via the website or by contacting **CustomerService@BracingBooks.com**.

BRACING BOOKS
5921 River Drive
Lorton, VA 22079-4128
USA

Printed in the United States of America
Signature Book Printing, www.sbpbooks.com

CONTENTS

ILLUSTRATIONS

ILLUSTRATIONS (cont.)

PRONUNCIATION GUIDE

PEOPLE
Borlaug	BOR-LOG
Calles [Rodolfo]	KY-es
Eva [Villegas]	EH-vah
Gallardo	guy-AR-doh
Harrar	ha-RAH
Hope [Pablo]	HOO-PAY
Narvaez	nar-VY-es
Patrón [sponsor]	pa-TRONE
Pepe	PEP-ee
Stakman	STAKE-man
Stak	STAKE (short for Stakman)

PLACES
Bajío	bah-HEE-oh
Cajeme	cah-HEM-ee
Calle	ky-YEH
Chapingo	cha-PING-oh
Ciudad (city)	see-oo-DAHD
Coahuila	coh-ah-WEE-la
Irapuato	eer-a-PWA-toe
Michoacán	mich-oh-a-KAHN
[La] Piedad	pee-eh-DAHD
Puebla	PWEB-lah
Saltillo	sol-TEE-oh
Tehuacan	TEE-wah-kahn
Texcoco	TESH-coco
Toluca	tol-OO-kah
Torreón	tor-ee-OHN
Yaqui	YAH-kee
Valle [valley]	VY-YEH

PLANTS
Lerma Rojo	LEHR-mah ROH-hoh
Kentana	ken-TAH-na
Marquis	MAR-kwis
Marroqui	marrow-KEE
Nazas	NAH-zas

ORGANIZATIONS
CIANO	see-AH-no
Ejidal	eh-HEE-dal
Geneve [Hotel]	HEN-eh-vah
Patronato	pat-ron-AH-toh
PRONASE	pro-NAH-see

INTRODUCTION

Humanity's Achilles heel is the quantity of quality farmland. Sadly, Planet Earth provides only a meager supply. Even the wonders of modern science have added little more. Basically, we must feed ourselves with the good land we've got . . . or go without.

This fundamental limitation on human existence became clear in the middle of the 20th Century. Prime farmland was then functioning at full capacity and barely feeding 3 billion. Yet births were rising at a pace to double the population by century's end.

Clearly maxed-out quality cropland could never support *an additional 3 billion*. A collapse of catastrophic consequence impended. Farms would soon fail to supply the sustenance for half humanity.

That denouement was not in doubt. Had farm output continued to flatline, modern times would have mirrored the time during the Dark Ages when Black Death (bubonic plague) halved the number of Europeans, a devastation still eliciting dread a thousand years later.

In the 20th Century's second half, however, human numbers failed to fall. Scores of countries saw food stocks soar. Their stressed-out soils turned into grain gushers, spouting staples in quantities never before conceived of, let alone seen.

The pages ahead detail the human drama that led to this miracle. They highlight a single scientist's travails between 1944 and 1959, revealing the lively chronicle behind his lonely campaign, which at the time was appreciated by few and approved by fewer.

Herein you'll read how this unsung loner discovered the hinge that reversed humanity's seemingly inexorable plunge toward peril. Despite our twenty-twenty vision, his mission still seems impossible: He first must overcome a fungal disease that threatens to savage even the miserly midcentury productivity. He then must reframe mankind's major food plant with a radical new architecture that more than doubles its efficiency. He next must fend off friendly fire from fellow beings who insist he do things differently or desist altogether. And finally he must save his own job. You see, during those 15 years he's several times scheduled for dismissal; once he's within days of being deported; and his funding is finally withdrawn and his research left to wither. The plants were then only halfway home, and in no state to avert famine.

Moreover, the pages ahead expose the surprising fact that he never dreamed of making history. He just made wheat, and then grasped each opportunity the newest model let him see. The food supply's overall progress thus arose not from plans or charts but from plants and chance.

But was it really chance? His advances seemed to spring from nowhere known to man or mathematics. Could some invisible entity have directed his progress along a concealed but coherent pathway?

Indeed, the presence of a Hidden Hand may explain why he so often branched out in unexpected directions, cutting new trails, regardless of conventional wisdom, convenience, or commands from his superiors.

Though he merely followed the trail the plant provided, his weird behavior propelled professionals to place obstacles in the path. His seeming lack of reverence for peers, precedent or procedure also provoked the cessation of his support.

Eventually, however, every quirky move he'd made—the very ones for which he'd been charged with dereliction of duty and ultimately denied his job—averted a new Dark Age.

His trust had been well placed; the plant had known best all along. By exposing its inner secrets it handed him the priceless insight that it was capable of producing several times more than anyone knew.

A rguably the greatest contributor to modern times, Norman E. Borlaug [the middle name is Ernest and the pronunciation is BOR-LOG] dedicated himself to the wheat plant. As you'll soon see, they met by accident in 1945, and it's not giving away much to reveal that after two decades of ceaseless struggle and sacrifice he gifted the world revolutionary pint-sized wheat plants that matured quickly, resisted disease, thrived under wildly divergent climates, and yielded at least three times more than any before. Thanks to that special combo of qualities the world's top crop gained the strength and stability to pour out staggering amounts of grain at the pivotal point in the human parade.

Breeders of other food crops quickly followed his example, generating pint-sized, fast-maturing, disease-resisting, geographically unfettered versions of corn, rice, potatoes and other staples, which together with his power-wheat detonated the explosion of food from farmlands that had seemed maxed out.

Nowadays crops everywhere bear the hallmark ensuing from the hard work and happenings you'll encounter right ahead. Though a product of the 1940s, 1950s and 1960s, his "Cornucopia Combo" lives on in the breads and wheaten products people eat in at least 100 countries. And that includes those we eat.

It's important to know that Borlaug did all this in the spirit of human decency. Despite the chromosomal creations' immense value, he lived frugally and donated his super-charged seeds as well as sage advice and savvy insights without reluctance or recompense.

Indeed, throughout his long life he's forever made light of his legacy. That's why few people recognize this humble and self-deprecating hero, let alone realize their daily debt for having something to eat.

The few who are aware of his accomplishments remain awestruck. Even they, however, are unaware that his personal life ranks among the most complex, compelling and inspiring of all time. The general feeling, which he actively encourages, is that he was a hard-working guy who just happened to stumble over some pretty good plants while doing his duty and doing his best.

In reality, as you'll soon see, his narrative of fantastic feats arose out of a seemingly never-ending sequence of horrors and heartaches.

The second in a series divulging all the setbacks and successes that led to the huge uplift in food supplies in the latter half of the 20th Century, this book continues the chain of coincidences, quirks, surprises and strange revelations that filled Volume 1 with fascination.

That prequel, a popular account of Borlaug's first 30 years, exposes how he acquired the spirit and skills to handle hassles. Reading it will deepen understanding of the hundred surprising stories presented in the next 16 chapters. Meantime, though, here's a rapid recap showcasing four of the themes interlocking the first hundred stories that framed his three formative decades.

Theme 1) How a youth born without prospects survived the troubled time when history hovered between ancient days and modern ways:

Borlaug's birth (March 25, 1914) fell within what we might call the pre-modern times. During his early boyhood rural America was not unlike what people today dismiss as a "developing country." In the absence of engines and electricity he inhabited a mostly silent society. It was also unhealthy: malnutrition and dysentery, to mention but two Third World disorders, blighted most years. It was a closed society: his village considered itself more an outpost of Norway than any part of North America. Nearby villages in Iowa's northeast corner were equally tribal, clinging to their individual Old World ways so zealously they employed their own languages and telephone systems. Moreover, families were of the extended kind. Borlaug himself was just one of seven members from three generations crammed into his grandfather's 3-bedroom cottage.

In those un-modern years food was far from abundant. For instance, when he was 2 years old (1916) the national wheat crop succumbed to black stem rust. This microbial marauder forced his family, like others in America, to spend miserable months trying to live on cornbread.

When he was 5 (1919) and trudging through a blizzard the tired little tyke surrendered his exhausted body to a seductive snowdrift. His rescuer was cool calm cousin Sina Borlaug, who was all of 12. Thank goodness the social mindset then demanded children be grown up and police themselves.

That same year the so-called Spanish flu, which had been killing up to 100,000 Americans a month, chose to check out his village. With viruses yet undisclosed to the mind of mankind, this mystical killer was seen as a celestial visitation sent to punish the wicked. Strangely, though, it targeted many too young to be wicked, including cool calm Cousin Sina, who just weeks before had saved the life of the little boy who'd eventually save millions of lives.

Like today's poor-country farmers the Borlaugs fed only themselves. They relied on animal power for the fieldwork and the heavy lifting. Every other task was done by hand. As a result, child labor undergirded existence. Farm children were born to work and had no choice in the matter. Thus, when he turned 8 (1922) little Norm had to dedicate his drive, dynamism and dreams to helping feed his family. That was preordained; other callings were neither possible nor permitted.

All this was considered normal and natural to the species; boys followed their father. But coincident with Borlaug's youth a new age dawned. In the 1920s technological marvels began toppling the timeless landscape, and ratcheting existence to heights never before possible.

The first marvel arrived when he was 9 (1923), upsetting the world of silence with sounds that emanated from nowhere and everywhere. Those supernatural echoes opened rural minds to alien and very weird wonders beyond understanding. They had an alien and very weird name: Radio.

When he was 11 (1925), the second transforming technology appeared. Those who witnessed it in Cresco were upset by the sight of lifestyles beyond belief. It wasn't absolutely clear whether the lives on that movie screen were make-believe or whether their own were. Clearly, though, there was more to American culture than cultivating corn.

When he was 14 (1928) a third uplifting miracle came within 10 miles of the farmstead, bringing with it the astounding possibility of wet-weather travel. Before that concrete strip crawled past Cresco all roads were dirt, and wet spells meant you couldn't drive without getting mired in mud holes.

When he was 15 (1929), a miraculous modification of horsepower showed up. Henry Ford's 20hp tractor freed the family from continually having to care for horses; it also freed half the farm from the need to grow feed. By letting the Borlaugs harvest twice the corn with half the effort the tractor leavened life fourfold.

Also during that 15th year, the high school Vo-Ag teacher exposed the clueless kid to plant nutrition. With a sprinkle of white powder the class members produced 50 bushels of corn an acre when their folks seldom attained 25. This magical multiplier also had a funny name: fertilizer.

Yet of all that era's time-warping technologies the most sweeping was high-yield hybrid corn. Although its seeds had to be purchased, they catapulted the Borlaugs into prosperity. Their turbo-charged chromosomes changed the family from farmers who fed themselves and got paltry paychecks to the kind that fed the world and got paychecks that were more than paltry. That's when he discovered what happiness meant.

By the time he's 15, these technologies had built a bridge to possibilities beyond the farm gate. His generation was rural America's first to enjoy the freedom of opportunity. Indeed, the chance to make something of himself unfolded like a flower.

Sadly, though, the blossoming season got cut short. That October, just after he'd he entered his senior year of high school, the Great Depression sprang from nowhere to hog unto itself every legal lifestyle option. And for the decade when he aged from 16 to 26 (1930-1940) rotten work and rotten weather combined to keep America's rural resurgence down in the dust.

Because of opportunity's rapid retreat history failed to recognize this home-grown Green Revolution. Borlaug, though, never forgot how high-yield seeds had plucked him from poverty and provided a few glorious months standing at the gates looking in on utopia. Sure, the view hadn't lasted long but it provided the zest behind all he did thereafter. Down the subsequent decades, he strove to help poor farmers experience that very same miraculous opening to the high life.

Theme 2) How the kindness of strangers fashioned a young life for humanity and for history.

During Borlaug's formative years a dozen insurmountable barriers got placed in his path. Yet each time his progress got blocked somebody popped up to move him forward against the odds. In addition, each time his career veered off track a stranger came from nowhere to correct his missteps. This is why his narrative seems preprogrammed, with some director behind the curtains making sure he sticks to the script. Consider:

At age 14 (1928), having just finished grade school, the need to work the family farm required he remain home rather than attend high school. Then the local teacher **Sina Borlaug** appeared at the house and pressured her uncle and aunt to jeopardize their own survival and *send little Norman to Cresco High.* "As a scholar he's no great shakes," his now 21-year-old cousin declared, "but he's got grit!"

At Cresco High he showed little aptitude until his sophomore year (1930) when **David Bartelma** arrived. The new principal, who was also wrestling coach, awakened the slumbering soul. On the wrestling mat the 16-year-old found his inner self, and the resulting taste of talent and attainment lifted his eyes to the stars. Bartelma also promoted a five-point strategy for good living that his pupil would use as a guide through a long, hard, adventure-filled life journey.

At age 19 (1933), after the Great Depression forced him back to farming, a state-sanctioned wrestling meet happened to be held in tiny Cresco. Norm beat everyone but the reigning All State College champion, whose awed coach offered him the chance to attend teachers college and pursue a career as a high school teacher.

Just in the nick of time, however, a hometown football hero he'd never met, set him back on course by chivvying him into attending the University of Minnesota. **George Champlin** didn't care that Borlaug hadn't applied, had only $61 dollars to his name, was scheduled to go to teachers college *in one week*, and would have to leave for Minnesota *the next day*!

After failing the U of M entrance exam he prepares to crawl back home a complete loser. But rookie professor **Frederick Hovde** keeps the chain of coincidence from parting by welcoming him into the Junior College, a new venture the university is trialing as a way to redeem young lives devastated by the Depression.

College dining halls being unknown, he waits tables in an off-campus cafe in exchange for morsels of food. While thus slinging for his supper, he meets **Margaret Gibson**, who survives by the same method of eating.

In subsequent years she'll keep him from quitting college. She'll become his wife. In time, too, she'll sacrifice much to his success.

When he is 20 (1934), the restaurant goes out of business, eliminating his ability to eat. **White Castle** then comes to the rescue with a 10¢ coupon for students. Thanks to that he exists on two tiny hamburgers and a small bottle of milk twice a day. For 20¢ he can stay in school and stay alive another day.

After the coupons run out famine again ratchets up the pressure to return home. This time relief arrives in the form of a sorority house mother who offers him the position of bus boy in the **Alpha Omicron Pi** dining hall. For pay, he can have "all he can eat." His greatest ever compensation, it keeps the ultimate world champion food supplier from starvation at age 20.

Now accepted into the university proper, he commits to forestry but cannot pay the tuition. **Eleanor Roosevelt** then keeps the chain of circumstance alive by pressuring her husband to help the nation's needy kids. FDR establishes the National Youth Administration, which provides a grant to pay destitute students 18 cents an hour for handiwork around campus. Norm can cover his tuition by devoting (over and above his studies and bus-boy duties) *15 hours a week* to pinning insect specimens onto boards in the Entomology Department or scrubbing cages in the Veterinary Medicine Department.

Despite his fabulous $2.70 weekly income, insolvency threatens to force him back to where he seems to belong. Then when he's 22 (1936) **Edward Behre** pops up to hand him responsibility for revamping a derelict forest in western Massachusetts. The job is for the summer; the pay is $100 a month. Norm performs so well Behre retains him for six whole months and sends him home $600 richer! It's the only fortune he'll ever make, other, of course, than the Nobel Prize.

In the summer of the 23rd year (1937) he ventures to central Idaho where **Hank Shank** trains him as a forest firefighter and assigns him to the nation's most isolated fire lookout. Living apart from all human contact, he must find water as well as cook, care for himself, and maintain mental balance in the middle of the boondocks. Mercy, he must even battle a wildfire with just a hand tool for help. Shank is so impressed he offers a fulltime job. Borlaug accepts with alacrity. In just 3 months, right after graduation in January 1938, he'll become a junior forester in the U.S. Forest Service.

Our story would here have died and gone to Hell except that, with just days to go, Shank plays out his anointed role by withdrawing the offer.

Norm and Margaret are distraught. They've been married less than three months. Now he's out of work and out of wild cards because even in 1937 the Great Depression shuffles and deals everyone's deck.

The Samaritan who now jumps into this Horatio Alger-like parable is a distinguished University of Minnesota professor who'd never met this misguided undergrad who now finds himself both lost and at loose ends. **E.C. Stakman** spots the promise in the ice-blue eyes and offers the ultimate lifeline: tuition for graduate school. He requires, however, that Borlaug abandon forestry and adopt agricultural science.

Only now, when he's 24, does the proper career come into view. In 1938 he experiences his first ever classes in soil science, crop science, plant pathology. A year later, for a PhD degree, he begins investigating a fungal disease of flax, provider of linen and linseed oil.

Still and all, in the summer of 1941 a further roadblock looms. The flax research is ending on a high note, he's about to graduate, he's got to leave school. But no job is in prospect.

Then, **Frank Kaufert** pops up with a truly weird offer. He's returning to become Dean of Forestry and wants Norm to take the position he's vacating at the famous DuPont Company in Wilmington, Delaware. Chemical industry is a devilish departure from celestial strategy. However Margaret urges acceptance, and the young couple reach their wondrous new locale along with the war: December 7, 1941. Within weeks, Norm is the giant company's go-to guy on military microbiology. Indeed, he spends the next three years solving pressing problems being dished out by bugs on battlefronts around the globe.

Despite the hellish goings on around the war-torn world, Wilmington is close to heaven. A daughter is born in 1943 and the next year Norm commits to a career as an industrial microbiologist.

His future course is finally set.

In 1944, however, the path ahead yet again lurches sideways when **George Harrar** bursts his burly frame and bullying personality into the storyline and entices Borlaug to abandon hope of wealth and the good life, move to the destitute country next door, and lift the burden of hunger from the backs of the rural poor.

Only now does everything fall into proper place. It's October 1944. He's 30 years old. He's headed for a hungry country to help produce more food. He's going to Mexico, where paychecks will be small but payoffs might be huge.

And the Hidden Hand is finally satisfied!

Or so it seems.

Theme 3) How despite never-ending difficulties and improbable rescues from false steps a sterling character developed.

Although the above recitation makes Borlaug seem like a puppet on a string, he was at every stage, gathering experience, building character, steadying himself, preparing for a life of service rather than servitude.

Of all his innate strengths the most fundamental came in 1918 direct from the Borlaug family patriarch. Though in that hopeless old era no one foresaw any prospect of farmers achieving freedom Granddad Nels boldly declares that a finer future was coming to uplift his brood from its dead-end existence as subsistence farmers.

Though that was nothing more than an old man's fantasy, the boy primed himself to meet the unknowable, improbable but still incredible apparition. He did it using the old man's recommended recipe for ripping open opportunity's door: schoolwork. "Think for yourself, Norm Boy," the old man had said. "Fill your head now to fill your belly later!" That mantra would color his character and make him forever upbeat no matter how gloomy the future would appear at the time.

With no opportunity for child's play, work became the venue for friendships. And he worked mostly with Bob, the youngest of the three plow horses. They'd been born the same day and grew up inspiring one another. Bob was very mischievous, and often encouraged joint misdemeanors such as a ride to the creek when they should be cultivating corn. On the other hand, in caring for his four-legged buddy Norm learned the joys of togetherness, loyalty and respect. Thanks to his huge and gentle helpmeet he was forever tolerant towards others even while being incredibly demanding on himself.

Thanks also to the extreme weather in the 1930s he's no stranger to discomfort. Largely forgotten now is the fact that that decade delivered the worst weather—hottest, coldest, driest, wettest, windiest, dirtiest and most devastating—in American experience. Coming on top of the Great Depression, gritty conditions molded Norm into a founding member of the generation nowadays often called The Greatest.

Political turbulence toughened him too. At age 20 (1934), during his first weeks in Minneapolis, he got inadvertently entangled in street violence and learned how a hungry mob can shred the social fabric. His hairbreadth escape from corporate deputies swinging billy-clubs at every head within reach imprinted on his soul the impulse to prevent hunger.

Disease may also have helped fashion the Greatest Generation. In those days most people succumbed to infections. That same year when he was 20 he faced his own deadly infection: strep throat. Though the first antibiotic had been revealed two years before, it was bottled up in Hitler's Germany awaiting a patent. Fortunately he proved one of the few with the fortitude to defeat the deadly bacterium unaided.

Throughout this time he studies forestry. His training was, however, quite low class for a center of higher learning. Yet it too fit the grand scheme: His skill at surveying land and laying out test plots seems almost pre-programmed for what he's about to face.

Foresters, such as his Idaho boss Hank Shank, also conveyed to him the can-do spirit then prevailing among Forest Service ranks. Through them he learned to lead with clear vision, commitment and, above all, courage. He also learned to be hard bitten and not beyond bad language. All in all, forestry molded the moxie and motivation to be a maverick for mankind.

For all the can-do qualities, his strongest character traits are emotional stability and an amazing ability to suppress sentiment. Actually, at his core there lies a streak of Scandinavian stubbornness. It arises partly from his roots in the village of Saude, Iowa. But the 1930s separated a special generation of self-reliant stoics. That doomsday decade demanded responsibility at a young age. And President Roosevelt contributed by exuding optimism during the darkest moments and by his try-anything experimentation, which at least kept hope alive.

All this induced in Borlaug a great sense of responsibility, especially to the strangers who helped his career. He forever goes out of his way to pass similar benefits forward to young people. Indeed, the pages ahead show him providing opportunity to what will eventually number hundreds of youths from dozens of countries, most of them poor and lacking any chance of furthering themselves.

Also in this volume more than a dozen more Good Samaritans join the parade and help him stay on that seemingly predestined course. Indeed, because of them he'll forever wonder if he's measuring up to expectations, and making himself work all the harder, just in case.

This commanding sense of thankfulness sometimes turns into an abject fear of failure that he'll occasionally force himself to ridiculous extremes, some of which prove critical to the final outcome.

Noteworthy too is the fact that he's not your stereotypical scientist. Thanks to Stakman, he's a generalist with a broad grasp of agricultural science. Thanks to the wartime work he fixes tough problems with speed and verve, targeting progress rather than perfection.

All in all, he's no theoretician. He's no academic. His respect is not for science. Only for solutions.

Theme 4: How a furious fungus forever threatens famine.

When Borlaug was born stem rust was prevalent and virtually unstoppable. Though he'd been but a toddler in rural Iowa, he remembers the awful interlude when this crop killer forced his family to exist on cornbread. Now in Volume 2 he himself confronts this age-old nemesis he'd once heard Stakman denounce as the "shifty, changing, constantly evolving foe of the food supply."

Although many diseases devastate food crops, this one is unique in launching trillions of spores onto the winds of summer and using the planet's great atmospheric currents to spread its malignance. With stem rust on the loose vast expanses of earth's greatest food crop die together.

This ruinous rival will dominate the present book, not to mention Borlaug's life. Only one practical antidote exists: a special wheat with the exquisitely rare, mysterious, almost mystical, ability to deny *every spore* access to its innermost tissues.

Can this rookie find such a variety to match the fungal foe that has spawned famines since at least Biblical times? Read on to find out.

That then is the back story behind the 30-year old researcher as he heads south in 1944 on a bizarre odyssey to fight hunger. To this point he's never developed a food crop. He's never worked on stem rust. He's never worked with wheat. He lacks the requisite training. And he knows nothing about the mysterious place he's headed for.

On the other hand he's not forgotten what it was like to be a poor farmer. He's not forgotten the power to be found in a seed. He's not forgotten his days doing land surveying. He's not forgotten how to live alone and cook for himself in the trackless waste. He's not forgotten the sight of hungry masses getting their heads bashed in. And he's not forgotten the wartime skill of solving problems promptly rather than perfectly.

Above all, he's neither forgotten the lessons learned on the wrestling mat nor Coach Bartelma's five-points for better living:

Give your best . . .
Believe you can succeed . . .
Face adversity squarely . . .
Be confident you'll find the answers when problems arise.
Then go out and win some bouts!

In the end those will prove enough.

BORLAUG

VOLUME 2

Wheat Whisperer, 1944 - 1959

1940

PROLOGUE

Norman Borlaug's decision to move to Mexico rested on a fantasy fashioned four years earlier by the very same daydream believer who brightened Volume 1 by conceiving corn-husking contests in his twenties, breeding hybrid corn in his thirties and conquering rural uprisings in his forties. Now in his fifties Henry Wallace soars all the way up to presidential running mate!

On November 5, 1940, when the voters honored FDR with a 449 to 82 Electoral College triumph, they also elevated Wallace to a title accorded barely a score of citizens a century: Vice-President-elect.

Sad to say, though, it was the least auspicious moment for entering Executive Service since Lincoln slipped into Washington by the backdoor four-score years before. This time, war is coming from the outside; indeed, from almost every point of the compass:

To the west, half of China is shadowed by war clouds that in a year will edge close enough to darken Pearl Harbor.

To the east Nazi U-boats command the coastal waters, where the pickings are plentiful and Americans help by keeping the lights on and adhering to the 1939 Neutrality Act that (to avoid infuriating the Fuehrer) forbids arming merchant ships. Britain-bound freighters and tankers explode in fragments and fireballs close enough for the crews to curse the shoreside lights that exposed their ships to destruction and themselves to death.

To the south loomed the worst of all perils, terrorism: "Hitler had been nourishing 'fifth columns' of Nazis in many Latin American republics," explains historian Samuel Eliot Morrison, "and the gravest danger to the Americas at that time appeared to be German subversion."

That November when Wallace's charmed career took him to the top of the Third Term ticket Hitler's proxies were already pricking America's big soft underbelly. Deep within the heart of darkness below Texas Axis agents were running clandestine radio networks, fomenting pro-fascist factions and smuggling oil to Caribbean hideaways, from whence it fed U-boats preying along the Gulf and Atlantic Coasts.

Coincidentally, Mexico conducted its own presidential contest in 1940. To observers peering down from the dreamland atop the border a happy outcome seemed impossible. Mexicans mistrusted gringos; many preferred Hitler to Roosevelt; most welcomed their Nazi neighbors. The presidente-elect, however, boldly bucked his backers. Manuel Avila Camacho pledged support for U.S. policies and fidelity to the free world.

In gratitude for eliminating the long-feared distraction of Mexican mayhem FDR announced that his running mate would attend Avila Camacho's inauguration on the final day of November. Problem was, having resigned as agriculture secretary and with six weeks to go before becoming presidential understudy, Henry Wallace lacked the status for so formal a Federal responsibility.

This impasse would have nullified the rest of our narrative had not common sense exerted its calming balm. Certifying Citizen Wallace "Ambassador Extraordinary," the State Department promised $50 a day for expenses, 5¢ a mile recompense for his car, and shooed him off. A driver was supplied but no aides, advance team, security staff or public-relations personnel. The man who'd soon be but a heartbeat from "Hail to the Chief" was flung *helpless and forsaken* into the neighbor's fascist ferment. He had to drive all the way to Mexico in his own car.

Seeing Wallace on this bizarre odyssey, you'd never guess he supplied the seed for his country's top crop or that he'd soon be president-in-waiting. From well-scrubbed, well-brushed good looks to happy handshake and humble green Plymouth he personified the common man.

Not surprisingly Mexicans took to him. And he to them. In fact when the outgoing presidente, the legendary Lázaro Cárdenas, suggested a tour of the nearby heartland, Ambassador Extraordinary Wallace extended his stay with joy, not to say jubilation. Mexico, you see, was the birthplace of the physical support beneath his worldly success: corn.

L ázaro Cárdenas was jubilant too. Heaven had sent an agronomic genius just as farm yields were sinking and food needs soaring. Mexico in 1940 was flirting with famine, a phenomenon that had formerly detonated disaster. During Cárdenas' youth, fear of starving had spawned crimes, cruelties, and chaos ranking among the worst in the woeful profile of human perversion. Now at age 45 the ex-presidente could feel the tension returning. The recent election had been the deadliest. The loser was plotting armed rebellion. Partisans were purchasing weapons in the open-air U.S. market. And Spanish fascists were sending arsonists to ignite the social tinder and fan the flames.

In suggesting Wallace turn tourista Cárdenas hoped the wizard of Iowa might expose a cornucopia of comestibles, and cool the countryside before Lucifer could light the social tinderbox.

This then is why on Sunday, the first day of December, America's Vice-President-elect tootled off into Mexico's murky midlands with his wife and friends. They should have exercised more care. The natty green Plymouth made perfect sniper bait and Henry Wallace was a high-value target: assassinating him would harden America's heart against entering yet another worthless war between the hopeless Europeans.

Yet who could blame the Iowa innocents for feeling carefree amid Central Mexico's stunning scenery. Only after they ascended the central hump known as the Bajío [bah-HEE-oh] did concern conquer complacence. In this upland plateau, big enough to encompass much of six states, Mexico's most basic dilemma was on dreadful display: Millions of the poor were hungry; children were malnourished; toddlers were typically stunted—some were starving. *And the Bajío was the national breadbasket!*

Wallace meandered through this misery a month before hastily heading home for his date with destiny on the Capitol Steps. Yet even then—at the peak of his public life—the misfortune he'd seen amassing just over the back fence had him mesmerized.

Realistically, though, what could he do? With Hitler's U-boats tormenting the territorial waters just 100 miles east of the Capitol Congress couldn't spare a care for another country's concerns.

Thus on January 21, 1941—within 24 hours of his elevation and with the crack of doom widening between the continents—the brand new V.P. dialed New York and posed a simple proposition: That the Rockefeller Foundation help the neighbors nurture more nourishment.

S uch a proposal was both unprecedented and unseemly. Back then, not even governments dared dabble in another country's farming. How a nation fed itself was an internal responsibility, a seal of sovereign status, nobody else's business.

Wallace, however, radiated both personal energy and the potent ether of the White House. Moreover the foundation happened to be seeking replacements for pet programs in China and Europe, now sadly shattered by war. Its president, Raymond Fosdick, loved Latin America, and had

CAREER SAVER #13

Fate's 13th facilitator, Henry Wallace during his tour of Central Mexico. Carl Mydans took this picture for *Life* magazine on January 1, 1940. Within three weeks, Wallace will be Vice President of the United States. Though his suit and tie are wildly out of place, he's soaking in the hopelessness pervading the Bajío. The sight inspired Wallace to overcome hunger and poverty here in Mexico's main farming area. Next, the discerning dreamer put his finger on why Mexico's food supply was in meltdown mode: deficiencies in the seeds, soils and farming skills.

What's more, the 51 year old Iowa prodigy knew just what to do: "Eighty percent of Mexicans live on the land," he wrote, "and the poorer people depend for their sustenance very largely on corn, together with some beans. From the standpoint of the great bulk of people who live on the farms in Mexico, I can't help thinking that efficient corn growing is more important than almost anything else."

This comment led four years later to Borlaug's bizarre odyssey to Mexico.

already begun a modest effort to lift the twin burdens of malaria and malnutrition from the backs of Mexico's country kids.

That project had triggered Wallace's call. He thought that country kids also needed a program to help them eat well: "Without improving agriculture," he explained, "the inevitable result of a declining death rate would be a lowered standard of living."

As a result of this series of surreal serendipities the Rockefeller Foundation loosened its purse strings just enough for a tiny (though grandly titled) "Survey Commission on Mexican Agriculture."

Then another fluky factor of fate muscled into the saga when a senior foundation official suddenly recalled hearing about a University of Minnesota professor who studied something called wheat stem rust. That hazy recollection led Fosdick to call Elvin Charles Stakman and ask if he'd lead the survey commission to Mexico.

Would he ever! Canceling all commitments, the U of M professor undertook the second of the three bizarre odysseys. This one was during the summer his student Norman Borlaug was completing his research on a fungal disease of the flax plant and his PhD.

Commanding a brand new station wagon Stakman crossed the Rio Grande in July 1941 and plunged into the darkness beyond the edge of the known world. With him in that GMC Suburban Carryall, which had been fire-engine red but was now sober green to satisfy scientific sensitivities, were Harvard's Paul Manglesdorf, a corn specialist, and Cornell's Richard Bradfield, dean of that era's soil scientists.

Squeezed between the professors was the boy botanist Richard Evans Schultes. Co-opted for his fluency in Spanish, young Schultes (his doctoral diploma still damp from last month's Harvard commencement) would find this a trip of a lifetime. It got him halfway to the Amazon, whence he'd emerge years later among the 20th century's great biologists.

Cramming a communicator into an already crowded conveyance may seem silly. But Mexico didn't go in for signposts in English. Indeed, it wasn't great on signposts, period. Rural roads commonly died and disappeared without trace, leaving travelers to navigate deserts, negotiate forests and skirt misty mountainsides by polling passersby.

All too often no passerby appeared; leaving vehicles to weave through the wilderness guessing which of the wandering tire tracks would get them where they were going. Rivers provided the supreme test. Bridges had yet to appreciate the joys of Mexican country living, so to cross a river you drove into the current, threading the wheels through unseen underwater obstacles and holes that sometimes were too deep to dodge.

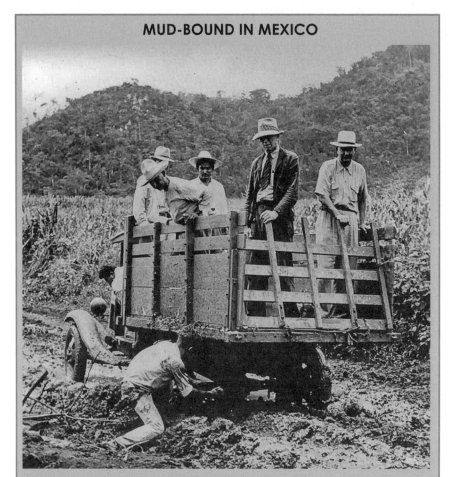

MUD-BOUND IN MEXICO

The Survey Commission on Mexican Agriculture. Three top American scientists learn the realities of Mexican country life. E.C. Stakman (leaning over side), Paul Manglesdorf (incongruous in tie and sweater), and Richard Bradfield (sporty white Panama hat) survey their plight in Veracruz state. With situations like this the distinguished professors found that wheels often had to yield to better modes of movement. Indeed, they described their two-month inspection tour as: "5000 miles—from the Texas border to the Guatemala border, by station wagon, flatbed truck, horse-drawn or mule-drawn buckboard, train, plane and, occasionally, horseback or muleback."

Stakman's involvement in this venture was another of the fluky factors that would fuel the food supply several decades into the future. It precipitated Borlaug's participation in Mexico.

Having inspected more than 100 locations in more than half Mexico's 28 states, the peregrinating professors condensed their conclusion into three sensible, scalpel-sharp statements:

It is at once apparent that the great majority of Mexican people are poorly fed, poorly clad and poorly housed. Sanitary conditions are much below the standards to which Americans are accustomed; as a consequence both pests and pestilences flourish. Illiteracy is common and adequate education is relatively rare. Transportation, communication and marketing facilities are far from satisfactory. Political standards are deplorable. In short, the general standard of living of the Mexican people is pitifully low and the country has many of the aspects of an over-populated land.

One wonders why such a condition should exist. Mexico is about a fourth the size of the United States; and yet its population is less than a sixth as great. The amount of arable land per capita is higher than in many much better off countries. The climate over much of Mexico is stimulating and a great range in climatic conditions permits the culture of a wide variety of crops. There are substantial mineral resources, including petroleum, silver, gold, lead, zinc, copper and antimony.

All these facts pose the question: Why is the living standard so low? There can be no simple answer. However, since Mexico is predominantly an agricultural country, with 77 percent of its employed population engaged in agricultural and other rural industries, it is obvious that at least part of the answer must be sought in the field of agriculture.

The body of their report noted that crop diseases and worn-out soils undermined Mexico's farm production. The puzzle's missing piece, so the authors claimed, was a cadre of competent researchers. Of all the country's agriculturists, only a handful had a Masters degree; none had a PhD. The authors then urged that the Rockefeller Foundation dispatch four young Americans to:

- Breed better varieties of the main food crops;
- Improve soil management and crop protection; and
- Train Mexican students in the agricultural sciences.

To lead this grand quartet Stakman privately touted his onetime graduate student, George Harrar.

He also suggested Norman Borlaug's inclusion, based on the singular insight that: "He has great depth of courage and determination. He will not be defeated by difficulty and he burns with a missionary zeal."

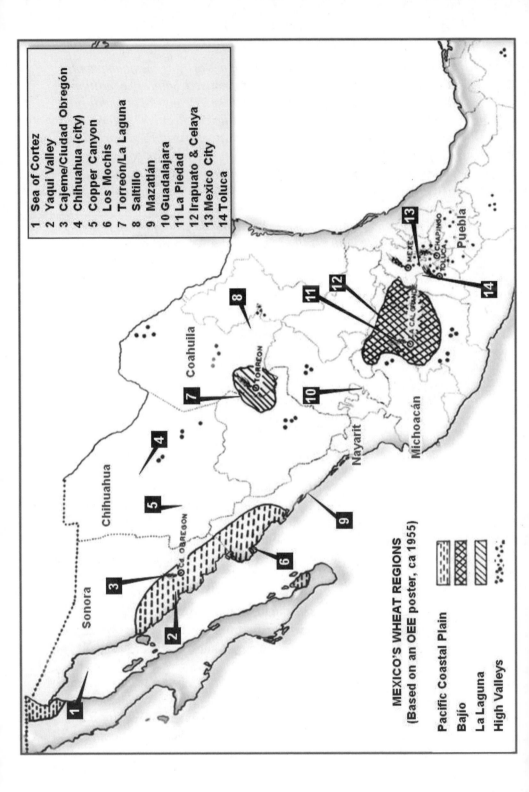

MEXICO'S WHEAT REGIONS
(Based on an OEE poster, ca 1955)

Pacific Coastal Plain
Bajío
La Laguna
High Valleys

1 Sea of Cortez
2 Yaqui Valley
3 Cajeme/Ciudad Obregón
4 Chihuahua (city)
5 Copper Canyon
6 Los Mochis
7 Torreón/La Laguna
8 Saltillo
9 Mazatlán
10 Guadalajara
11 La Piedad
12 Irapuato & Celaya
13 Mexico City
14 Toluca

1

1944

Heartbreak

With Wilmington fading in the rearview mirror of his wife's ancient Pontiac Norman Borlaug feels sick at heart. It's September 11, 1944, and he's abandoning Margaret in her time of need. She is 8 months pregnant, far from family and friends, and has no one to help her care for their year-old daughter, Jeanie.

He's moreover abandoning a job of infinite promise and income potential. While ahead there's a mission impossible, an alien culture, a language beyond understanding, a society suspicious of everything American, pitiful paychecks, and the potential for Montezuma's revenge, malaria, and mindless mayhem.

Deepening that Monday morning depression is guilt over forsaking his own nation. World War II has nearly a year to run, victory remains elusive, quitting seems cowardly.

Yet more unease comes from his aging vehicle. Since 1941 Detroit has produced only machines of war. America's 27 million cars and 5 million trucks are therefore wearing out. Spare parts are scarce. Tires are unobtainable; every passenger vehicle has run on its last set for at least two years. Blowouts are the commonest killers on the road.

Gasoline is a separate worry. Two years back, the Feds rationed families to 3 gallons *a week*, explaining that "Non-essential driving is one of the luxuries all of us will have to give up for the duration." Borlaug's been honored with a special coupon book. But should his stamps run out he'll be stuck for want of a slip of federal scrip.

On the bright side, though, Washington has lifted the 35 mph national speed limit (imposed in 1942 to preserve tire treads) all the way to 40 mph!

The man behind the wheel has by now morphed into a slim, poised, PhD, with a direct gaze, friendly manner, fair complexion and film star features. Despite a natural ability to charm the camera, this 30-year-old

CROP CRUSADER

Young Norman Borlaug. When he goes to Mexico in 1944 the 30-year-old is bone-lean, modest, quiet, youthful . . . with a temperament mingling scientist and adventurer. The empire-building eyes are as blue and sharp as ever; so too is the compulsion to perform that has driven him since childhood.

is no celluloid sophisticate. His manner and bearing still echo the tiny towhead who'd scampered about an Iowa farmstead whistling for wild joy a quarter-century back.

A year earlier, the foundation had dispatched three members of Stakman's suggested quartet. On site already are George Harrar, the leader; Edwin Wellhausen, a corn and beans authority from the University of West Virginia; and William Colwell, a soil specialist newly graduated from Cornell. Borlaug will be the final cornerstone.

Regardless of the Rockefeller connection, the venture is underfunded. Indeed, it seems utterly vacuous. Four agronomists couldn't modify a modest Midwest county . . . let alone a massive foreign country. Moreover, these are novices. Their average age is 33; none has celebrated a 40th birthday. Only one has ever before stepped outside the continental U.S. Three know no word of Spanish.

Such an ill-conceived, ill-prepared and ill-funded project suggests it was merely a sop to Henry Wallace who, when it was authorized in 1943, was Oval-Office heir-apparent. Why else would the Foundation cast four callow, clueless kids to catch a falling foreign food supply?

Maybe it's only from the modern mountaintop that these nonentities seem predestined for a stupendous success. Harrar, Borlaug, Wellhausen, and Colwell possessed a mix of survival skills, practical knowledge, and real-life experience that endowed them the means, mindset and mojo to make sound judgments, take summary action, transcend tight situations and triumph over impossible odds.

As head of this compassionate cavalry corps George Harrar proved picture perfect. From the start, he challenged his staff to: "*Make Mexico capable of feeding itself.*"

Anyone daring so much would today be denounced as deluded. But this was before caution and cowardice engulfed human endeavor; Harrar remained misguided enough to embrace confidence and courage. The only one knowing anything of the wider world, he'd capped his doctoral degree with a couple of years teaching in Puerto Rico. Now 37, he projected personal presence like a searchlight, thanks to an athletic frame, powerhouse mind, stubborn sense of purpose, and a larynx that loosed words with machinegun power and penetration.

Despite endless battles with local functionaries, Harrar remained on surprisingly good terms with his hosts. His tart tongue, imposing persona, and fluent Spanish actually mesmerized Mexicans. And the feeling was mutual: Harrar really did want to help, and he pressed his staff to: "Train the students and ease them into your own jobs!"

CORPS COMMANDER

George Harrar. OEE's team leader was a luminous character renowned for broad-shoulders, manly physique and a polished appearance. He brought energy to every room. Typically, he sported sharply pressed army slacks (popularly known as suntans), crisp khaki shirt, fat brown tie, and shiny work boots. That unique office armor together with the upright carriage contributed to the magnetism that radiated like a personal nimbus. As an undergraduate at Oberlin College he'd been dubbed "Flying Dutchman" after setting the Ohio state record for the quarter-mile dash. For better or worse, the nickname stuck and Harrar remained "Dutch" to intimates.

To conceal the unseemly collaboration between a foreign foundation and a prickly proud nation the program was disguised under a plain-Jane code name: Office of Special Studies. Perhaps for deeper cover, everyone used its Spanish acronym, OEE.

Begun without hype or hope, this very small, heavily veiled venture was launched ever so quietly on an ambiguous course to unknown places beyond the edge of the known world. Only providence knew how much time would pass before it failed of its own volition. And providence wasn't about to reveal the surprise it was holding for history.

OEE began as a scattering of tiny, totally inadequate facilities: The main office comprised three hot and dusty rooms on the third floor of a rundown edifice located in San Jacinto, on Mexico City's northern outskirts. There, Spanish was spoken.

A separate downtown secretariat handled the mail and phone calls to the U.S. Located in Calle Viena #26, it was merely a couple of rooms borrowed from the Rockefeller Foundation's medical unit—the one suppressing malnutrition and malaria among Mexican country kids. There, English was spoken.

The research facility occupied 160 acres of long-abandoned farmland 25 miles east, near the old Aztec capital of Texcoco [TESH-coco]. This worthless tract crouched in a quiet corner of the sprawling National Agriculture School popularly known as Chapingo. It was the only facility with open communications. There, science was spoken.

When Borlaug dropped by his future worksite he discovered . . . well, nothing: no greenhouse, laboratory, equipment, technicians, field hands or even fields. The sole structure was a crude adobe cabin Ed Wellhausen had thrown up in 1943. Because its roof was felt-paper impregnated with heavy oil and because there was neither floor nor foundation everyone called it the Tarpaper Shack.

Although four adobe walls without floor or solid roof may seem ill-suited to superior science, the surroundings were worse. The worn-out land radiating out roughly 500 yards (five football fields) from the Tarpaper Shack had reverted to dry, tawny, tortured tangles of weeds.

Six months earlier, a small portion had been cleared for test-plantings of the finest U.S. varieties of beans and corn. Borlaug could see the results: the beans were battered by insects and diseases and barely alive; the corn had been mauled by leaf blight and killed by early frost. Hybrids were sick enough to make an Iowan lose his ardor or maybe his lunch.

This failure seemed downright un-American, as Norm notes:

This was our first inkling that raising crops in Mexico might differ from anything we'd expected. We'd assumed our seeds would perform as they did back home. Suddenly it seemed we shouldn't be so sure of ourselves. This place was smarter than we thought. It had certainly outwitted us.

A s resident specialist for beans and corn, Ed Wellhausen was the OEE's point man. Borlaug, by contrast, was its handyman. Despite official designation as Plant Pathologist, he spent October 1944 peering through a transit and staking out boundaries for fields, roads, fences, waterlines and drainage ditches.

Surveying skills made him employee of the month. Still and all, his efforts seemed futile because taming a third of a square mile of tumble-down terrain required a tractor. And none was available.

Then, early in November, someone mentioned seeing a farm-equipment graveyard behind the farmers' bank in Texcoco. Wellhausen and Borlaug immediately descended and, amid a mass of repossessed discards, discovered two TD8 Internationals. Though not farm tractors, their weight, power and crawler treads ideally fitted the immediate need. Because neither ran, both were readily released into OEE's care.

The sudden appearance of two rusty wrecks precipitated even more frustration; no one knew beans about live bulldozers, let alone dead ones. But a week later someone idly mentioned that a mechanic living nearby had once repaired tanks for the Mexican army. Ed Wellhausen raced to the village of Boyeras and right there, on the man's own doorstep, hired him onto the support staff.

Dismantling both behemoths, Vicente Guerrero quickly commanded a daunting muddle of metallic body parts: large ones strewn outside the Tarpaper Shack and small ones—screws, nuts, chains, belts, bolts, cables and springs—strewn across the hard-packed dirt inside.

In their enforced impotence the scientists lounged around, helpless, disheartened. Borlaug's second month thus passed in angry fretting while, with the care of a surgeon transplanting tissues, a one-time tank doctor reassembled the best bits from two comatose crawler tractors.

On the day of reckoning the uneasy onlookers gawked as the improbable medicine man climbed aboard, pulled the decompression lever, engaged the starter, and got his heavy-metal patient breathing on gasoline fumes.

After observing five minutes on life support he chose to test the vital signs: pushing the decompression lever, he eased out the throttle to switch fuels. In its Lazarus moment, the iron giant coughed and

GRINGO DISGRACE

Ed Wellhausen and the collapse of America's greatest corn varieties. When the all-American crops failed in 1944, the grandiose mission to feed all Mexicans suffered a reverse. Having derided the local corn, the four aggies found their Yankee superstars were worse. These sickly, slanting, scrawny plants bore no food at all. The young men had arrived confident they could transform food production. This fiasco ended their faith in themselves and in their cherished beliefs. Mexico had taught them humility!

spluttered and then began happily inhaling its standard fare, diesel.

Finally, Guerrero selected first gear, hauled on the lever that lifted the blade from its place of rest, and inched back the main clutch lever.

Here was the moment of truth. The anxious observers stood silent and stock still; the long-inactive treads, by contrast, protested their loss of leisure with metallic squawks and screams. Then by grabbing the ground the chimera began crawling.

The observers first relaxed. Then they jumped and clapped and cheered. Their euphoria erupted less from pleasure than from relief. The Mexican military mechanic had supplied their first success. More than power, he'd given them purpose.

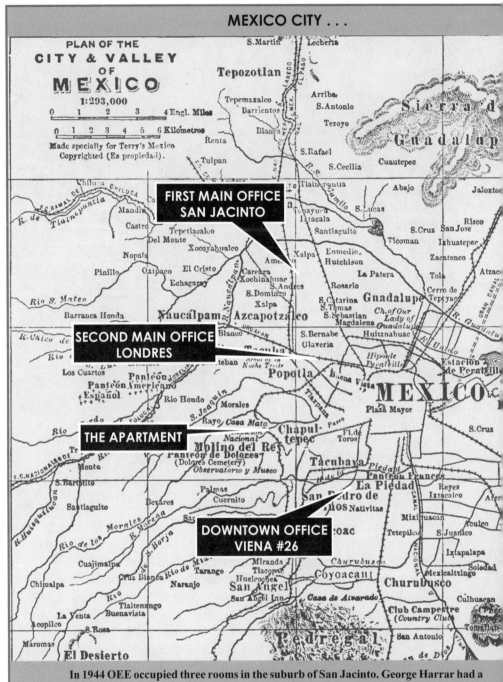

MEXICO CITY . . .

PLAN OF THE
CITY & VALLEY
OF
MEXICO
1:293,000

Made specially for Terry's Mexico
Copyrighted (Es propiedad).

FIRST MAIN OFFICE
SAN JACINTO

SECOND MAIN OFFICE
LONDRES

THE APARTMENT

DOWNTOWN OFFICE
VIENA #26

In 1944 OEE occupied three rooms in the suburb of San Jacinto. George Harrar had a separate office in Viena #26—two rooms borrowed from Rockefeller Foundation health program.

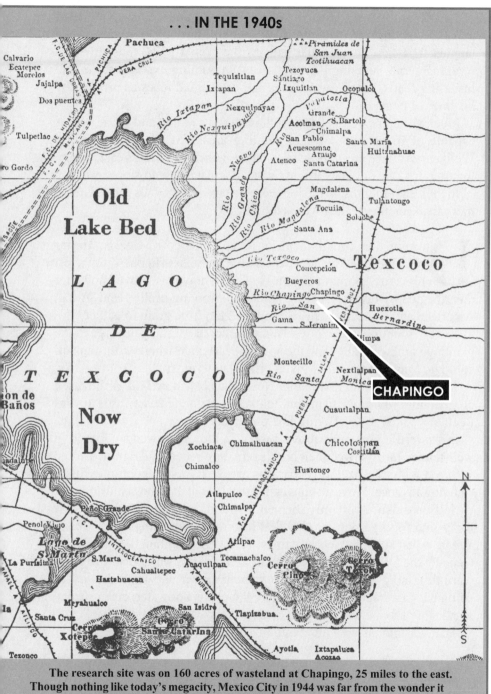

. . . IN THE 1940s

The research site was on 160 acres of wasteland at Chapingo, 25 miles to the east.
Though nothing like today's megacity, Mexico City in 1944 was far from the wonder it
had been in Aztec times when, like Venice, it was built around water.

As the group's designated go-fer, Borlaug spent December 1944 maneuvering that yellow rust-stained machine through the tawny weedy tangles. His first step on the path to the Nobel Prize thus involved scraping scrub, leveling planting areas, smoothing exposed earth, and installing roads, fences, waterlines and drainage ditches as profiled by his lines of pegs.

Meanwhile, the others dug a well, installed a pump, and affixed pipes capable of irrigating the main planting areas. At the same time Ed Wellhausen added an adobe lean-to on the Tarpaper Shack's eastern end, trusting that one day they might need someplace safe to store seed.

In their first months on the job these scions of the 1930s proved much more than scientists: they were laborers.

Despite the formal focus on beans and corn, George Harrar remained wedded to wheat. Three months earlier he'd sown test plots of Stakman's top picks. Those, however, proved no better than the nearby beans and corn. Although growing healthy and strong, American and Canadian wheats produced too little grain to gather.

Never doubting the cause, Harrar ordered Borlaug to repeat the planting somewhere beyond the Valley of Mexico where worn-out soil could no longer trump God-given gringo superiority.

Thus it came about that late in November Norm and Ed Wellhausen climbed into Margaret's ancient Pontiac and trundled eastwards toward Puebla, a sunny state offering fine prospects.

In the fertile highlands above Tehuacan they borrowed a corner of a well-tended farm, sowed their boss's remaining seed, and returned home suffused with satisfaction: Their all-star wheats were about to unfold a stunning advance. Mexican hunger had met its match. Who could doubt it?

Self-confidence certainly seemed justified. This was Borlaug's first foray into food production, his first hands-on happenings with wheat, and he'd just sown the world's finest varieties. Marching into the Hotel Geneve, the OEE's designated downtown digs, he was aglow thanks to warmth arising both from his flourishing career and from the joy of being back in the lap of luxury where there was hot water, clean sheets, reasonable food, and folks who could follow what he said.

That warmth lasted a mere minute:

> As I picked up my room key the desk clerk handed over a note that had been waiting several days. The first words shunted aside all sense of elation. The clerk's crabbed scribble summarized a phone

call from Wilmington. Margaret had given birth to a son, Scott. She was well. But there was some trouble. A letter was on the way.

After an agonizing hour of desperate dialing and cajoling operators in two languages, one of which I couldn't understand, I finally got through to Wilmington General. The hospital staff made no effort to help: Margaret was unavailable. Her ward had no phone. She was sleeping. No, they wouldn't wake her. No, they wouldn't provide personal information. Nothing could be done. Call back tomorrow!

Next morning in a state of panic I visited the downtown office and discovered Margaret's letter. It had been written under great stress. The sentences were rough and broken. But my eye latched onto two strange words: *spina bifida*.

These I didn't understand, so I hurried down the corridor and collared George Payne, the physician managing the foundation's malaria team.

"What is spina bifida?" I asked.

In turn, he inquired why I wanted to know. He was usually outgoing and very friendly but on hearing of Margaret's note, his manner turned stony and strictly professional. It was a birth defect. In some cases the spinal column was exposed. There was danger of sudden movement paralyzing the legs and bodily functions. There was risk of infection . . . and of hydrocephalus. "I'm terribly sorry, Norman," he added, "but I have to say that at best it's bad. At worst, it's tragic."

This knowledge was almost impossible to bear. It emptied my mind of everything else. Mexico be damned, I had to get to Delaware. Fast.

There was no option but to fly. Trouble was, I was out of cash. So was everyone else. Though George Harrar could advance a loan from operating funds, he was traveling in the U.S., and well beyond reach.

This was as big a frustration as I ever faced. It was agony sitting in the office that morning and confronting the phone. Knowing I couldn't get to Delaware for love nor money made everything so much worse. Another age passed before the various operators got me through to Margaret.

Sadly, I explained that there was no way to get out of the damned place until the boss got back.

"That's okay, Norman," she said. "Don't worry too much. Being here won't help. I can cope. But come as soon as you can."

Three long days later Harrar returned, and Norm caught the next plane out. Another day passed before he touched down in Philadelphia. Then, having taken a train to Wilmington and a cab to 1407 Delaware Avenue, he climbed with leaden feet to the second floor and knocked on the door marked 3B.

As the door opened he saw Margaret's face reflect palpable relief.

They stood and hugged, saying nothing for an age. "I made the decision, Norman," she finally whispered through the tears. "There was no more time. They wanted to cut Scotty up . . . but the operation sounded too desperate . . . I thought it best to let nature take its course."

A lifetime onward, he still has difficulty relating any of this. Although born in Wilmington General, the baby was scheduled for transfer to the Alfred I. du Pont Hospital for Children, a brand new state-of-the-art pediatric facility located in a park-like setting just beyond the city limits. The exposed spine, however, precluded even so short a trip.

Indeed, that open wound effectively barred both Norm and Margaret from touching, talking to, or even approaching their child. Moreover, the isolation ward was restricted to hospital staff. The distraught pair could thus do nothing but pray and pass the time. Most to be feared was an accumulation of water on the brain. That so-called hydrocephalus would turn their fragile offspring into the condition so commonly and so unkindly called "vegetable."

Then a lining spun of purest silver gleamed through the dark clouds of despair. Norm had dropped by DuPont for a chat with his former co-workers, and over lunch Wendell Tisdale offered him his job back. This brought a flood of relief. Norm grabbed the opportunity: "Yes," he exulted to Margaret that night, "I'll be a microbiologist . . . or a chemist. I'll work here in a laboratory. We'll stay in Wilmington. We'll be with Scotty. And we'll all have proper medical care!"

By now, however, Margaret knew him better than he knew himself. His heart was no longer in industry, or even the U.S. His passion for helping the hungry had taken wing; he'd only be happy toiling in foreign soil. "My husband has a future," she said in her calm, self-assured, almost ethereal manner. "My baby has none. You go back; I'll come when I can."

It was another selfless decision by which she'd uplift the future.

Two days after Christmas 1944, for the second time in three months, Norm headed for Mexico. This time he was high in the sky in a cramped, bucking, noisy DC-3 probably newly released from carrying troops into battle.

His mind this time was trebly troubled by the albatross of guilt.

L ate in January 1945 he tracked down a rental apartment in the colorful housing complex of Colonia Virreyes (Viceroy's Compound). Having handed over a deposit, he bought a bed and four chairs, and moved right in. "We have our first home in Mexico ready and waiting," he wrote his wife. "Come when you can."

Although Margaret had resolved to remain in Wilmington to the end, frightening forces were sapping her fidelity.

One was the state of the family finances. Despite DuPont's support of the medical expenses for its *ex-employee's* very sick child, Norm's new salary was too niggardly to sustain apartments in two countries.

Another was the Wilmington General Hospital's refusal to let her enter the pediatric isolation ward. Mother and son still had had no contact, and the worsening spectacle refracted through plate glass was making evermore difficult her twice-a-week visits.

Then, halfway through February, the specialist called Margaret into his private office. Hydrocephalus had begun. Her baby might last a month . . . two months . . . a year at most.

During the last visit the doctor gently guided her away from the glass divide. Rest assured, he said, little Scotty would receive good care.

Margaret then had to confront a wrenching, staggering, stupefying amalgam of loss and guilt. Later she said the hardest part was walking onto the platform, climbing aboard the train and staying seated as it pulled away from Wilmington. There she sat, hurting, hunched and head down, holding little Jeanie tight. That animal contact, according to her recollection, was all that saved her sanity as the wheels thrummed away the miles separating her from her suffering son.

Forever.

A week later Margaret reached the City of Mexico, exhausted less from the trip than from the tussle with scruples and self-control. Though heartsick at the awful march of events, she took an immediate liking to the spot her husband had selected. The apartment lay almost in the shadow of the ancient citadel of Chapultepec, which the Marine Corps Hymn elevates to "The Halls of Montezuma" but whose name literally means "Grasshopper Hill." Harrar, Wellhausen and their wives lived nearby, providing both companionship and convenience for the long commute to the worksite way out beyond the sprawling city's farther edge.

For Jeanie the new home was protective, pleasant, nearly perfect. Now a year-and-a-half old, she'd become the link that kept the family circle complete. Through their love for their toddler each parent came to cope with the horror of having another child—one they'd never hugged, kissed, caressed or even cooed to—slowly succumbing in cold-hearted confinement far away, alone, and unaware it had a family and was loved.

Also helping them heal was Mexico City's sunny upland clime, then among the world's most salubrious.

Moreover, they were enjoying luxurious living. Can you believe they had a separate kitchen, a separate dining room and *two* bedrooms? Such excess elevated Great Depression graduates into something akin to millionaire eminence today.

Upon her arrival Margaret had found the apartment flaunting all the base barrenness of bachelorhood. Within days, though, it had been scrubbed and washed and tidied and decorated—not to mention fitted with furniture.

Making those rented rooms family friendly was more than formality. Housework provided the very first rung in the life-long struggle to climb the ladder from the lower depths of heartbreak.

2

1945

Meeting Wheat

In November '44, following the debacle with corn and beans, Borlaug helped Ed Wellhausen plant more than 1000 forms of corn as well as 1800 distinct beans. Each was sown in a little row of 10 to 15 seeds. As OEE's designated pathologist, Norm settled into caring for these 30,000 to 40,000 plants. He'd finally found his calling: corn and beans doctor.

In March 1945, however, the career course was reset yet again. This correction was heralded by a peremptory summons that echoed across the fields. Peering up from his calm, quiet world amid bean seedlings, he saw his leader striding toward him, back straight, suntans immaculate, boots shiny, shirt smooth, tie regulation brown.

As always, George Harrar's persona preceded him like a big brass band, and in standard parade-ground bark he broke the news: "Norm, I've got too much administrative work to handle . . . I want you to take over the Wheat Program . . . Run it any way you want . . . I'll give you all the help I can—when I can!"

This took Norm aback. He didn't really want the job. Wheat was less an institutional priority than Harrar's personal interest. And he doubted he could meet his boss's unstated order: *make Mexico capable of producing all its daily bread!*

That command could cause a colossus to quake. Though Mexico planted over a million acres of wheat, it posted almost the world's lowest grain yield. Whereas the U.S. and Canada averaged 1100 pounds an acre, their southern neighbor averaged about 750—a double disgrace because much of its wheatland was irrigated. Moreover, Mexico's production yo-yoed year by year. In '39, '40 and '41, to mention but three cases, stem rust *halved* the already slim output.

Worse, doubling a nation's output was too much for even an expert. Yet Borlaug had never worked with wheat. He had nothing more than the lessons learned at Stakman's knee.

Moreover Mexico could contribute no literature, no equipment, no trained staff, no seeds for scientific research. There was not even a wheat specialist to explain previous experience. During the 1930s the government had employed a wheat scientist but in 1943 it abolished the position. The crop clearly had no future.

Did any of this affect the fresh-faced greenhorn? No. Armed with his first independent commission, he recalled his high-school wrestling coach's admonition, and reached for his bootstraps.

First up, he visited the agriculture department whose imposing high rise happened to be near the apartment. The agricultural authorities, however, received him with disdain, both because wheat was unworthy and because he was too dim-witted to speak Spanish.

Then on a whim he entered the building next door and dropped by the irrigation department. Here, he was received with rapturous enthusiasm. Plans were laid out for a massive project that would vastly expand the capacity to irrigate the Yaqui [YAH-kee] Valley. That wide, dry, alluvial plain was in Sonora, a remote and unruly state generally considered Mexico's Wild West. The water engineers, however, considered it a wonderful place to grow wheat.

On exiting the towering building on Paseo de la Reforma Borlaug experienced an epiphany: He'd learned how and where he could uplift the country's food supply:

> We established great working relations that day. Irrigation was probably the most efficient government department; its engineers were professionals who really knew their stuff. From the start we both sensed we could work together toward a great end. They could irrigate vast tracts of good wheatland but couldn't keep the crop healthy. That's where I might make a difference. And without healthy plants their great project would be next to worthless.

His exultation was, however, tinged with exasperation. Sonora, you see, lay hundreds of miles north of the zone where the OEE was contracted to work. The Rockefeller Foundation's agreement with the government restricted it to the Bajío, the area Henry Wallace had worried about back in 1940. No one had thought beyond that.

Back at the office he raised this disquieting dichotomy and was summarily squelched. "Listen, Norman, keep your mind on the job!"

Harrar barked. "Our problem is in the Bajío. This is where the poor farmers are. You must get that clear!"

What to do? Borlaug confronted perhaps the most basic question in hunger fighting: Target the most needy? Or the most numerous?

We mortals may find that a no-brainer but he decided to uplift *everyone*.

■ LESSON ONE: Feed Everyone

Although it wouldn't be recognized for years to come, the decision to confront his esteemed boss produced his first principle for building an embracing and enduring food supply: *Opt to feed the whole populace, not just the hungry. That way every citizen has a stake in overcoming the inevitable obstacles.*

This policy would become a benchmark of his genius and set him apart. But at the time, he'd merely sought to circumvent an asinine rule banning him from the one spot where he might avert hunger nationwide.

In early April he decided to challenge his boss:

> Dutch, the Yaqui Valley is Mexico's most promising wheat area, and I'm going to take a look. If we can lick stem rust up there everyone will be better off. We should at least consider working in Sonora. It's the right thing to do!

In this case, however, neither cogency nor common sense could alter cast-iron conviction. Harrar nixed the notion. Still Norm persisted. The irresistible force representing consumer interests thus met the inflexibility of a contract.

Indeed, both psyches were heated by mental friction until—surprise, surprise—the one who blinked was the dashing, sartorially correct director. "Okay, okay," Harrar said resignedly, "Take a quick trip to the Yaqui Valley and look around. Nothing more than that, though."

Despite all the wonders this decision would eventually open to the world, something of the collegial marrow ossified that day. George Harrar would never again view his junior partner quite the same. This naïve newcomer was disruptive; he wouldn't stay within the designated limits; he was no team player.

Sonora was severed from Mexico's main stem by the Sierra Madre Occidental, once described as "a land on end, a tumbled down world." Though only a thousand miles from the capital, the road trip required a roundabout trip involving at least a week of pothole

OLD LOOK . . . NO GLORY

Cajeme. When he arrived, the town where Borlaug would develop wheats for the world was swathed in insignificance. It had begun 32 years before when Southern Pacific engineers plunked Estación Cajeme in the open desert. Anyone wanting the train to stop had to wave a flag. In 1944 it remained a small forgettable outpost with no claim to fame and no particular future. The place was so raw it lacked a graveled road; the main street was just a dusty drag.

persecution, not to mention a long stretch driving in the U.S. Rail was more direct but hardly friendlier and not much faster. Flying seemed unlikely, given Mexico's barely fledged airline system but he learned that an air connection had just opened. Best of all, it covered that thousand miles in just two days!

Thus it was that, early in April, he clambered aboard a United Airlines DC-3 for a hop north to Torreón in the country's dun and dusty core. Then a second DC-3 lifted him over the awesome mountain massif to Mazatlán on the blue Pacific shore. Following a night in a cheap hotel, he boarded a venerable Fokker Tri-motor for the haul up the coastal plains and into the western wilderness known as the state of Sonora.

As that amalgam of plywood, fabric and corrugated steel took to the skies over Mazatlán Norm peered through the tiny frosted window at the brilliant coastal plain—green and lush in the dawnlight. But as the 350 miles slowly unwound the color drained away leaving a sepia expanse that seemed more mirage than mirror image of the seaside city he'd just left. Though this so-called Yaqui Valley touched the same blue sea, it was in reality little more than desert. Being barely airborne, he could see endless cacti, agave, yucca, mesquite, rocks, sand. Nothing more.

At noon the winged boxcar settled gently back to terra firma and the tops of a wheat crop crowded the gauzy glass. The runway, you see, was merely a sliver of dirt carved from a living farm a stone's throw from a tiny town known to most maps as Cajeme [cah-HEM-ee].

Having written to a local research facility, he was glad to find its assistant director waiting beside a dilapidated government pickup parked next to the guard hut that was the airport terminal. Behind it sprawled a settlement radiating the frontier feel experienced mainly in matinee movies. Indeed, its unpaved streets and false-front stores evoked an elaborate stage-set erected for, say, Roy Rogers.

As Norm had no interest in sightseeing, they drove down the dusty main drag and out into the flats stretching all the way to the blue jewel known as the Sea of Cortez. That pinky of the Pacific lay fifty miles farther west, however, and the scenery resembled those in cactus-clad advertisements touting Arizona vacations.

Half a bumpy hour later, the cracked windshield exposed his destination. Plopped out there in the middle of nowhere, the Yaqui Valley Experiment Station had been the brainchild of a dotty governor who'd envisaged it as a vehicle for driving Sonora up and out of dust and destitution. Though its stone-pillared entrance suggested it had once been a showplace, Norm saw only desolation:

> The place looked like hell: Fields sprouted more wild oats than wheat . . . canals hosted weeds rather than water . . . cattle, sheep and hogs had gone for someone's dinner . . . farm machinery had emigrated in an equally mysterious manner . . . fences had fallen . . . and a large experimental orchard had shrunk to a few figs and oranges and a solitary grapefruit.
>
> The buildings were in no better shape. From the outside they resembled bombed-out Berlin: windows shattered, doors askew, screens tattered, roof tiles torn off. The laboratory block was befouled by rusting equipment, rotting seeds and musty mounds of moldy old documents.
>
> I never saw a more dismal scientific facility . . . and I've seen plenty of dismal ones.

The director was away and the driver quickly dumped the awkward guest who was so clueless he couldn't even converse, and disappeared in a lather of distaste and discomfiture. Norm then dropped his bedroll and pasteboard suitcase and set out through the shimmering surroundings.

Having never encountered such an apparition, the farmers met his advent with silent stares. Then as he drew near, their eyes widened in surprise, not to say suspicion. Why was this weirdo walking alone out here in the white heat and asking questions in such atrocious Spanish?

As to wheat, they expressed only disgust. A few years back stem rust had focused its bile hereabouts, being cruel enough to deliver *three* crop failures running. In 1939 the destruction was total, in 1940 nearly total, and in 1941 moderate, though only by comparison.

In April 1945 stem rust still had this place strangled. Farmers grew Barigon, an almost worthless wheat variety, just because it survived.

Though the ripening crop looked healthy, the fungus had not been forgiven. Farmers were shifting to flax, a more reliable and more rewarding option since it underpinned domestic tranquility the world around. Flax, you see, provided linseed oil for house paint.

That first afternoon ended in full-blown frustration. Having come north to learn great things, he'd found nothing worth learning. Although Barigon withstood stem rust, it made poor pasta and bad bread. Most of Sonora's harvest ended up in soda crackers. The growers, being more embarrassed than anyone, meekly accepted pitiful paychecks.

When Norm trudged back to the old experiment station in the gathering dusk he was depressed. And despite fatigue, he faced a bad night:

> The communal kitchen was so filthy I took over a long-deserted staff house, arranged a few stones outside, then lit a fire and

heated a can of beans by burning old corn cobs. Finally, after sweeping some dead rats out of the staff house I unrolled my bedroll on the stone floor. During the night live rats ran over the bedroll. I pulled a coat over my head but slept very fitfully.

Next day, stepping out into the soft dawn glow he set off to explore farms farther out across the khaki countryside. There, late that morning, he stumbled across small fields of a pair of obscure wheats named Mentana and Marroqui [marrow-KEE]. Neither looked promising. Only later would he learn they were his predecessor's discards. The wheat specialist whose position had been abolished two years before had first thrilled to this pair; then abandoned them due to Mentana's abject surrender to rust and Marroqui's abysmal lack of yield.

Borlaug nearly rejected them too. Lacking any other booty, however, he stashed a head of each in two of the envelopes he'd brought.

That second evening he returned to the research facility thirsty, hungry, dusty, sweaty . . . and no longer depressed. He'd come to the realization that Sonora had flat terrain, full-sized rectangular fields, farm machinery, irrigation—features seldom seen in Central Mexico.

Moreover Sonorans seemed a scrappy lot, shrinking neither from a stranger nor silly questions. Disenchanted, stubborn, skeptical, maybe even small-minded, they seemed committed to bettering themselves. Indeed, they were not unlike Iowans, and among them he felt at ease.

Thus, despite failing to accomplish anything of consequence, he headed home on the third day with spirits soaring:

> When we rose out of Cajeme I looked down on the vast expanse of the Yaqui Valley and my mind wrestled with a new concept. The OEE wheat program needed to change . . . we had to rethink our strategy. By solving the Yaqui Valley's stem rust problem we really could give Mexico all the bread it could eat!

Back in Mexico City, he touted Sonora's astounding possibilities like one obsessed. For the moment though he had to focus on the more than 1000 forms of corn as well as 1800 distinct beans whose health was his responsibility.

Together with George Harrar's small wheat planting, this monster corn and beans trial provided Norm's professional induction into hunger fighting's most basic demand: drudgery. For three long months he had to scrutinize all three plantings for signs of disease or pests.

This was too much for even this genie of demonic devotion, so he was grateful when Harrar assigned him two Mexican students.

HOME-MADE . . .

Chapingo was not your normal experiment station. Finding no facilities when they arrived, the scientists built their own from scratch. Borlaug laid out this site with an old bulldozer built from scavenged parts. The Ford pickup that will play a part later in the story can be seen on the left. This is where the Borlaug saga with food crops

. . . WORK PLACE

The only structure was this Tarpaper Shack, a crude adobe structure with a tarpaper roof and dirt floor that Wellhausen had built it in 1943. This work place was expected to make Mexico capable of producing all its own corn, beans, and wheat. In the fullness of time, it would be the staging area for much more than that.

One was José Guevara, who studied agriculture at the nearby school, and knew no English. Though already in his twenties, Guevara seemed neither so old nor so wise. Having escaped a painful existence in the poverty of backwoods Coahuila, a rugged northern state whose top holds up much of Texas, he expended prodigious energy in Borlaug's cause. For coworkers unable to converse, the pair got on famously. Even today, Norm can't mention his friend without a grin. From the start, they were joined at head and heart and needed no words.

The other was José Rodríguez. A 23-year-old plant pathologist, "Pepe" (as everyone called him) was short, sharp, spirited and very savvy. Because he was bilingual Harrar used him to help mediate with the Mexican government. Pepe would come to work in Borlaug's fields to sweat away the stress induced by the clash of American bravado and Mexican bureaucracy.

During the winter the three colleagues helped Wellhausen keep his corn and beans healthy. Then in April, right after Norm's return from Sonora, the willowy pair marched into the plantings ringing the Tarpaper Shack to assess the 15 separate specimens of each of the 1000 special corns. For almost two weeks the former farm boys squatted side-by-side on little folding stools, inspecting corn plants one-by-one and deciding how best to categorize:

- Leaf-blight damage;
- Root-rot damage; and
- Stem-rot damage; and
- Insect damage.

Their conclusions were penciled into a loose-leaf, binder—the spiral-backed kind beloved by college kids.

At the same time, they yanked the ears off the healthiest plants, sealing those seed-laden prizes in strong envelopes labeled with the code number inscribed beside the plant's notebook entry.

By the time they'd finished the last plant in the thousandth row the fall season's first frost had hit, which meant Wellhausen's 1800 mini-rows of beans awaited attention. The task now was to inspect each plant for manifestations of two devastating diseases (bean rust and leaf blight) and two destructive insects (Mexican bean beetle and Mexican pod weevil).

Day after day for two more weeks the American scientist and Mexican student pulled up bean plants by the thousands, laying each on the ground and conferred under the high sky to record:

- The number of lesions on the roots;
- The number of blemishes on the pods; and
- The number and size of the seeds.

Again the standout seeds got stashed in envelopes marked with the plant's code number.

As the improbable companions raced to finish the last few specimens their souls were suffused with satisfaction. Crammed with 105 closely inscribed sheets, the notebook was near bursting with promise for boosting Mexico's most nutritionally crucial crops.

Even before applying statistical analysis they sensed certain of their seeds possessed the power to foil some pathogen or pest. Through crossbreeding those could share their talents and transform Mexico.

Guevara was particularly excited. The promise residing between those black covers could fill out a fine thesis, earn him a degree and maybe a Rockefeller Foundation scholarship to study for a Masters in the U.S.

But it was not to be:

By noon we needed maybe an hour to complete the fieldwork but decided to take a quick break for lunch and finish up leisurely during the afternoon. When we reached the end of a row nearest the Tarpaper Shack I placed the notebook on top of one of the stools and then placed the second stool on top of that. Then we retired to the shade of an old ash tree that stood near the edge of the field.

The day was hot and dry, and while we enjoyed strong coffee from my thermos flask and the bacon-cheese sandwiches Margaret had provided a dust devil swirled up about a quarter-mile away to the west and came skimming toward us. The strange sight of a tornado-like cloud of dust was fascinating, and we watched as it swirled through our piles of corn plants, sending the dried leaves flying.

Then that brown whirligig wind suddenly ducked right and headed straight for our bean field. It blew away the top stool, and José and I stared in horror as the notebook came free and lifted into the air. It went up and up, and was high above us when the binding opened and pages blasted out like confetti from a circus cannon.

That was among the most agonizing experiences of my professional life: Seeing that data circling away into the heavens was dreadful to behold. With it went not only our hopes but our hearts. The whole season's work literally had taken wing, and there was nothing we could do. The figures and codes explaining exactly which of the thousands of plants had disease resistance and insect resistance were gone.

Together, we slunk over to the Tarpaper Shack and moped away the afternoon overwhelmed by despair.

In subsequent days the despondent duo posted reward notices. They circulated flyers among the students at the agriculture college. When nothing came back after a week they doubled the reward to about a dollar a page . . . a fortune. Six pages got handed in.

Finally, they had to face reality: The fantastic accomplishment of individually planting, supervising, inspecting and evaluating nearly 3000 distinct forms of two separate crops had gone for naught.

Any reinforcement for Mexico's food foundation would be delayed, maybe denied. Guevara would have to spend another year redoing everything. And there was no longer any chance of a scholarship to the enchanted alternative universe he longed to experience for himself.

Even the Master Plantsman was jolted. "When you do agricultural research in a new country," Wellhausen opined dryly that evening, having just learned that his year's research results had gone with the wind, "you'd better not be too conceited."

Now Borlaug was convinced he'd made a disastrous career choice. What a fool he'd been to throw away all his stateside prospects on the delusion of helping this peculiar purgatory. What could have possessed his mind? Here he was adrift in unfathomable mysteries—troubled, confused, out of his depth.

Indeed, to his glazed eyes there seemed no possible way forward . . . or backward. Paradise couldn't be regained.

He'd let the group down.

He'd let himself down.

He'd proven unworthy of his leader's grand challenge.

Worst of all, he'd let his suffering family down.

With the winter-season work completed, he switched full attention to wheat and to the upcoming summer season.

Regardless of anything else, he needed to immunize Mexico's wheat crop against its fatal foe, stem rust. For that, there's but one option: sow seed of every different plant type and see which (if any) endured the showers of stem rust spores that will later fall like red rain.

With the previous winter's crop then ripening across Central Mexico, Borlaug, Rodríguez and Guevara toured hill farms in several nearby states. Wandering through randomly chosen fields, they yanked heads off any plant that seemed at all unusual. The task was complicated because the fields were mixtures of Spanish wheats whose seeds the farmers saved and sowed year after year. The area was an unholy mix of tall and medium stems, bearded and beardless heads, red and white grain.

Some were overripe, others still unripe. Most were diseased; many dead.

Following ten days of search, 8500 seemingly distinct healthy wheat seedheads were safely ensconced in the lean-to newly affixed to the eastern end of the Tarpaper Shack.

Come May, this amateur and his assistants grabbed the bags from the lean-to, threshed the samples individually, and prepared to sow the resulting 8500 distinct seed lots. To observers that seemed sacrilegious. In Mexico, wheat was a winter crop; summers generated more rust than the species could withstand. Borlaug, however, *wanted* his plants attacked. He hoped it would expose the rare specimens possessing the mystical means to resist the red rain.

Actually, though, his faith seemed foredoomed because he had no way to prepare the fields. Given its weight and steel-ribbed treads the giant TD8 was useless. Absent any alternative, the three tyros became their own beasts of burden. Fastening a strap about his chest, each in turn tugged a small nursery-plot cultivator while another guided the tines that tilled the turf and tore out the weeds.

This was truly incredible. Although the soil was loose and the furrow shallow, acting the ox seemed the ultimate low for a human being. Beneath the unfeeling Mexican sun at 7000 feet altitude the body rivered sweat, the back burned, the rope flensed the flesh. Yet these boys of burden persevered until two short rows (each featuring 10 to 15 seeds) had been sown for all 8500 selections—a task absorbing more than two weeks and involving over 5 miles of sod-busting by biceps.

In addition, a small "crossing block" was sown with 49 wheat varieties selected for their potential to build Mexico a better *mañana*. These 49 very short rows were clustered together for convenience when he'd mingle all their genes after the flowering began in July.

Slated for that ménage were:

- The Mentana and Marroqui samples from Sonora;
- Three commercial Mexican varieties gathered by Harrar;
- Seed from 38 envelopes Stakman had mailed from Minnesota; and
- Six lots from an obscure Texas professor named Edgar McFadden.

Late in May Borlaug was standing beside the Tarpaper Shack when he received a jab from a bony elbow: "Let's go to the Bajío," Ed Wellhausen urged, "and put in a breeding nursery."

Norm agreed with alacrity. While his seedlings were getting their grip

BEASTS OF BURDEN

Pepe Rodríguez pulls the plow, Jose Guevara pushes, Ed Wellhausen awaits his turn. With neither tractor nor animals to plow the land at Chapingo in 1945, the researchers harnessed themselves to the plow. Enduring heat and insects, they turned the soil for the miles of rows of corn, beans and wheat that began the enterprise that would end up changing the world's food supply. Rodríguez and Guevara made up the first of what would become Borlaug's many hunger-fighter squads.

on the ground he could spend a few weeks investigating the OEE's designated target zone. Though the Bajío had furnished most of Mexico's food for centuries, he'd not yet set foot there.

The sight of the six pastoral plateau states seemed to end the gringo observers' last hope. The region teetered between the modern and the medieval. Infections, diarrhea, malaria and malnutrition were rampant enough to rank child mortality among the worst ever recorded. Nearly half who died had yet to enjoy a fifth birthday. And kids lucky enough to beat the odds faced forlorn prospects. Parents typically yanked them from school at the age of eight or nine and yoked them to family activities, including caring for younger siblings, collecting firewood, tending animals. As a consequence, from every five Bajío inhabitants only one could read or write.

The acceptance of poverty's cruelties was the most discouraging feature. Women and girls spent their days collecting water and preparing food, mostly corn, which they ground between two flat stones. Seeing they were going to marry and churn out children along with the butter, what point was there in hoping for more out of life?

To Borlaug the farming operations were both foreign and familiar. They were basically those his family had gleefully jettisoned more than ten years before.

Men and boys in May 1945 were planting corn, beans, chili, and squash. Some used a wooden plow pulled by a burro or an ox. Most remained manacled to the machete, the hoe, and the sickle for the weeds.

This experience chastened. They'd come to strengthen crops. But culture was the more corrosive factor, quashing prospects for progress and keeping the society trapped in poverty.

With this disquiet disturbing their minds the two agriculturists prepared to sow Wellhausen's corn nursery on the contours of a borrowed hillside high above the city of Celaya.

Although their mutual attachment was tightening, the sun was attempting to tear them apart. It burned on and on with atomic zest. Bajío summers normally supply regular afternoon showers, and the pair awoke each morning hoping for rain. Each evening, however, arrived without hint of cloud shadow. Nowadays we'd call it the *El Niño* effect, and it was frightful. Land cracked. Plants shriveled. Reservoirs, rivers and lakes disguised themselves as mudflats. The nearby city actually ran out of electricity until the U.S. military railed in a power plant mounted on a train for Celaya's 100,000 inhabitants.

Though weather's willfulness affects all farmers, this endless wait showed Borlaug just how low life could go:

> For a week we stayed in small hotels. The food was bad; the water worse; the flies were terrible. I got sick. We boiled our water but could do little else; sulfa drugs were coming onto the market in the U.S. but not in Mexico. I got sicker. Some nights I lay in my bedroll writhing with pain and faint with nausea.

One evening he sat leaning against the car's dusty wood paneling and penciled Margaret a note explaining why he hadn't returned on schedule:

> These places I've seen have clubbed my mind—they are so poor and depressing. The earth is so lacking in life force; the plants just cling to existence. They don't really grow; they just fight to stay alive. The levels of nourishment in the soil are so low that wheat plants produce only a few grains. Even the weeds and diseases and insects lack the food to be aggressive. No wonder the people are the way

MEXICO'S BREADBASKET . . .

Wheat farmers in the Bajío before Borlaug arrived. This vast upland (which included parts of six states: San Luis Potosí, Guanajuato, Querétaro, Michoacán, Jalisco and Aguascalientes) comprised Mexico's breadbasket. These so-called "scrub wheats" were miscellaneous mixtures differing in qualities and needs. The stands were thin, susceptible to disease, and hard to manage and harvest. Every operation was done by hand. Yields seldom reached 500lb an acre.

. . . RUNNING ON EMPTY

The Bajío in the mid-1940s has been described as a lost world, without clocks, calendars, cinema, newspapers, books, electricity or appliances. It also had no sanitation. Even farmers lived hand to mouth. Millions went hungry. Out of Mexico's 22 million citizens, 16 million suffered extreme poverty. More than a million went barefoot; more than 4 million had only *huaraches*, a crude sandal. Mexico had only 1 bed for every four people; only 1 radio for every 70.

they are. Can you imagine a poor Mexican struggling to feed his family? I don't know what we can do to help but we've got to do something.

Back at Chapingo Borlaug settled in to managing almost 9000 rows of wheat plants, and he was mighty relieved when Harrar assigned two more helpers.

The fact that the newcomers wore skirts was a surprise; *never before* had women been allowed to participate in agricultural research. Machismo barred females from the professions (the modern ones that is), and naturally never trusted a woman with the vote. By now, though, sexism had begun triggering shame. Within 12 months—that is, in 1946—Mexico's other half would finally get to cast a ballot.

Still and all the right to vote didn't mean the right to work, so Harrar took it on himself to bring gender justice to agricultural research. His problem was finding candidates. OEE recruited its trainees from the nearby agriculture college but being partly operated by the Army it remained a mainstay of manhood.

Lacking any alternative, Harrar approached the National Polytechnic Institute as well as the Autonomous University of Mexico and hired two recent biology graduates. Angela Melendez and Marta Zenteno made their mark on history surveying endless rows of Borlaug's wheat plots during the long hot summer of '45.

Through a seemingly endless summer Pepe, José, Marta, Angela and Norm moved up and down thousands of mini-rows, searching the stems for the eruptions known as rust pustules. They also felt the leaf tissues, seeking signs of leaf rust, stripe rust, smut or scab. And they recorded thousands of observations and measurements in their notebooks.

During that growing season Norm ruthlessly ripped out every obvious loser, thereby exposing his most important talent: the ability to assess a plant and act instantly. His trigger finger remained forever itchy, and in time he'll unceremoniously end the lives of plants by the millions. Ousting underperforming specimens is called "roguing," and it's a major reason why so few farm acres can feed modern mankind.

Between Borlaug and the students the vital team spirit developed slowly. Although he attracts devotees like a diva, the youngsters who signed on that summer of '45 started out defiantly distant. He chuckles at the memory:

In the beginning they came to work dressed in suits and shiny

TECHNICAL CHALLENGES, 1945

Round 1 (May-October, 1945). He is 31 and a food-crop research rookie.

STEM-RUST RESISTANCE. In Round 1 Borlaug aims to find a way to keep stem-rust from mugging Mexico while he creates better replacements. During this summer in Chapingo's newly formed fields he'll plant and manage 8500 separate local types as well as the best commercial varieties from the U.S. and Canada. Toward the end of this summer season billions of rust spores will descend. He hopes some of his plants will survive. Those he'll use to hold the food frontier.

In addition, he'll organize a planting in which (when the flowering season arrives) he can breed building blocks for more productive wheats. The small and special planting involves:

- Mexico's top commercial varieties (Aguilera, Candeal, Pelon Colorado);
- Mentana and Marroqui (discovered by accident in Sonora);
- 44 stateside varieties possessing good rust resistance; and
- Canada's brightest stars (Regent and Renown).

He hopes to eventually combine Mexican climatic compatibility, Gringo rust resistance and Canadian flour quality into varieties that are safe from stem rust and yield more food and better food than any wheats Mexico knows.

At this point Norm and wheat are strangers who've met but not yet worked together.

shoes. By going to college they'd earned a place in society, and they wanted everyone to know.

His own battledress was khakis and shabby work boots, and his first lesson was that working with your hands rather than your head was honorable. Even the privileged should soil their fingers for the food supply. Dignity could be found in fieldwork—not to mention muddy boots and sweat-stained shirts.

For a while it was a hard sell. "Dr Borlaug, we don't do these things," Pepe Rodríguez growled in frustration. "You should draw up the plans and take them to the foreman and let the *peones* do the work."

At that point Borlaug lost his temper. "If we don't do things ourselves," he snapped, "how can we advise anyone? How can we ever be certain of our ground?"

Thanks to the power of his words and the power of his work ethic, the students took to wearing khakis and boots. Nonetheless on the bus to work they toted the embarrassing evidence in a bag. Soon, though, it turned into a personal trademark. Freed of the mental fetters of societal conformity, those hunger warriors were walking tall. Casting off style, they took on substance, and wore their dusty work clothes for all to admire.

D rudgery's demand for daylight required that he sleep in the Tarpaper Shack to devote the hour-and-a-half commuting time to more drudgery. Typically, he waited a week before heading home for a change of clothes, a change of diet and a hot bath—all by then long past due.

The Tarpaper Shack had not been designed with sleeping in mind. His lodgings therefore resembled those occupied during nightmares:

> The only place to lie down was the dirt floor, and I got fairly used to feeling mice scamper over the sleeping bag. I cooked on an open fire fueled by corncobs. With no hotel or restaurant nearby, there was no alternative. José Guevara sometimes stayed too. We'd rise before the sun jumped over the eastern mountains and begin working while the leaves were still heavy with dew. That was less than ideal but daylight was too precious to squander.

Insects made the subsequent hours so inhumane some ardent agency or activist would nowadays outlaw this workplace:

> As the heat rose, we'd have flies buzzing our faces and maybe a mosquito or ten biting our ankles. Beyond those aggravations, there were *rodeodores*—tiny flies that imbibed so much of our blood they could no longer fly; we'd watch them roll off our arm and flop to the ground. Worse were *no-see-ums*, a kind of gnat that prefers eyes but often zooms up the nostrils. They made life more miserable than mosquitoes, which at least had the sense to stay in the shade during the heat of the day.

Mexico's overwrought sun, a fireball that glowed from misty dawn until merciful dusk, delivered the ultimate misery. For those sweatshop scientists perspiration poured by the hour. And the chronic afternoon winds kicked up almost unbearable clouds of dust that hovered head-high, mixed with sweat, and caked the brow with mud.

Given the lofty elevation and limpid skies, the group needed protection from the sun. Initially they adopted the local favorite, a wide-brimmed straw hat. Later they moved to baseball caps, which bettered the blustery afternoon breezes and could be swung to meet the sun as it surfed the sky. Shocking to a society mistrustful of all things gringo, baseball caps became the Borlaug team's badge of honor.

S triding the lines at season's end, he found that rust had won Round 1 by a knockout. That October, *every* Mexican plant—all 8500 scrub wheats as well as the best formal varieties displayed angry red, yellow, orange or black rust pustules.

The implications were scary to contemplate. Those plants occupied most of Mexico's 1.25 million wheat acres, and all were rotted to their roots. Therefore whenever the weather turned warm and moist the microbial manipulator could maul every wheat-growing region upon which the capricious breezes chose to fling the flying stem-rust spores.

That knowledge stabbed like a knife. The country's food supply was on life support. Even during the winter season it was unsafe.

This is a silent crisis that only he recognizes. He's Mexico's sole wheat scientist. Solving it is his responsibility.

Sadly, most of the American wheats were goners too. Of the 49, only four withstood the summer sizzle and fall spore showers. Despite their modest yields and other faults, Norm is more than satisfied. These, his Foundation Foursome, can hold the fort as well as be the bricks for the dike he needs to build to keep the microbe from mugging Mexico:

> That summer of '45 four plants showed good resistance to stem rust. By our later standards, they were not high yielding but they surpassed Mexico's existing wheats. So I decided to start with them.

Two of those living dead arose from Stakman's seed packets. A matched pair, Kenya Red and Kenya White, were named for their country of origin and their seed colors. A wheat breeder named Gerald Burton, working in the East African highlands in the 1930s, had created them by cross-pollinating various European, Australian and Moroccan varieties. Their rust-resistance likely derived from durum, the wheat species that produces pasta. No one's sure of that because records had burned along with the Kenya Experiment Station's field house. Only by luck were a handful of seeds saved from the blaze. And only by dumb luck did a few of those reach an Australian who by happenstance had studied with Stakman and felt obliged to share a few with his venerated mentor. On such a slender chain of coincidence rests our own food.

The other Round 1 survivors arose from the obscure Texas professor's six envelopes. These will also influence history's course, so with the calendar curving over toward 1946, we interrupt the main story for a detour of indebtedness to a wheat-gene genius no one knows: Edgar McFadden.

L ike most of those peopling these pages, Edgar McFadden didn't look like a Hunger Warrior. In a wheatfield it was easy to miss this rather nondescript academic whose head barely topped his seedheads. Typically he sported rimless glasses, a fedora, a sharp stare and an aura of bitterness. This last habiliment arose from a career spent fighting for respect. His sin: no PhD followed his name.

McFadden discovered his calling when he read about Luther Burbank developing the Idaho potato (a variant of which provides our French fries even today). That epiphany occurred in 1904 when McFadden was a prototypical prairie boy helping out the family on its farm near Webster, South Dakota. Later that fateful year the family bull gored his father, so little Edgar had to step into the big shoes, become man of the house, and tend the wheat crop. He was all of twelve.

As the growing season advanced the pre-teen protege reveled in the joy of witnessing wheat heads swelling with the gilt-edged promise of 40 bushels an acre. For him, it was a personal high and, like most such highs, proved a hoax. That fall, the stem rust fungus delivered its worst fury in a quarter century. The kid in knee britches, his mind on fire and his skin charred from a season in the sun, watched as the silent spook laid waste to his fields, his folk's fortunes, and his fantasy of being as fine a figure as his father.

Though any breadwinner bears a fearsome responsibility, this impressionable kid with his kinfolk's future on his back found the setback mind-bending. The eventual harvest—5 bushels an acre—forced his family to flee the familiar world. Trusting they'd find better circumstances in heathen lands a thousand miles southward, they headed for the hill country of West Texas.

Forever after, Edgar dreamed of foiling the fungus that had felled his family. Then in 1911, when he was 19 and in yet another devastating rust epidemic, he spied a patch of emmer vibrant with strength and vigor.

A distant wheat relation, emmer ranked as little more than a weed. However in ancient days it had fed Greeks, Romans, Egyptians and more. At the time of Christ it was the main wheat of the world, so the bread broken at the Last Supper probably was baked from emmer flour.

In the Middle Ages emmer fell from the food supply. Its first fault was to produce flat bread, which lost out to the astounding raised loaves produced by the modern interloper. Its second fault arose late in the growing season when a spell of hot weather caused the stems to break, dropping the grain onto the dirt.

But in 1911 those seemed mere trifles; McFadden was mesmerized by the fact that wheat's country cousin stood tall in the face of stem rust. Alas, the genes conferring that immunity were beyond reach. Emmer (*Triticum dicoccum*) and bread wheat (*Triticum aestivum*) belong to different branches of the family tree. They flower at different times. Moreover, their pollen is incompatible, since emmer cells contain 28 chromosomes to bread wheat's 42.

Nevertheless, the obdurate 19-year-old determined to test Nature's separation of the species. Others considered him crazy. He himself doubted his sanity, once likening his chances to a nickel cigar: "because only one in a thousand is worth a nickel."

Craziest of all, he chose to go for the gold by mating emmer to the greatest bread-wheat of all time: Marquis.

Marquis, like many crop varieties, arose more by accident than actual intent. Its formal beginnings hearken way back to 1842 when a Scottish immigrant decided to cultivate wheat at his new homestead 80 miles north of Toronto. Writing to a friend he'd left behind in Glasgow, David Fife requested seed wheat. It was a forlorn hope: A crucible of the Industrial Revolution, Glasgow was a place where seed wheat was less common than silverware. However, when strolling the city's Clydeside docks one evening, the friend spied a few grains spilled during the unloading of a ship (likely just in from Ukraine). Thinking they looked like wheat, he slipped a few into the lining of his cap.

On Fife's place near the village of Otenabee, only five of the mystery seeds produced plants that flowered. Then, according to the best story, a wandering cow ate two and was about to enjoy the rest for dessert when Mrs Fife happened to glance out the window. Charging from her kitchen, flapping her apron and screaming abuse, she changed the course of history because the three saved plants went on to provide the first blockbuster cereal. Indeed, in the second half of the 1800s Red Fife, as the variety was called, provided the plinth beneath Canada's success, including its 1867 elevation from British Dependency to self-standing Dominion.

Despite buttressing a burgeoning nation, Red Fife was far from faultless. A miller's delight? Yes. A baker's dream? Yes. A farmer's fancy? No. In Canada's latitudes, where Jack Frost often sneaks in early to enjoy a few weeks of fall, the fields sometimes died before their time. For the growers that was too much to bear. Having invested dollars, dreams and drudgery only to have everything freeze in the final fortnight was more than frustrating . . . it was fatal to the finances.

To circumvent this elemental flaw, Canadian scientists crossbred Red Fife with wheats hailing from the general vicinity of Mount Everest which, so they figured, should know how to handle Jack Frost. In the 1890s, for example, the brothers Charles and Arthur Saunders interbred Red Fife with Hard Red Calcutta, and the winning merger they named "Marquis."

From the start Marquis proved a star. As the 20th Century got underway, the great wheat-growing provinces Manitoba and Saskatchewan embraced it not just because it matured before Jack Frost could come a-calling but also because it out-yielded Red Fife and its super-elastic dough raised loaves to the heavens. Indeed, the soft and spongy bread was so delectable the public could hardly stop eating it.

Although wheat was already Prince of the Prairies, this billion-to-one gene jewel propelled Canada into the top ranks of food-producers. By 1915 trains totaling a thousand freight cars trundled through Winnipeg *daily*, slowing just enough for giant grain silos, properly spaced out alongside the tracks, to dump in a load of Marquis in one huge whump!

The sight of such prosperity was not lost on the otherwise purblind viewers over the southern horizon. "Farmers and also millers, bankers, and real-estate dealers have had their attention attracted to it," a Department of Agriculture bulletin reported in 1913. Within a year Marquis had colonized half a million acres of American heartland.

All this demonstrates yet again that civilization is only as good as a seed. In 1904 the Saunders brothers had given the world 23 pounds of Marquis seed; a decade onward, hundreds of thousands of farmers were annually providing almost 7 million tons to millions of consumers in dozens of countries were enjoying fluffy fabrications bakers fashioned from the classy new upwardly mobile flour.

This is why Marquis's downfall in 1916 forced the Feds to impose wheatless Mondays and Wednesdays. North American—perhaps even Western—society then depended on this crusty Canadian. When rust ripped out that societal support the resulting collapse sent ripples running around the globe. For one thing, thousands of farmers abandoned wheat. For another, thousands more shifted to durum wheat, which previously had satisfied a strictly ethnic segment of North America's diet. "Macaroni," you see, had been widely scorned. Now, solely because the durum plant could withstand the 1916 rust, this ethnic specialty ascended into the mainstream. Eventually, it would become a darling of the Western diet, producing what we nowadays prefer to call "pasta."

In his quest to mate the modern high-rise wheat to the almost forgotten flat wheat beloved by Jesus and Judas, Edgar McFadden sensed progress in 1917. A few years earlier, while at college in Brookings, South Dakota, he'd coaxed the landlady into donating a section of the garden behind her rooming house on the southwest corner of 8th Avenue and 9th Street. In that tiny plot between the peonies he'd planted short rows of emmer and Marquis. That particular year the plants inexplicably, bloomed at the same time. One day that July, tweezering with urgent fingers he removed every pollen sac from half the emmer flowers and half the Marquis flowers, leaving those plants solely female. Then a few days later he brushed Marquis pollen onto the feminized emmer flowers and emmer pollen onto the feminized Marquis flowers.

The result, that fall was several hundred horribly shriveled seeds, which for safekeeping he stashed in a coffee can.

When the coffee-can's contents were sown in the spring of 1917 only one plant emerged. This single progeny of original cereal sin flowered, self-pollinated properly, and by season's end had ripened 100 seeds of its own making. Those still-shriveled scions were unique in bearing genes of two biologically incompatible *Triticum* species.

In the spring of 1918 the now 26-year-old student sowed his manmade misfits at the Webster farm, which his folks had retained. Within weeks, though, his prospects for furthering the freaky seedlings hit a snag when he graduated from college and was rewarded with a call to the colors.

With McFadden doing Army duty on the Pacific coast, the five-score specimens hiding in the hills of South Dakota should have been lost to history. Luckily for us the new recruit persuaded his commanding officer to bestow a "harvest furlough." Apparently, he neglected to explain that unlike other farm boys he needed to get all the way to South Dakota to harvest four rows 12 feet long. His furlough was for science, not society.

Back in Webster that October, McFadden found that his specimens had segregated into two basic forms—some resembled emmer and were practically stem-rust free; the rest resembled Marquis and were practically dead. He'd gotten nowhere. However, by checking plant by plant he located two Marquis lookalikes that remained rust free. Against all odds, the 27-year-old dabbler had done the unthinkable and got emmer genes into bread-wheat chromosomes. Under his identification system the magical pair were H49-24 and H44. Lovingly storing their 200 seeds in two carefully labeled coffee cans, he dutifully returned to boot camp for more training to fight, perhaps to die, in France.

However, within a month it was World War I that died. McFadden shuffled back to South Dakota to join the U.S. Department of Agriculture. On the side, though, he kept building his brainchild.

The offspring should have been as sterile as mules; instead, H49-24 and H44 flowered and fertilized themselves as if free of original sin. That fall, with eager gaze, he scrutinized the resulting segregates. Every plant expressed the genetic havoc inherent in its hybrid heritage but a few showed portent of potential. Their seeds he saved.

For two more years he sowed his perverted prospects, each time using seed only from the most precocious and most perfect looking plants. Then in 1921 disaster struck when the USDA abolished his day job.

Newly married, McFadden should have sought gainful employment. Instead, he retreated to Webster to continue the quest. He was betting his family's future that he could farm normal wheat to pay the bills.

During the early 1920s farming wheat in South Dakota was far from easy. In 1921 his fields succumbed to drought . . . in 1922 to hail . . . in 1923 to rust. Each was a bad experience but the 1923 epidemic proved Day County's worst calamity. For the world, though, it proved a godsend. The sight of his small test plots growing tall and strong amid the deluge of rust spores that had collapsed the commercial crop re-energized McFadden. He now knew he could beat wheat's greatest foe.

Nonetheless, there was still far to go. His creations could foil the fungus but had no other redeeming quality: The grain was light, the chaff black, the flour dark. A sane person would have quit. Instead, McFadden mortgaged the farm to finance a course of backcrossing. For five more growing seasons he struggled to improve his progeny by punching up Marquis's contribution without knocking out emmer's rust-fighting role.

Obsession was now in charge. Neighbors saw him at night sitting in the small plots beside the house, communing with his creations until he dropped off to sleep on the dirt. No wonder they considered him unhinged.

And worse was to come. The quirky crank next descended to the despicable depths of a plant abuser. Having pampered his prized specimens inside a greenhouse, he then ramped up the heat and humidity to help the fungus do its damndest. He even carried diseased wheat stems into this chamber of horrors and drenched his cherished beauties with the vilest cocktail of contagions he could cook up.

It all worked. By the spring of 1925 Edgar McFadden could show the world two wheat varieties that reliably resisted stem rust while also producing quantities of quality grain.

Despite having invested almost 20 years of effort, the eccentric recluse didn't try to cash in. Dividing the seeds into packets of 25, he mailed them to wheat breeders across the U.S. and Canada—*without charge.*

That's how things were done in those backward days. On perhaps a dozen experiment stations grateful researchers sowed the seeds and throughout the 1926 season scanned the plants with anxious stares. As the summer advanced their spirits soared, buoyed by an overwhelming sense of deliverance. McFadden's bequests remained robust.

Of the two strains, H49-24 outperformed its brother. McFadden christened it "Hope," and in 1927 formally released its seed for commercial cultivation. It seemed like a miracle, being so rust-resistant that seed firms offered a dollar for every rust spot any farmer could find.

There were no takers.

Nonetheless history soon found a way to hijack Hope. The early '30s happened to be the time when Stakman and Hayes were creating the bread wheat designed to resist the four killer races of rust. They too started with Marquis but added extra defiance from durum, which, although a separate species (*Triticum turgidum*), occurs on the same branch of the family tree and shares many of bread wheat's chromosomes. This Minnesota-bred gene combo was released in 1935, the year that dealt yet more disaster to the food supply. That fall, United States and Canada together lost 8 million tons of grain as rust reached out and turned the genetic key one more turn and retook the house of wheat for its own habitation.

By that time Marquis's successor, Ceres, dominated northern wheat belt, and its demise left the Midwest even more depopulated and destitute than the Depression. In 1935 U.S. railroads hauled 75,000 fewer freight cars of wheat to market and hauled almost nothing back. Stuck in survival mode, Midwesterners had nothing to spend.

Yet amid the square miles of dead wheat two sturdy ramparts stood tall: one stemming from McFadden, the other from Stakman and Hayes.

McFadden's Hope lost the popularity contest owing mainly to emmer's bad genes. Farmers cursed whenever torrid fall weather caused the stems to snap and drop the year's prospects into the dust. Millers freaked out whenever the grain was shriveled, which meant the mills were often in turmoil. And bakers denounced the flour for insufficient gluten to bestow the high-rise delights demanded by the millions of Marquis-mavens.

By contrast, Midwesterners quickly embraced Stakman's miracle plant named Thatcher.

But no wheat breeder ditched McFadden's creation. They adopted

CAREER SAVER #14

Fate's 14th facilitator, Edgar McFadden. Though nowadays forgotten, this self-taught amateur helped protect the world's wheat crop from stem rust for the better part of a century. By breaking the most basic rule of biology, he introduced genes from emmer, an ancient wheat that hadn't been eaten for a thousand years. In 1945 the self-effacing and soft-spoken McFadden donated seeds to a supplicant in Mexico he'd never heard of. Without that gift Borlaug could not have succeeded. In the end, Norm introduced the genes McFadden had teased out of ancient emmer into the wheat crop worldwide, thereby improving the security of modern mankind.

TECHNICAL PROGRESS, 1945

By the close of Round 1 in November '45 he's trialed almost 9000 distinct plants. Four have survived their life-or-death final. This Foundation Foursome includes two gifts from Edgar McFadden (a Texas A&M professor) and two from E.C. Stakman (Norm's former professor at the University of Minnesota). Though far from great, Frontera, Supremo and the Red- and White-seeded Kenyas seem capable of holding the line against rust for at least a few years.

That fall's haul also included seeds derived from his first fumbling attempts at mating wheat. That stash of 500 separate seedheads (containing about 100,000 seeds) constitutes his Generation-1. He'll not know what gems it might contain until he's planted and replanted the seeds season after season for several years, each time identifying the best plants and replanting *only* their seed.

Also in this rookie season Borlaug has discovered his first basic lesson on hunger fighting: *help the whole society eat better; you'll then have many supporters when difficulties and demonizers try to prevent your success.*

By the end of their first time together wheat and Borlaug are still species apart. Indeed, wheat seems to be treating him with doubt, maybe disdain.

Hope not just as a gene supplier but as a savior. Although a poor performer, it proved a powerful parent. Blessed with wheat's normal 42-chromosome set, it could endow other varieties additional anti-fungal protection. The genes a college kid had combined in a single seed in the borrowed backyard of a South Dakota boarding house eventually spread to millions of farms worldwide. In time, this improbable botanical baby provided humanity's top crop a uniquely powerful body armor.

Despite all this, McFadden continued to be treated with disdain. Stakman was the only wheat scientist Norm knows who openly admired this diffident, defensive almost deadpan colleague. But by then Stak had personally experienced the man's worth. In the late 1930s he crossed Hope to his famous Thatcher. The result was Newthatch, which—due to its double dose of rust resistance—became the main gene-mix sustaining society and bestowing the huge grain surpluses during World War II. To take just one of the war years, 1943's wheat production in the U.S. totaled almost 23 million tons—an increase of almost 3 million tons over blissful peaceful 1939.

After transferring to Texas A&M University in 1935 McFadden crossbred his brainchild with wheats from around the world adding extra rust-protection to each. Among Hope's many marriage partners was a collection of Mediterranean winter wheats, whose matings spawned wildly dissimilar offspring. The six seed lots the meek matchmaker mailed to Mexico nine years later actually derived from a complex cross between Hope, Mediterranean, and Frondoza (a variety from Brazil).

Whilst packing up that envelope McFadden surely considered it a waste. Of all the wheat breeders he'd supplied during his career, this was by far the least promising. Borlaug was not only a nonentity, he was misguided enough to work in a country lacking any prospect for wheat.

For Mexico, though, the gift would prove a godsend. As we've said, when Norm surveyed the outcome of his preliminary trials in the fall of 1945 McFadden's specimens stood tall by surviving both the stem-rust spore showers and the summer heat of Central Mexico.

These two are key greeters in the momentous meeting between Borlaug and wheat. They were, however, far from perfect. The seeds came from experimental lines, and the plants surviving Round 1 were each unique. Thus when the Day of Judgment arrived in October Norm had to check each individual plant. All but two were junked, and the specific seeds he carried forward came from the 209th and 211th plants he happened to check. He called the pair Frontera and Supremo.

3

1946
A Change of Latitude

Throughout the summer of '45 Norm pressed his case for Sonora. That northern wilderness, he explained to all and sundry, offered nearly a million acres of flat land ranking among Mexico's most fertile. Yes, the annual rainfall was merely 7 inches but irrigation was expanding. Yes, rust was rampant but suppress that disease and Sonora farmers would grow more grain than the national granary could hold.

Beyond challenging contractual obligations, his proposal threatens bankruptcy. OEE's budget was too limited to encompass work in a remote backwater. Borlaug couldn't possibly go!

On that decision, management was adamant. Twice he was chided with firmness—not to say finality. "Sonora doesn't need our help," Harrar declared in his most armor-piercing tones. "Our focus is the Bajío . . . *That's where the poor farmers are!*"

Between these two, relations were getting rockier. Harrar's sharp stare now turned passive as he pulled up the poker face previously deployed only against pushy Mexican officials. Norm still puzzles over it:

> Sometimes I couldn't tell what George was thinking behind that cold glare.

Still the fact remained that he was forbidden to work where he might place Mexico's food supply on a firm foundation. Then one night the answer sprang to attention. By using the old experiment station he could fit in a second round of research *during the off season.* Following the fall harvest at Chapingo he'd rush the winning seeds north for replanting in Sonora. By late spring he'd have a new generation of winners, whose seeds he'd rush south for planting on schedule at Chapingo. He'd thereby complete his designated duties in full accord with contractual demands

TECHNICAL CHALLENGES, 1946

Round 2 (Nov 1945-April 1946). First stint in Sonora. In March he turns 32.

Here's where Borlaug and wheat must work together:

STEM-RUST RESISTANCE. His prime effort is a make-or-break test for Round 1's winners—the four that survived last summer's sizzle and rust storms.
The season is also about building a backup generation. For this, he grows out the 140,000 seeds produced by the flowers he crossbred last summer, merely letting the plants sort out their mixed up juvenile genes.
Also he plants a new crossing block wherein (at flowering time) he'll cross-pollinate Round 1's winning quartet with wheats that might improve behavior.

MULTI-LOCATION ROAD-TESTS. Besides Sonora he sows the promising quartet in three locations scattered across the country (La Piedad, Torreón and Saltillo) using the exact same seed and set up. This is their final exam. At season's end, on his way home from Sonora, he'll visit each site, and make his go/no go decision.

Round 3 (May-October, 1946). Second stint in Central Mexico.

MULTIPLICATION. This summer, he'll bulk up the four winners (assuming they've aced their finals).

STEM-RUST RESISTANCE. At Chapingo he'll also let his crossbred plants sort out their inner genetic conflicts. And he'll make yet another generation of candidates for the even farther horizons.

while also squeezing in twice as many rounds with rust, and working where he might foil any possibility of a new visit from famine.

For the family, this sequence would be hurtful. He'd be separated from Margaret and Jeanie for months on end. He'd be at the other end of the country from his colleagues *for half the year*. He'd never get a vacation. For a few midwinter weeks, when the plants needed no attention, he might dash home for Christmas with the family. That's all.

Everyone else, however, could benefit hugely. By perfecting varieties in half the time he'd likely forestall the return of rust and possibly calm the volcano rumbling beneath the restive society. Moreover, just maybe the top brass behind the barbed-wire in New York wouldn't realize he was "moonlighting" off the reservation half the time.

The fact that his six-month jaunts would be off the books made the difference. George Harrar agreed to a test run. However, Norm would have no financial support, no staff, no facilities, no accommodations, no farm machinery, no vehicle. In the distant desert he'd be alone, without help, without implements, and without anyone knowing.

That November he flew north for this clandestine test. Along with the clothes in his suitcase were carefully packed the 200 seeds from Frontera as well as the 200 from Supremo. In there too were a couple of thousand seeds harvested from the dozen or so Kenya Red and Kenya White plants. Beyond those are numerous small packets carrying seed from the winners of his first cross-breeding experiments.

In total, the seeds add maybe 5 pounds to his luggage. They also carry the weight of the world.

Already hearing footsteps, he resolves to give full responsibility for rust-proofing Mexico's wheat to the Kenya pair and the wobbly duo called Frontera and Supremo. After one more season of testing he'll begin bulking up their seed for release to farmers.

This took courage. On the basis of brief trials at Chapingo and Sonora he's betting his reputation these four will perform for farmers.

It took courage too because he's bucking professional principle. You see, breeding crops sequentially in separate locations and different seasons is absolutely, positively verboten. Professors and textbooks are in complete accord: varieties *must* be developed where they'll be grown by farmers. Indeed, research plantings must be sown *on the same day farmers use*. Every agricultural school hammered that message home. To ignore such a seminal commandment was to squander all hope of success.

Since his initial visit nine months earlier Sonora is unchanged. The facilities remain foul; creature comforts a fantasy. This time, though, he's here for several months. He's a thousand miles from family and friends. He's unable to communicate, since there's no phone and he knows no Spanish. He's trapped, since George Harrar's denial of a vehicle means he can't leave. There's no access to a market, or groceries. And there's no safe water for drinking or hot water for bathing.

Heck, there's not even a bathroom or a bedroom. The best spot for sleeping was the loft above a ramshackle storage shed. Climbing the ladder, he unfolds a canvas cot amid a décor that includes moldering sacks of long-abandoned grain. As one of the ground-floor walls is merely wire mesh, he must share his shelter with mosquitoes, mice, rats and snakes. He still shudders at the recollection:

Thank God I'd been a forester and learned to live alone in the wilderness. Without that I'd either have quit Sonora or gone completely mad.

Though austerity and sacrifice are central to his being, it helps that he returns each night exhausted. Having pried open a can of food, heated it

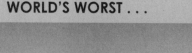

WORLD'S WORST . . .

El Yaqui Experiment Station. For his stints in Sonora, Borlaug chose to live and work all by himself in this remote research station. Here, he had no help, no tractor, no equipment, no sanitation, no running water or stove and no accommodations other than a tumble-down building with no windows but an abundance of rats, among which he spends his nights with a sleeping bag pulled tight over his head! The photo was taken in 1951, after the place had been tidied up. His wheat plantings occupy large blocks on both sides of the road.

together with some coffee over smoldering corncobs and snatched a moment to eat, he collapses into the sleeping bag—regardless of the debris or the denizens sharing his abode.

Actually, the field facilities limited his activities even more. Without machinery, the plots must be planted and managed by hand.

On the third day, as he hoed lumpy soil over the rows, he noticed a visitor striding purposefully toward him. An imposing character, the newcomer towered almost six feet, with a powerful build, barrel chest and rough strong hands. Between the lines on his face there was much to read, though Norm didn't divine that fact till much later. Despite advancing age, the old timer seemed in ruddy health. Strangely, under the sombrero, steel-rimmed glasses and somber stare, he wore a suit. Stranger still, a pair of dusty work boots peeped from below his properly pressed trouser cuffs.

"Buenos días, Señor. I am Aureliano Campoy." The English was good

. . . WORKSITE

In 2008, he recalled his life here: *"When I arrived in 1945, the original Yaqui valley experiment station was in shambles. There was no machinery left, no electricity, and the windows were broken. Nevertheless, that's where I stayed, sleeping on a cot and cooking over an outdoor stove. The station superintendent, Ricardo Leon Manso, had little or no budget but was still eager to support our work."* **The cabin Norm occupied is one of those down the left hand side. The loft in which he slept is behind the trees in the center.**

but accented and ponderous. "I live there," he jerked a finger back over a shoulder. "I see you work like a peon. What is it you do here? And why do you work on the Lord's Day?"

The young scientist explained he hoped to create better wheats for farmers, a claim that elicited a scornful snort. That evening in a letter to Margaret Norm wrote:

> I don't think he believed me but I know he was very curious. I had seen him watching me work from across the road. I told him I was making new wheats for farmers and—glory be—he will let me have his tractor and some implements next weekend.

Two Saturdays later Norm was perched on Campoy's dinky little Farmall tractor focusing on getting straight rows when a surprisingly modern Chevrolet sedan swept through the stone gates. He watched in fascination as the driver extricated herself. Big-shouldered, heavy, with strong, bare, freckled arms, the lady was no longer young but nonetheless oddly eye-catching.

As the tractor clattered to the end of the row the newcomer turned and waved a beckoning arm. Her confidence and ease were appealing, and he guessed she'd be in her late 60s. "You must be the crazy American my foreman has been telling me about," she yelled. "I'm Cathy Jones, and I hear you're without transportation. I'm heading to town for groceries. Care to ride along?"

There and then he grabbed the chance to not only acquire the week's meager needs but also converse in colloquial English.

B y November's end Norm had sown the five-acre nursery. By mid-December the seedlings were emerging, strong and healthy. Now with a three-week window of freedom from fieldwork, he headed south for a quiet Christmas with the kinfolk.

As the Panini plane took to the skies he relived his previous exhilaration: The winter trials are underway. He's found a couple of friends. Although still unsure of himself, he's making acquaintance with wheat. And Sonora is the perfect place for him.

The exhilaration proved fleeting. On reaching the apartment all sense of satisfaction subsided when, in Margaret's strained face, he read the sorrow beyond words.

They held each other, close in their grief . . . and relief. Margaret slowly disengaged herself. "I prayed he'd go in his sleep, without pain. And they said he did. He never had a chance, poor little thing."

She described wanting to rush to the airport, to fly off to be at her baby's side. But the doctor who'd phoned told her not to come. It would be best, he said, to keep the memory as it was. Besides, she knew that after paying the fare there'd be nothing left for the funeral and final hospital bills.

Borlaug consoled her. "It will get better with time," he said. But each knew their scars were carved on conscience.

That night he lay sleepless and again perilously close to cracking. This was another testing time: He'd not had a single professional success. He'd jeopardized his family's health, happiness and hopes. He'd alienated his esteemed boss. And now there was this engulfing sense of loss for the child he'd neither touched nor talked to—and who'd died so far away he couldn't even attend the funeral or pay his last respects.

Tears smarted in his eyes.

In a scientific paper written decades later, he recalled his unhappiness:

> Many times during the [first] four years, frustrated by unavail-
> ability of machinery and equipment, without the assistance of
> trained scientists, traveling over bad roads, living in miserable hotels,
> eating bad food, often sick with diarrhea and unable to commun-
> icate because of lack of command of the language, I was certain I
> had made a dreadful mistake in resigning from my former position.

Scientists are not supposed to possess (or at least expose) sentiment.
Never in formal scientific publications do they admit personal secrets.
Unless maybe the memory still sears the soul.

That Christmas break served to soothe the psyche. During those few
weeks the family was together in a condition outsiders might judge
"uneventful." Deep down, though, Margaret was reassembling
her emotional topography. Jeanie, at two and a half, was mastering the
mechanics of motion. And the man of the house was by slow degrees
gaining back pride and self-respect. He nevertheless lagged far behind
his daughter in a singular talent: Spanish. Jeanie effortlessly imbibed
phrases and feelings from the neighborhood kids and conversed with all
whom she encountered. He still could gab only with gringos.

Late in January 1946, having managed to extend his homestay to a full
month, Norm headed north for the action section of the second season.

Early in February, when the crossing-block began flowering, he
swarmed over the precisely arranged rows, cross-fertilizing each of the
12 lines with all the rest and doing it both ways—i.e. with half the
specimens employed as female and the other as male. There being at
least a dozen plants in each lines, he makes 144 crosses, each demanding
an hour of frenzied, focused, finger work.

Having completed his second stab at wheat breeding he flew home,
leaving each of his precisely fertilized flowers to sort out just which of
the 25,000 gene pairs will dominate.

Back in the City of Mexico he found the scientific staff augmented by
the reticent forester who'd trailed him in grad school. Joe Rupert had
settled into the Hotel Geneve. But as friendship ripened Margaret offered
the spare bedroom, and Joe moved into Chez Borlaug.

For a product of Minnesota's Iron Range—where the wind arrives
pre-frozen and the North Pole seems a mere horizon or two away—Joe
Rupert seemed surprisingly committed to tropical agriculture.

Actually, he'd come mainly for mental health. Three years earlier, just
after earning his MS degree, he'd been drafted, hastily trained as a

combat medic, and dispatched to North Africa with the new and naïve forces led by an obscure and somewhat suspect general named Dwight David Eisenhower. During the botched Battle of Kasserine Pass the shy agronomist tended GIs extracted from Sherman tanks shattered by Rommel's high-penetration artillery shells. The sight shattered Joe too, and Stakman arranged the posting to Mexico trusting it would help grow scar tissue over the impressions of broken, burned and disemboweled bodies branded on his brain.

Helping an ex-student reclaim his mind from mayhem was typical of this plant-pathology professor with the hard shell and soft heart. Did he know his students would form a dream team? Maybe so. After all, Rupert and Borlaug were alike in age, appearance, training, world outlook, social values, enthusiasm for the daily grind, impatience with red tape. They were, indeed, commonly mistaken for each other. Mexican officials swore they were brothers, even to their faces.

As friendship ripened the pair became a mutual support group. For Joe's nerves there was no better therapy; for Norm their closeness supplied solace too. He and Rupert became brothers in all but surname.

Their potential would, moreover, be magnified by two Chapingo students who during the spring of 1946 signed on as part-time assistants. Both Teodoro Enciso and Alfredo Campos began as "weekend warriors," contributing Saturdays, school vacations, and other brief interludes that their college advisors couldn't veto. Both approached their assignments with reluctance, loath to commit their inner selves. Soon, though, they caught the Borlaug bug, ditched the egghead existence, and sweated their hearts out amidst heat, flies, dirt and diseased plant tissues. In those fields they were working for a cause not a course.

April arrived. Time to head north to finish up the Sonora tests. Joe offered his services. Norm also invited Teodoro Enciso, who possessed the power to converse with the locals.

As Panini's flying machine was too flimsy to haul home several hundred pounds of seed, George Harrar allowed Norm to take the boxy Ford pickup the Federales had assigned the OEE. It was the only truck at his disposal and Borlaug could borrow it only until the end of the month.

Road travel to Sonora required careful planning. From Mexico City you drove north to the U.S. frontier, tumbled into Texas, skittered across New Mexico and half of Arizona, hung a left at Tucson, and dropped down into the Yaqui Valley from the wrong direction. If all went well, this 1500-mile mission over mostly miserable roads would take but a week.

Anticipating trouble inserting a foreign-government's vehicle into the United States Borlaug dropped by the Ministry of Agriculture and the American Embassy. Both assured him the border crossings would be quite uneventful. A special treaty allowed Mexican government vehicles free passage of U.S. territory for purposes of reentry.

Then, with their spirits and confidence soaring, Norm, Joe and Enciso loaded all they'd need for the trip and the field trials, including:

- Four extra tires;
- A 60-gallon drum brimming with gasoline (for the many stretches lacking gas stations);
- Two pint-sized thrashers—a tiny one for stripping grain from individual plants and a slightly larger version for handling nursery plots containing perhaps a few dozen plants;
- 200 paper bags (for small seed samples); and
- 50 gunnysacks (for the huge harvest that might prove mythical).

Margaret brought little Jeanie downtown to send the strange expedition off in style. Norm kissed them both, waved cheerily from behind the wheel, and maneuvered the old green Ford along the bumpy boulevard leading out of the city.

As they disappeared Margaret tried to quiet her concerns. How many times would she watch her husband head out into the unknown like this? And merely for a crop everyone said would never work in Mexico.

For three excruciating days the trio sharing the bench seat of that pre-war contrivance bucked their way over worn-out roads. On reaching the Texas border at four o'clock on the third afternoon they were battered, blown, bothered and desperate to cross into El Paso for a bath, a beer and a bed.

But after glancing at the dusty pickup with DF license plates and doors emblazoned with silver-eagles, the border guard threw a tantrum. "Well, this is a real complicated procedure seeing that there's a Mexican government vehicle," he snapped. "No use even talking about it now. Come back in the morning."

An hour later he closed the gate to America, forcing the three to snooze the night away on the dusty pile of gunnysacks beneath a blanket of Mexican stars all winking derision.

Next morning Norm referred to the treaty. To such impertinence, the official invoked a border bureaucrat's prerogative for pettiness: this cross-border criminal was clearly attempting to sneak into the United States two thrashing machines and four tires for purposes of personal financial gain. Full duty must be paid in advance!

Norm noted that the thrashers were used only by cereal scientists and had no commercial value. Moreover, in two days they'd be back in Mexico. But the customs officer remained unswayed.

After much of the day had disappeared in successive rounds of verbal fencing, the federal functionary conceived a final riposte: the United States would permit citizen Borlaug free entry if, and only if, his personal paraphernalia were shipped to Arizona by a bonded trucking company. Nothing could then be peddled for profit without the Treasury getting its rightful recompense. He could recover his belongings at the border in Arizona. Everything would be fine. No worries.

By now Norm was mad enough to commit mayhem. Harrar's coolness toward this Sonora silliness meant he had no funds for emergencies. Worse, the harvest season was already nigh; he should be already in Sonora. Making thousands of field measurements, entering data, and crunching numbers to confirm the winners would take two weeks. Collecting and thrashing the superior seeds would require a further fortnight. Drying and packaging those seeds would absorb yet another two weeks. And after all that was behind, hauling the bounty home would wipe out another week.

That schedule was seared into his brainstem. The whole intricate sequence *must* be completed before the end of May at the absolute latest. If the next generation seedlings weren't quickening in Central Mexico's soil by the beginning of June they'd be deep frozen in September before ripening much—perhaps any—grain. Should that happen he'd lose not just momentum; he'd lose his mind. So he grumpily handed over personal dollars, unloaded the equipment for the trucking company and headed west for Arizona with Joe and Enciso in an alien truck bearing a few personal belongings.

At Nogales, Arizona's main gateway to Mexico, things got worse. When asked about the thrashers, tires and sacks the border authorities laughed. The bonded warehouse had nothing remotely like that.

This time the normally self-effacing scientist discarded all sense of decorum, not to say decency. Overcome by rage, he provided all within earshot voluble insight into the U.S. Customs Service's competence.

An official then scurried to a phone and scurried back. So sorry, there'd been a little problem . . . the trucker had made a mistake. But don't worry: The equipment was quite safe . . . in Los Angeles!

For almost two days Norm, Joe and Enciso slouched round the Arizona side of Nogales. Then when their weird wares returned to the fold they scuttled into Mexico thankful to be back where things worked and people could be trusted.

Driving hard they hit Hermosillo about midnight. Pressing on they ran out of roadbed around 3 am and for 200 miles trailed tire tracks weaving between mesquite and cactus, jouncing through dry arroyos and slithering through wet ones—all in pitchy gloom with not even a compass for counsel.

Dawn was breaking when Cajeme thankfully showed itself. The travel had subtracted two weeks from the tight-wound timetable. More than half a century onward he's still furious. Many incidents crop up in general conversation as "the most miserable in my life." This particular mix-up with officialdom *in his native country* is among the commonest. Unlike most of the others it emerges with no wry smile.

Ultimately, however, everything turned out okay. Seen in the dewy dawnlight the old experiment station's plots proved a joy. The red orb rising above the spiky shoulders of the Sierra Madre made a glorious backdrop to the panorama in which row upon row was holding out against stem rust. Frontera, Supremo and above all the Kenyas were heavy with grain and ready to reap.

In his long and loopy career this was *the* defining moment . . . the divide between general education and genuine experience. Finally he could see the sky from the dungeon of despair. You might almost say (like Winston Churchill did just five years earlier after the Battle of Alamein that turned the course of World War II) that up to this point he never enjoyed victory . . . and after this point he never suffered defeat.

That last claim would prove true at least on the *scientific* battlefronts: from here on, Norm's defeats will be delivered by malicious mankind.

During the next six weeks the three scientists drove themselves demonically, and by the middle of May they'd gathered the harvest, separated and threshed the outstanding plants' seeds, and logged the data into the notebooks—all nowadays bound with screws and including thousands of pages crammed with neat tight handwriting. The winners' seed, moreover, had been winnowed, dried, and packed into the 50 gunnysacks and the 200 paper bags for the next phase of their journey through space and chance.

When it came time to head back south, the little green government truck was burdened with the botanical booty, not to mention the spare tires and the 60-gallon gasoline drum.

Then Borlaug realized that entering the U.S. carrying all that seed would bring more grief. So he chose the direct descent. He'd entrust their fate, not to mention their nerve endings, to the road of greater evil.

The southward passage started out uneventfully. They dropped down the state of Sonora and entered long, thin, dusty Sinaloa. Paralleling the Pacific shore, they ran into Nayarit, a small state where the road died. Cutting southeastwards through the uncharted boonies, they plunged blindly across the lookalike landscape hoping to hit Mexico's second largest city, Guadalajara. On this stretch maps were mere moonshine. Wiggling through the wild scrub was best done by guess and by golly . . . though, once again, a compass could have offered comfort.

Beyond the absence of maps, roads, signage and geographic reference points, there was also the acute absence of gas, oil, replacement parts, mechanics and air pumps for the far-too-frequent flats.

Worst of all hazards were river crossings. These were unavoidable since a surprising number of sturdy streams tumble across Nayarit, headed for the Pacific from the tall sharp spine of the Sierra Madre. In 1946 most flowed free of bridges. On discovering a river in your windshield you turned and headed along the bank in search of help. Ferries were common enough, most comprising a couple of rowboats lashed side-by-side with planks laid over top. You paid the owner, drove up onto the planks, and let a cluster of kids on the far shore tug you over on a rope.

When nothing so safe or satisfactory was possible you sought a spot on the near bank where the most tire tracks met the murk. The key was to aim for the muddy scars on the far bank and hope nothing, least of all a hole, lay in wait. Sadly, destiny did not always deliver on a driver's prayers, and during the rainy season river crossings were so perilous it was pointless entering this state on wheels.

That year, however, the rains overslept, and the intrepid trio bested even the most energetic streams. With neither nerves nor spirits unduly frayed, they struck the sprawling metropolis of Guadalajara dead center.

Getting home was a relief, and he'd certainly earned a rest. But it was the third week of May; Central Mexico's wheat-sowing window was beginning to close. Thus, following a quick stop at George Harrar's downtown office to sketch out the latest discoveries, he headed for Chapingo and began preparing 10 acres to host his third bout with black stem rust.

A few days later a youth wandered by and asked if Borlaug needed help. Pablo Maurer attended Texas A&M and was home for the summer. He hoped to experience field research. No pay necessary.

Extra hands without an extra hit on the budget was a signal blessing, and the pair soon struck up a friendship. Two weeks later, when the soil and the seeds were all set, Maurer quietly spilled his personal story. He and Norm were then relaxing beneath the old ash tree and the peaceable surroundings made the Maurer misfortune seem all the more melancholy.

During Pablo's boyhood his family owned a fine estate in Puebla. It was near Atlixco de las Flores, which is not merely the city of flowers but the city, so the locals brag, with the best climate. Life had been idyllic until, during the presidential election of 1928, a mob invaded the farmstead, killed Pablo's father, divvied up the land among themselves, and brazenly erected dwellings and began sowing crops.

Norm already knew what that signified. Farmland thieves inherited a patriotic penumbra from the revolution, which had been heated by hatred of hacendados [landowners]. Indeed, back in 1913 the illiterate Indian revolutionary Emiliano Zapata had coined the republic's modern motto, "The land belongs to those who work it," with the express purpose of encouraging the poor to "repossess" rural property.

During the subsequent decades Zapata's seductive syllables inflamed the mass-mind until every farm became bandit bait. Thefts occurred most notably during presidential election campaigns, when political and patriotic sentiments were high and policing low. Thousands of worthy families thereby saw their heritage heisted.

In the Maurer case the authorities refused to oust the squatters and dithered nearly a decade before offering 250 acres of sun-scorched, sea-level soil almost a thousand miles north of the family's shady birthright. Understandably, the members were distraught. Their patriarch had given his life for their lovingly tended ancestral sward with the wonderful climate, not some swatch of pitiless plain in the Wild West.

Despite the tragic outcome, Pablo seemed less disturbed over past wrongs than present realities: "My brother is trying to farm the new place up there in Sonora," he finally blurted. "Roberto's trying to grow wheat. But he doesn't know much. Maybe you can help him."

Borlaug took note. When he next got back to Sonora he'd look into it.

D uring that summer young Maurer proved his bona fides as both peon and plant breeder. He, Borlaug, Rupert, and the student team sowed the seeds from the 50 gunnysacks and 200 paper bags brought from Sonora. Then as the season advanced they checked, rechecked and rogued the tens of thousands of glistening green specimens, shedding the losers like bow-waves.

After the flowers blossomed late in July, Norm performed more pollinations. Outsiders assume the process to be simple and secure but building a better plant is neither perfect nor predictable.

That was especially true in the 1940s, when the composition of chromosomes remained mired in the mists. In those pre-DNA days, plant breeding was a kind of biological magic. No one could identify genes, manipulate genes, tag genes, or detect the presence of recessives hiding behind dominants.

Crops then advanced less by system than serendipity. Civilization's most basic ground force—the food-plant fashion designers—suffered endless days of disquiet. Skewing the mating game to produce a useful variety was not unlike decrypting a cipher: a comparison here, an assumption there, a flash of fancy somewhere else. Crop builders absorbed myriad intimations and figured out how each might fit within the grand vision occupying their mind.

Strange to say, the greatest enemy was imagination. Success demanded lots of data and strict scholarly detachment. Absent the microprocessor, the big pull-down handle on Norm's little adding machine got a merciless workout. Yet, he couldn't march strictly by the numbers. While focusing close up he still had to peer past the horizon to a magical new wheat world that would be protected and prolific.

The plant breeder's problem is that genes expose their effects in their own sweet time. Nature slows things down by exposing the qualities arising from the clash of wheat chromosomes only after several cycles of sowing and re-sowing.

Typically, the first set of seed—known as filial one or F1 for short—grow into plants that are intermediate between the parents. Planting their seeds gives rise to a second set, F2 for short, whose qualities are normally dominated by pushy genes from just one parent. But when those F2 seeds are grown an amazing efflorescence of individuality often occurs: each plant expressing its own being. Only here among the grandchildren, F3 for short, do the randomized gene-combinations find the confidence to show their inner nature.

The polyglot painting the F3 pretenders portray—an occurrence known as segregating—is the crop-breeder's goal. Segregating fields provide a palette of possibilities. As the season advances each separate specimen is checked and rechecked in hopes it might express the perfect combo of qualities to make a masterpiece.

For these reasons the crosses made here in 1946 will not reveal their true colors until the 1950s.

In targeting rust Borlaug happened to be in the vanguard of human progress. Few others knew about this fungal scourge. In 1946 the Technicolor wonderland north of the border is enjoying wheat's golden age, and hardly any American or Canadian remembers or cares to remember the old wheat killer.

True, Stakman keeps warning that the infernal infection will reappear. Yet the rising generation of plant pathologists ignores the now emeritus prof. Many are unaware of just what he'd accomplished; most relegated stem-rust epidemics to the ashes of a primitive past best forgotten. No epidemic has been seen since 1935. Modern science has conquered rust!

Despite mass denial, Norm remains committed to confronting the red menace. He's unfazed by floundering alone in obscurity. Nonetheless, he must proceed cautiously. Immersed in the amorphous world of genes it's easy to chase mirages. To his team members he said:

> If we split our effort up into splinter projects we'll never get anywhere. We can't wander off on sideshows; we have to do one thing first, **and that one thing is beat stem rust!**

That season's prime interest was the Generation-1 plants he bred himself the year before. In July, when flowers began forming in Chapingo's irrigated fields, he begins the process of introducing one plant's male parts (pollen) to another's female parts (stamens). Even under the finest conditions this is a maddening mind game. But Mexico's searing summer heat squeezes the flowering season into three brief weeks, turning the mental marathon into a sprint.

Genetically speaking, the method differed little from breeding roses or apples, not to mention show dogs or Arabian thoroughbreds. Nevertheless, the act of creating wheats of predictable pedigree is so complex that Borlaug had to endure three weeks of frenzied fandango. Twice a year.

THE FUNGUS THAT HOLDS HUMANITY HOSTAGE

For wheats, if not for the overall food supply, stem rust represents what military planners call the "decisive theater." Before tackling anything else Borlaug had to conquer this wheat-destroyer that winters over in the warm lands of Mexico.

His battle is fought in the dark. Being both ingenious and invisible, the fungus resides inside wheat stems giving no hint of its presence until the damage is done.

Having settled on a wheat stem, stem rust spore sneaks moisture from a handy raindrop or dewdrop and rapidly (before the sun can suck it dry) sprouts a threadlike germ tube that squirms around in search of one of the plant's stomates. With those microscopic breathing holes occurring by the thousands over the stem surface, it soon worms down into the comfort of this convenient crevice and, by swelling yet more, splits apart the cuticle to gain access to the world of succulence inside. There, in the stem's luscious living center, it punctures cell after cell, sucking up nutrients and squeezing through cellular passageways like an amorous amoeba prowling the corridors of happiness in search of a blind date.

After a couple of weeks enjoying the good life secluded from the outer world this furious speck, too small to see without an expensive microscope, converts itself into spores with such abandon that it balloons into a cellular congregation easy to spot with the naked eye.

The amazing feat of swelling from the world of microbe to that of mankind builds enough pressure to burst the stem and open a path to freedom. Then through that jagged rent, the so-called pustule, the fungus calmly puffs out its accumulation of infective particles and sends them onto the winds of the world.

The scale of the resulting assault is hard to fathom: pustules can contain a quarter million spores; wheat plants can contain dozens of pustules; and an acre typically contains 100,000 wheat plants. A single acre of rusted wheat therefore can cast 300 billion infective agents onto the wings of the breeze, creating mass mischief over square miles of wheatland.

In epidemic years earth is said to have more rust spores than blades of grass or grains of sand. Soaring upward and outward, perhaps hitching a ride on a handy jet stream, each malevolent microdot carries the keys for opening a new disease cycle. Indeed, with its genome as mutable as influenza's, every spore is potentially a separate disease. That's why this fungal species is arguably Hunger's greatest weapon of mass destruction. In a single season it can putrefy half the fields of the world's number-one food plant, as it had on America's Great Plains in 1904, 1916 and 1935.

One evening in August 1946 he returned to the apartment to find Margaret's large brown eyes more troubled than for nearly a year. She was again pregnant.

Although that news should have brought a glow of happiness, the older heartbreak had not yet healed. The couple considered the implications and discussed the consequences. Both affirmed there was no reason for concern but in this case common sense proved neither convincing nor comforting. Their minds fell prey to private panic.

Throughout the soul-shaking months ahead the horror of history repeating itself hid in their hearts like some persistent poltergeist.

Then in the fall as the seedheads matured a new crisis arose from an unexpected quarter: the heavens! Hungry birds suddenly descended on his precious grain like kids for cotton candy.

This was no small threat. Seasonally great flocks of sparrow-like seedeaters fill the sky as they swing back and forth between the Americas. For them, Mexico makes a convenient dinner stop. Moreover, through secret bush telegraph they advertize the whereabouts of the best eats. One day a few scouts find the field; next day, fluttering hordes enshroud the glorious smorgasbord.

This presented an unforeseen predicament. If he couldn't prevent the beaks from digesting his grain he wouldn't have any results to digest himself. Every measurement would lose meaning; a low yield might signify a bad plant or bird patronage. He'd never know, and every datum and every decision would be shadowed by doubt.

But what to do? Hungry birds transcend human control. Only one possibility presented itself: "Joe," he said, "we need bird boys."

That was easily arranged. The foreman now overseeing the fieldwork at Chapingo offered to recruit three youngsters from his village, Boyeras. They'd be there at dawn, he said but only if they got five pesos a week *paid in advance*. Without that, their parents would find a better employer.

Norm handed over 15 pesos.

Next morning he and Rupert discovered the bird patrol on the job. In ragged shirts and frayed cotton pants, their heads hidden within sombreros barely topping the plants, three little scamps darted hither and yon on shoeless feet, tossing clods, cracking whips, yelling Spanish infelicities at the offending feathers.

Borlaug shouted a greeting, and the boys approached slowly—shy and circumspect. Then one stepped boldly forward. His face was square, his frame solid, his back straight. "Mi nombre," he said, "es Reyes Vega."

Norm has a knack of putting young people at ease. Placing his hand on the skinny flat shoulder, he said. "Reyes Vega, you and your brothers do a good job. Come every morning and every evening, okay?"

"Okay, Señor."

The youngster seemed smart beyond his years. To his parents, however, he was too valuable to spare for any luxury such as learning. A couple of years earlier they'd yanked him from school and set him to work. Five pesos a week trumped any self-improvement their son might entertain.

As the boy disappeared down the path, shyly peeking over a shoulder at his strange new *patrón*, the glint of his gaze flashed a spark of intuition to the onlookers.

"Did you see those bright eyes, Norm?" Rupert asked.

"Yes, Joe," Borlaug replied, "He'll do well, that one."

Even with the bird threat behind, many ambiguities and many causes for anguish remain. Indeed, facing so fuzzy a future, most plant breeders would have gone on experimenting until quite sure of their ground. Norm, however, begins readying his Foundation Foursome for the big time. Frontera, Supremo and the Kenya pair have passed their finals and earned his trust. Now he'll cast each headlong into the outer darkness where society takes over from science.

Nowadays few experimentalists would dare so much. Not only are Norm and his plants novices but no Mexican knows the fungus is around and ready to explode. The danger is neither clear nor present; this silent crisis is known only to him.

Thanks to Stakman, Norm understands rust's power and these four mediocrities have proven they can maintain good health. He'll advance them into farmers' fields. Should they flop, his repute and his future will just have to suffer.

That October, Borlaug and Rupert took the Foundation Foursome on a road test. They used the OEE's newly acquired station wagon, a brown, wood-framed, wooden-sided Chevy. For Frontera, Supremo and the two Kenyas it's the final performance check.

Driving 300 miles north, they established two small plantings on government experiment stations located in the Bajío. From the national breadbasket they then headed 300 miles further north to sow similar plots in La Laguna, a newly developed irrigation district near Torreón.

Finally, they ventured on another 300 miles into the heart of Coahuila, where they hoped to learn how their marquee foursome will perform under conditions like those in the paradise next door, Texas.

On reaching Coahuila's colorful capital, Saltillo, Norm and Joe visited a local agricultural college and asked where they might establish a trial. To their delight, an agronomy professor assigned two students to escort them to the perfect place.

In the outcome, the place would prove less than perfect:

At seven the next morning the four of us set out, heading southwards, back the way Joe and I had come the day before. An hour or so later, the students directed us to turn west into a remote highland. After maybe an hour's climb we came to a mountainside farm. The students introduced us to the owner, who pointed out a small field we could borrow for the trial. The plot clung to the south side of a very beautiful but also very deep valley. Despite its steepness, it seemed ideal for our needs.

The four of us prepared a patch about the size of a tennis court using hoes. After a while we noticed puffs of cloud crowning the hills at the head of the valley to the west. There, rain was falling; we paid no heed . . . it was miles away.

A couple of hours later Joe noticed that the nearby gully bottoms were brimming. Then things got serious. The little stream we'd crossed when driving into the field had surged over its banks. There was no way out—we were trapped.

The sky soon opened up on us too. October being still the dry season we were unprepared, and there was no possible shelter on that exposed slope. The four of us huddled together inside the station wagon. We were wet as sponges and had no way to dry off. Having put in a hard day's labor we were all famished but had no food. There was no heat either, and at that altitude the night air was cold.

We stretched out in the back of the vehicle. Even with my sleeping bag thrown over top we shivered, praying for daylight and clear skies while the deluge drummed on the metal over our heads.

Next morning, thank God, the rain stopped; but the floodwaters stayed high until late afternoon. By then all of us were thoroughly out of sorts. As I drove away no one was in a talking mood.

Back in Saltillo I rented a hotel room where we could clean up. Having hit the showers all four of us dashed for the dining room. Then to my surprise, as we crossed the lobby one of the students ducked over to the hotel piano and began playing and singing Mexican ballads. He was a muscular young man who'd already impressed me by his hard work. Now he showed the talent to lift our spirits. The tunes he coaxed from that battered old instrument were magical. With the assistance of a little tequila, the frustrations eased and for a while even the hurt of hunger subsided.

Taken all round, this young man impressed me so much that, a year later when he graduated from the Antonio Narro School of Agriculture, I offered him a job.

Thus it was that Ignacio Narvaez [nar-VY-es] manipulated a battered old bar piano to acquire a full-time position on the scientific staff.

During the decades to come he and Borlaug will share trials, tribulations and triumphs as they propel a wheat-short world into plenitude.

TECHNICAL PROGRESS, 1946

By the close of Round 3 in November '46, following two seasons' in Central Mexico and one season in Sonora, he's already one round ahead of schedule.

As the year of 1946 comes to an end the change of latitude is beginning to provide dividends:

- He's made the fateful decision that Frontera, Supremo and the Red and White Kenyas will advance into farmers' hands. He's got to the first Horizon in his mind. They'll hold the food frontier while he fashions better replacements.

Horizon 2, now coming into his sights, is the gene-dike he needs to build to keep Mexico from ever again being mugged by the microbe. The bricks for this barrier are his made-from-scratch creations:

- Generation-1—arising from the crosses made in mid-1945—is now in the F3 stage and starting to segregate.
- Generation-2—made in Sonora early this year is in the F2 stage and stubbornly sticking to one or other parent's pretensions.
- Generation-3—just created in Chapingo is still in the baby stage and unable to communicate.

Thus his fields exhibit age groups from adolescents to newborns. Despite an acute absence of grownups, there's something grand about the scene; it's his first evidence of professional competence. Wheat, though, remains unimpressed. It's acting standoffish, and keeping its secrets to itself.

In the 2 years since his arrival, the number of mouths in Mexico has risen by 1.2 million, or 5 percent, to reach 23.2 million.

Back in the fall of '46, though, such a dizzying possibility was unknowable. Indeed, to Norm the sole outcome from this soggy scrape was that from then on he never left town without stocking his vehicle with **three** sleeping bags, a 12-gauge shotgun, a fishing rod, a camp stove, and a cache of emergency rations comprising canned meat, peas and peaches; bags of dried beans and rice; and coffee.

For that foresight he'll all too soon have reason to be thankful.

4

1947
Setback

In November 1946 Borlaug and Rupert delivered the summer's winning seeds to the northern locale where they're officially forbidden to work. During the next three weeks they sowed hundreds of rows of seeds under the broiling desert sun. Nights were spent in the experiment station's rundown loft, which they shared with the weeviled grain, not to mention rats, mice, mosquitoes and snakes.

Borlaug still marvels that his friend didn't rebel:

> Thank God Joe could take it. If he hadn't been through combat in the North African desert, I'm sure he'd have left. Who could blame him?

Conditions were so terrible that even Norm might have left had not Farmer Campoy stepped forward. The old man, who lived directly across the road that ran along the research station's western edge, initially kept his distance. He was, however, intrigued by the strange goings on at the derelict research station. They often saw him peering from his front porch as if puzzled by the unfathomable ways of gringos.

That shyness soon eased, and from then on he'd appear several times a week:

> Campoy didn't have enough to occupy his time. He often came over to talk with us. He'd always show up after church on Sundays, when we were the only ones foolish enough to be out working!

Next, the curious neighbor took to volunteering his farm machinery. When the plots needed planting, disking, cultivating or harvesting, he'd appear on his Farmall or small combine without being asked or paid. In so doing he facilitated all that would soon unfold.

TECHNICAL CHALLENGES, 1947

Round 4 (Nov. '46-April 1947). Second stint in Sonora. In March he turns 33.

NURSERIES. The multi-location trials have morphed into nurseries. The plots sown (on his way north to Sonora) in La Piedad, Torreón, and Saltillo are for observing the performance of various plant lines, some still quite raw.

STEM-RUST RESISTANCE. In Sonora he'll primarily advance his own creations. The several thousand plants will be left free to expose their individual strengths. By season's end he'll rip out any falling short of expectations, which means almost every last plant. When flowering starts in February he'll breed a new generation.

Round 5 (May-October, 1947). Third stint in Central Mexico.

MULTIPLICATION. This summer he must increase the 2 tons of the Foundation Foursome to 50 tons. As the Chapingo site cannot accommodate so large a planting, he has no clue how he'll do it.

STEM-RUST RESISTANCE. When flowering begins in July he'll also advance his own creations (Generation-5). By now he's concentrating on backcrosses—mating his best seniors to one of their own parents so as to pile in genes for adult behavior. Primarily, he wants to boost behavior while retaining the newborn rust resistance.

Though reclusive by nature, Campoy quickly developed a concern for the strangers who'd come to help yet were forced to cook for themselves beneath the stars and sleep in a shabby attic amidst forgotten filth. Doubtless he considered them crazy to persevere without creature comforts, let alone peons, pickups or plows.

Cathy Jones, whose property adjoined Campoy's, adopted Norm and Joe like a broody hen taking in orphan chicks. On weekends they were required to join her trek to town for supplies. Sunday nights she demanded their presence for coffee, which always morphed into a meal. She did their washing and mending when common decency made those necessary. She listened to their talk and nodded approval of every plan and opinion. And bit-by-bit her own story emerged.

In 1905, 18 years old and newly married, she'd quit Connecticut expecting to find bliss and contentment in the Promised Land just past Arizona. For that she had good reason. American magazines displayed stunning photos of canals brimming with water and fields gilded with ripening grain. Having drooled over those lush images she and her husband Cappy sank their bottom dollar into their dream property—one otherwise far beyond reach.

Behind the magazine spreads was the Richardson Construction Company of Los Angeles, which had procured a Mexican government warrant to develop the Yaqui Valley. In exchange for providing water, it could people these otherwise dry plains with settlers. The company's advertising barrage attracted the desperate and the dreamers. "Five million acres of the best land on earth—with the best climate on earth," read an ad in the June 1910 *Overland Monthly*. Soil that "will grow anything," blared *Sunset Magazine* . . . . "Profits as high as $300 an acre from tomatoes and onions."

By 1909 the Richardson brothers had dug 50 miles of irrigation canals and peddled off 100,000 acres. By then about a thousand Americans had settled Mexico's western coast; many in the Yaqui Valley. Most were down-and-out Californians mesmerized by the money they'd reap shipping their tomatoes, oranges, melons, onions and cucumbers to Los Angeles and San Francisco via the Southern Pacific's shiny new tracks.

Sad to say, none of the glossy representations or glowing rhetoric applied to the clueless Connecticut couple's corner of cloud nine. Only summer showers watered their swatch of sand until 1936, when the irrigation department completed a new dam behind the dusty hills.

During their three-decade wait for the mirage to materialize, the plucky pioneers Cathy and Cappy lacked not only irrigation but income and alternatives. It took them five years to learn how to work their 50 waterless wilderness acres. Then in 1910 the trials got tougher when a spark from Halley's Comet seemed to ignite Mexico's social explosion.

In reality, the igniter was a gentle idealist who in 1910 chose to defy hard-headed Porfirio Díaz, the dictator who'd helmed the nation for 34 years and who'd welcomed gringos to settle in Sonora. An unlikely reformer, Francisco Madero came from a family owning mines, smelters, distilleries, wineries, banks and more than a million acres of land generating cattle, cotton, lumber and rubber from the guayule bush. For the Maderos the decades under the dictator had been exceedingly good, yet the 37-year-old Francisco was consumed by concern for societal iniquities. A vegetarian, spiritualist and social reformer, he lived like the poor, dissipated his inheritance creating cooperatives for penniless farmers, and wrote a book calling for free elections and open voting, a policy sure to destroy his family's fortune.

In that pivotal year of 1910 the young man's defiance of despotism seemed more fantasy than folly. In person, he was indecisive and wielded hardly more than dollars and dreams; Díaz on the other hand wielded bullets, business interests and the bluster of dictatorial empowerment. But when Madero's ragged disciples disobeyed explicit orders and stormed into the city of Juarez, the old despot's troops dropped their guns and rushed for the exits to save their fat necks.

Exposed as an emperor without the necessary clothing of soldiers, Díaz fled to Spain . . . to save his own fat neck.

Appointed the dictator's replacement, the champion of democracy became presidente without electoral legitimacy. Madero proved, however, much too good and much too soft. Absent an iron fist, mankind's old nemesis, Civil Strife, released a reign of terror. Within three years the romantic reformer was in his grave and Mexico was under the spell of four pretenders, each backed by his own private army and currency. Gutierrez claimed to rule from Mexico City, Carranza from Veracruz; Zapata ruled Morelos as well as the mind of the masses, and Villa controlled the main militia from Chihuahua.

None of these satraps possessed the title deeds to legality, so the command was turned over to Chaos. With four competing pesos in circulation, money turned to mush. Unable to convince farmers to swap produce for paper, those who needed to eat began raiding farm fields, not avoiding a massacre when appetite called.

Mexico now had no bread, only circuses. Finally, pillage ascended to the throne. "Violence bred violence and illegality further illegality," writes political scientist Eyler Simpson. "Lands were seized by peons without even the most sketchy compliance with the formalities of the law . . . . Hacendados with guns in hand desperately defended their property. The result was an epidemic of little wars, pitched battles and assassinations. Hardly was there a hacienda in the whole republic that was not in a state of siege, or a village that did not live in mortal terror."

Throughout this time bullets established the bylaws. Militiamen with cartridge belts stitching their chests roamed the rural regions, torching villages, trampling crops, stealing cattle, killing at will. Among notable atrocities, they blew up the Mexico City-to-Cuernavaca train, along with 400 passengers. Among lesser atrocities, half-mad militias turned their artillery on towns and hamlets, seemingly without cause or contrition. And along the country roads, bodies hung from trees and telegraph poles by the neck—many lacking hands, legs or genitals.

In turn, this maelstrom of murder attended the various presidential claimants. In surprising ways all met brutal ends: On February 22, 1913, Madero was gunned down in the dark of night, whilst being moved from the National Palace to a holding cell in a proper prison. In 1915, vigilantes in Texas ran down putative president Pascual Orozco and shot him in cold blood. In 1916 Victoriano Huerta died in U.S. custody at Fort Bliss, Texas, probably of cirrhosis of the liver. Two years later Emiliano Zapata arrived for a meeting in Chinameca to be greeted by an honor guard that first presented arms then deliberately lowered the carbines to loose the welcoming volley into his disbelieving body. In 1920 Venustiano Carranza was shot while sleeping on the dirt floor of an Indian hovel. One summer morning in 1923, three years after hostilities ended, Pancho Villa stepped from his Dodge sedan into a hail of machine-gun bullets. Finally, in 1928 Álvaro Obregón, a former Yaqui Valley farmer who'd ended the revolution, ruled for four years with decency and imagination, and been shot at a banquet honoring his triumphal election to a second term.

Moreover, for every prominent assassination there were at least 100,000 nameless murders. Indeed, the number who perished during the decade of despair is unknown. Guesses range from 1 million to 2 million and beyond. The reality is that from the 15 million Mexicans in 1910 about one in every eight was destined to die before the decade did. In 1920, despite a soaring birth rate and medical advances that were closing the door to child mortality, the population would shrink by a million.

Gringos being particularly prized as prey, Cathy and Cappy Jones' survival testifies to their courage, commitment, good fortune and probably their trigger fingers. Both remained rooted to the spot they'd selected as misguided teenagers. Even after Cappy died in 1931 Widow Jones stayed on, choosing Cajeme over Connecticut to raise her daughters.

When Norm arrived 15 years later both girls had moved stateside. Mrs Jones inhabited her cozy cottage alone. Solitude was perhaps what induced her to care for the poor creature occupying the disgusting dump across the street. Whatever the reason, her help was welcomed:

> I couldn't have survived without Mrs Jones. I was cooking my own food, sleeping in a grungy hayloft, seldom getting a bath. She provided comfort and a touch of home. Those kept me sane and made the Sonora work possible.
> Above all, though, Mrs Jones made me speak Spanish. On week nights she'd invite me over and then *force* me to brush up my grammar. By then I knew many words but couldn't make meaningful conversation. She was sure hard to please, and drilled me so relentlessly I at last learned to communicate.

That ability to converse allowed him to function in his new homeland and made him finally at home in his skin. By providing the key for unlocking his exit from the abyss of despair Cathy Jones earned the honor of Career Saver #15. Without her, he may not have made it.

January 1947. After his normal quiet Christmas with the kinfolk Norm headed back north where the swelling flowers will soon need pollinating. During his few week's absence the Round 4 fields—drum roll here—have behaved by the book. The spreading green acres of his Foundation Foursome are more than soothing, they are substantiation. Clearly, Supremo, Frontera and both Kenyas can survive in the winter wonderland that welcomes North America's rust races to party and procreate.

His immediate chore, however, involves introducing each of the four wheats to partners likely to perk up the pedigree and produce an even greater generation.

Three months earlier he'd sown those parents-to-be in a crossing block conveniently sited alongside the station buildings. These several dozen mini-rows each contain 20 or so separate plants. Beside them, the partners for the coming nuptials are lined up in a predetermined order to simplify pollen transfers. Now arrives the moment to submit each one to the carnal delights of cross-pollination.

Although the procedures have become routine, cross-fertilizing hundreds of plants in two directions—i.e. using half as mother, half as father—nevertheless absorbs nonstop activity from dawn until whenever the light dies at dusk. For three whole weeks!

Following those madcap days in early February 1947 he should have hastened home. However, he decides to tempt fate and sneak in an extra month before rushing home for the birth.

Thus until the middle of March he paced the fields, ruthlessly ripping out every specimen falling even marginally short of expectations. As before, he works with immediacy; decisions are split second; doubts are never entertained.

With the head of the household absorbed in some unfathomable enterprise over the rainbow Margaret and Jeanie live in something approaching solitary confinement. Despite close friends and neighbors, the separation was acute. Margaret's pregnancy was progressing and Jeanie's formative years were passing while their missing man preferred some ungodly place they'd never seen.

Norm was troubled too. But what could he do? To call home he mounted Friday-night expeditions to Cajeme. Trunk lines from this town of perhaps 10,000 were so few and so feeble that days could pass without a connection coming free.

On such occasions he stayed over at the Hotel La Colonial, a run-

CAREER SAVER #16

Fate's 17th facilitator, Joe Rupert (on left with Borlaug and George Harrar).
Although Joe had attended the University of Minnesota in the class a year behind
Norm, the two were much alike. Both had studied under Stakman. Both had been
foresters until succumbing to Stak's blandishments and taking up agricultural
science. They looked and acted like brothers and helped one other during the
depressing period when Borlaug's own colleagues were attacking his research. In
turn, Borlaug helped Joe get over the trauma of the frontlines in World War II.
Mutual friendship got each through critical patches in their lives, which is how Joe
Rupert did his part in keeping the Borlaug saga intact.

down hostelry on the dusty main drag. More than once he conceded
defeat Sunday afternoon and slouched back to work having wasted a
weekend. Without a lot of luck, calls from Cajeme could take a week.

Though none then realized it, the pattern of existence had been set.
Wheat would consume all three. For much of the year Margaret would
be minding the store while Norm lived like a monk in some fleapit
proper folks shunned. She was, and remained forever, sanguine about that
connubial sin.

This particular time, however, he strained her legendary tolerance by
arriving home less than two weeks before she entered the maternity
home in Lomas de Chapultepec.

Their third child was born March 29. It was a boy, and the sight of his firm back and fully formed body dispelled the fears that for months had flitted behind their smiles.

They chose to name him "William Gibson."

In no time he became "Billy."

W ithin days of the birth, Norm heads off once more. The sun is hastening north, and on the hot flat floor of the Sonoran Desert he finds that fate has handed him three surprises.

The first involves Mentana, which Mexico had previously dumped because it died during rust epidemics. In his first wheat-breeding efforts Norm had included it as a gene donor. Now, four seasons onward, descendants of Mentana/Kenya crosses are segregating, and exposing progeny undaunted by desert heat *or stem rust*.

The second involves the other reputed loser, Marroqui. This supposed wimp now proves itself a whopper. Years went by before this riddle unraveled. Turns out, the predecessor's field staff had failed to realize (or at least report) that half the crop had become sparrow bait. The variety's ill repute was quite literally for the birds.

Norm's third surprise is the discovery that Marroqui genes induce wheat to ripen two weeks earlier than normal. Eventually this natural turbo-charging will help secure the global food supply. By reducing the time spent under the sun, Marroqui genes help protect the world's wheat crop from fire, frost, drought, damp, heat, hail, wind, disease, insects, rodents, birds, loose livestock, wild herbivores, human error, human iniquity and the many other ills field crops are heir to.

Only now did he appreciate the snap decision during his first Sonora sojourn to save a seedhead from the mystery plants. The 200 grains from the Marroqui seedhead produced plants whose pollen becomes the genetic vehicle for the first of what would eventually become a dozen pillars of power sustaining the world's top food-producing plant. Together, those strengths comprise Borlaug's Cornucopia Combo.

Speed is the first pillar of power behind Borlaug wheats. In the event he'd merely taken a long chance on improving local agriculture; in the outcome the genes the *peons* let fall down the pecking order would speed maturity and facilitate the production of two or even three crops in the same land and the same year in hot and hungry countries around the world. Indeed, they'll lift life for millions and in time will contribute even to the security of our own storied amber waves of grain.

Soon, however, the scene in Sonora will take a disastrous turn. With March merging into April the sight of his fields edging toward maturity soothes the soul. But the arrival of spring sends the mercury soaring skyward and manic winds slashing downward. In the large multiplication plots Frontera and Supremo plants suddenly display distress. Given the imminence of the harvest, Norm considered it unimportant until one hot and blustery afternoon his horrified eyes beheld the curious phenomenon emmer farmers had seen and cursed more than a millennium before.

The few seedheads he spotted on the ground beneath amputated stalks signified a major setback. Emmer genes are at work, and desert heat and deadly winds are stripping the heads from his plants.

He must gather this grain immediately. But how?

Again Señor Campoy saved the program. Next morning he drove over his tiny combine, and within hours Norm had collected the remaining seedheads before the sharp-edged afternoon breezes could behead the rest.

A couple of days later Norm had 2 tons of Frontera, Supremo and the red and white Kenya grains, ready for threshing. For the first time he had enough to plant a farm—though just a small one.

In late April Norm hauled home the research winners' seed as well as the 2 tons of his Foundation Foursome. Never before has he needed to plant seed by the ton, and Chapingo lacks the land and equipment for so big a planting. He proceeds undaunted, however, and is soon back preparing the research plots around the Tarpaper Shack.

That May of 1947 sees the start of Year 3; he's now put in 4 rounds of research without a break, and his fields are attracting attention. Visitors seemingly pop up from nowhere to ask about the surprising emerald succulence bejeweling Texcoco's otherwise weedy wastes. Thus it came as no surprise that one day late that April, he looked up from preparing nursery plots and spied a small, round American staring down at him.

The man, who seemed to be in his thirties, was clearly agitated. His legs were firmly planted, feet apart, and he rocked from side to side as if unable to remain at rest. Indeed, from cowboy hat to cowboy boots he exuded a strange sort of raw energy—kinetic *and* potential—that seemed barely tamed.

After the briefest of introductions Richard Spurlock poured out a tale of woe. "They destroyed my cows last week," he said, choking over the words. "I'm stuck here for four years with nothing to do!"

In time, Borlaug would learn that Spurlock hailed from Wyoming and had contracted to manage El Cerrillo, an American-owned dairy farm high on a hillside in the wide valley called Toluca [tol-OO-cah], about 40 miles west of Mexico City. For several years his beautiful spread sustained the country's finest Holsteins. But a week earlier government officials had arrived with a bulldozer and a sharpshooter, dug a trench, herded in every cow, shot the lot, and pushed the soil back over top.

This act was not as mad as it seemed. You see, five months earlier, in December 1946, foot-and-mouth disease surfaced in Vera Cruz, about 200 miles to the east. Within weeks, panic pervaded that Caribbean coastal state, sending farmers hustling their cattle, pigs, sheep and goats westward to escape the wasting disease. Almost before anyone realized it, 250,000 square miles in 16 states spanning Mexico's middle were either infected or likely so. And the sickness would have spread further had not the government deployed the army to block the frenzied farmers with a cordon of military might.

Not knowing what to do next, the authorities turned northwards and asked for help. The response was rapid. Nine times since the mid-1800s United States had faced down this disease, suppressing each outbreak only with immense destruction of animal life and personal wealth. The thought of the scourge creeping back over the southern fence forced the Department of Agriculture to rush 18 veterinarians to Mexico City.

This small beginning in April 1947 evolved into that era's biggest public-health operation, aimed of course at animal health. During the next four years, the so-called Aftosa Commission employed more than 5000 professionals, including hundreds of livestock inspectors, sanitary technicians, appraisers, paymasters, secretaries and mechanics specializing in cars, trucks, heavy machinery, boats and a DC-3 airplane. Those support personnel would eventually sustain 2500 veterinarians sequestered in small zones of responsibility covering a swath of rugged terrain right across Mexico, from the Caribbean to the Pacific and from torrid lowlands to frigid mountaintops.

In those days it was nearly impossible to control this contagion that corrupts cloven-hoofed creatures' paws and maws. An airborne virus, it proliferates with the same alarming, almost mystical, momentum as the 1918 flu Norm had seen take down Cousin Sina's family. Its presence cannot be detected until the feet break apart and tongue tissues separate leaving lame, sick, salivating and very sorry looking creatures, a third of whom die leaving the rest to infect their brethren.

In 1947 slaughtering every susceptible creature was the only secure solution. That year, the veterinary teams scattered across Mexico's middle killed 900,000 cows, pigs, sheep and goats, not excluding the much-revered black stud—of fierce mien and wicked horn—used for breeding bulls to battle matadors in the *corrida*.

That seemingly mindless massacre loosed mass outrage. For millions of villagers a scrawny animal stood proud as the solitary asset acquired during a life of deprivation. The creatures slaughtered were more than flesh and blood; they were bank accounts, food reserves and four-footed tractors. Many were family. Further fuelling the anger was the peasant farmers' ignorance of infection or even of microbes. To them, the beasts looked perfectly healthy (as most were).

Despite generous gifts of horses, mules and cash, the operation morphed in the popular mind into a gringo scheme to impoverish families and distress innocent children. Sunday after Sunday, the rural clergy preached that seductive fiction until most rural minds were bent. To people still sunk in superstition the scientists became *Los Matavacas*, the cow killers! Rumor built upon rumor until righteous wrath triggered terrorism. At least seven American veterinarians were murdered. One, Robert Proctor, entered a village and was immediately stoned to death. Wielding machetes, village women hacked apart the earnest young inspector's body, buried the bits between boulders, and walked over and over the site until it resembled a well-worn trail.

Norm was affected too:

> This was a very scary period. The countryside was dangerous; we stayed in the city as much as possible. And we avoided the Aftosa Commission for our very lives.

Later the Mexican Army assigned a small squad of soldiers to each veterinary team (which comprised a local vet and an American vet). Not even rifles, however, could forestall every act of rural revenge. In the state of Michoacán, for example, one such squad escorted vets into the village of Zingue. They'd made it clear they wanted *to just look* at the livestock. But the villagers, who'd previously pledged that no outsider could enter, gunned them all down. Village horsemen then dragged the bodies of the army captain, six soldiers and the Mexican and American vets up and down the dusty road, to lusty cheers.

The scientists were actually as unhappy as the citizens. USDA recruiters had descended on veterinary schools from Maine to California and dispatched much of that year's graduating class to remotest Mexico to kill the creatures they'd just learned to care for. Their career opener thus provided neither satisfaction nor security. Beyond the seven who were murdered, 19 Americans lost their lives in highway accidents, 14 died in a plane crash, two were thrown to their deaths from horses, one was run over by a train and another was accidentally shot. Moreover, hundreds more were felled by typhoid, malaria or dysentery, and some of those also succumbed.

In its second year the Aftosa Commission adopted the obvious alternative: vaccination. In those days foot-and-mouth inoculants were crude and capricious enough to sometimes spread the sickness faster than nature ever dreamed. Further, in the tropical heat they quickly spoiled. Thus, wherever ice was unavailable, which meant almost everywhere in rural Mexico, the vaccine quickly turned worthless. But by 1948 great risks ruled every possibility; so a huge quantity of inoculant was ordered from Holland and extraordinary efforts were made to deliver it together with ice to every affected locale—not excluding airdrops from the DC-3 into remote and roadless regions.

Some sense of the commitment can be gained from the fact that during the next twelve months 60 million vaccinations were performed. The underlying achievement, however, can be better appreciated when you realize that *each* cow, sheep, goat and pig—16 million overall—had to be located, corralled, roped, tied up and inoculated precisely at four-month intervals. Just identifying individual animals across the wild wastes of inner Mexico was hard enough, especially as ear-tags, barcodes and portable computers still awaited invention and the locals did their best to mislead the *matavacas*.

Despite the odds the tough-minded technicians succeeded. In September 1950 the outbreak was officially declared over. When the bills were tallied, United States had spent $127 million for items as diverse as food, lodging, compensation to Mexican farmers, and hundreds of thousands of horses and mules. The dollars were deemed well spent.

T his then is the strange phenomenon lurking behind the distressed stockman's plea in the spring of 1947. Despite every appearance of good health, El Cerrillo's prize cows had been among the first dispatched. With most of his contract still ahead, Richard Spurlock faced a suddenly empty career. "I've heard you know about wheat," he said as he rocked back and forth that morning at Chapingo. "I've raised grass and alfalfa but never a food crop. Can you get me started?"

With nary a second thought Norm placed in this stranger's charge his most immediate and vital line of work: the multiplication of the 2 tons of seed just trucked down from Sonora.

We may consider that natural; in those days, though, it broke all precedent. Seed-multiplication was the prerogative of governments or great corporations. Borlaug, however, used this amateur—a cowpuncher who'd volunteered for a cause he couldn't comprehend.

Norm explained the difficulties: The goal was to produce 20,000 tons—enough to supply wheat farmers throughout the republic. For one thing, producing so much seed would take several seasons. For another, he didn't know how Frontera, Supremo and the Kenyas would perform when grown on such a scale, let alone on a fancy farm high in the hills.

These uncertainties thrilled the cowboy. He was another of those rare souls excited by challenge. Though his manner may have been coarse and his words direct, behind the bull-bluster lurked a questing mind eager to engage in great things. So, following the first rains in early May, Norm loaded up a pickup and drove the gunnysacks up the hill and onto the heavenly ex-dairy farm high in the Toluca Valley, a couple of hours and a couple of cultures away to the west.

With Spurlock having idle land, not to mention peons, storage barns, and farm equipment, planting 2 tons of seed was easy. Indeed, El Cerrillo possessed a complete line of Massey Harris tractors, plows, disks, harrows and a grain drill. None had yet been sullied by soil; they'd been bought to produce alfalfa and hay for the cows now so sadly absent. These shiny new Canadian-built implements made their mark with the first-ever multiplication of a Borlaug wheat.

Taken all round, Spurlock's loss of cattle proved yet another stroke of monumental good luck for us all.

At Chapingo each morning for three weeks during the height of summer Norm enters the Tarpaper Shack, pulls a pair of fine-nosed tweezers from his pack, ties them about his neck with a length of twine, stuffs his shirt pockets with paper tubes, paperclips, pens, and notebook, not to mention a hooked knife with a razor-sharp blade. Then he grabs his canvas-bottomed stool and marches into the serried ranks of crop conscripts for a twelve-hour tryst with the 42 chromosomes competing for control amid the passions of pollination.

Mating wheat taxes the brain as well as the body. The plant seems deliberately designed to keep humans from fiddling with its fertility. Male and female flowers are crammed together for their mutual satisfaction. First up, wheat breeders must dig into each tiny flower and deliberately excise every male part. And they must do that at the precise

BREEDING WHEAT . . .

. . . IS HARD TO DO

LEFT: Borlaug breeding wheat at Chapingo. His vest pocket is stuffed with the tools of his trade:

- *A hooked knife* to decapitate the top 40 or so florets, leaving about 20 and making the process manageable while still providing enough seeds for progress.
- *Tweezers* to extract the pollen sacs from the 20 remaining florets. With three per floret, 60 pollen sacs, each as small as a sprinkle on a sugar cookie, had to be carefully removed for every cross pollination.
- *Paper tubes* to shield the virginal remnant.
- *Paperclips* to clamp the tube shut and keep out stray pollen. And
- *A pen* to note the code number on the paper cylinder.

Having emasculated every plant selected for a "mother," he's halfway home. A few (two to five) days later, when the female tissues have swelled into readiness, the magical moment arrives: Moving down those rows of neutered-males, he reads the code number on each envelope, checks the notebook and strides to the individual plant chosen to sire this particular dam:

- Slicing open its florets to expose the bright yellow mature pollen sacs, he snips off the head and carries it gently to the waiting partner.
- At the new plant he removes the paperclip, opens the top of the cylindrical envelope, inserts the golden head, spins the stalk between his fingers to scatter the male cells evenly over the waiting females, and
- Reseals the top with the paperclip.

The rest is then relegated to nature—and, so to speak, proceeds discretely behind closed doors.

moment when those tiny appendages have formed but before they can do what comes naturally. Adding extraordinary difficulty is the fact that these pollen sacs do their thing *before* the flower opens. The breeder thus must violate each tiny floret merely to expose the secret specks of maleness. All this explains why Norm toted a stool into the plots. You can't stand all day when castrating wheat plants.

Beyond precision and exquisite timing each operation demanded dexterity, patience, concentration, speed and above all, steady hands. Even the simplest—providing the pollen—presents problems because heat damages pollen. Once opened to Mexico's broiling sky the pollen stays viable less than 5 minutes, which explains why the crossing block was arranged so precisely. During those hectic hours there was almost no time for wiping the brow, let alone walking.

One day the head bird boy, Reyes Vega, wandered by and asked what Borlaug was doing to the wheat flower. Ever the solicitous coach, Norm demonstrated the cumbrous and complex initial steps: shearing away the flowers on a stalk, slicing open the florets, pulling out the immature pollen sacs, and hiding the feminized remnant within a paper tube.

When the boy asked if he could try it, the request seemed a shocking impertinence. Since its nineteenth-century beginnings cereal breeding had been performed by eminent academics with scientific papers in their bibliography and learned letters lingering long after their names. The act of transferring pollen between the sexes of a crop seemed so sacred as to be consecrated solely by scientists. Letting an unlettered kid in on the secret rites stretched the limits of permissiveness past the point of blasphemy.

Norm, however, loved the notion, and quickly indulged the lad. And almost from the start, the school dropout whose eyes gleamed like stars in the tropics picked up the procedure as if born to it. Indeed, before 1947's three-week flowering season was over he'd become as adept as a modern microsurgeon. By then the world's most unlikely wheat-breeder, a village kid without formal learning or technical preparation, was wielding the knife, tweezers, envelopes, pens and notebooks with aplomb and operating on the intricate wheat flower parts with speed, skill, precision, and what amounted to saucy ease.

Thus the fourth outsider joined the team—of his own volition. The Hidden Hand had struck again!

Today we can admire all these intricacies and exertions but at the time Borlaug got no sympathy. Professionals were convinced that breeding crops sequentially in separate places was utterly wrong. This upstart, so they convinced themselves, operated not only outside the rules but outside his rights.

Previously he'd been such a nonentity that no one cared what he did; now, though, he was making progress and casting doubt on the dogma. The critics sharpened their claws. Public censure soon appeared in print.

The denunciation was difficult to refute. His peers possessed the power of precedent. Even the textbooks indicated that shuttling seeds a thousand miles (not to mention several thousand feet in altitude) between Sonora and Chapingo was unprofessional. Planting breeding stock out of season and in different climates rendered the work worthless. He should instead develop separate lines for each locale and sow the seed only when local farmers did.

Echoes of this misconduct soon reached the top of the Manhattan skyscraper. Rockefeller Foundation brass hats promptly dispatched experts to review its misguided minion's fitness. Being certified cereal-breeders, they carried home appalling accounts of this warmed-over forester's ignorance of fundamentals.

Within the OEE, too, Borlaug's folly stoked the fires. Both George Harrar and Ed Wellhausen felt their friend was frittering away precious funds directing his crop down a dead end. Only Stakman, who popped in a few times a year to keep an eye on things, showed sympathy. Yet not even Stak spoke out in support of his protégé's maverick approach.

Then when H.K. Hayes deemed the work defective Borlaug's incompetence seemed settled. Following his wife's death, the great University of Minnesota corn and wheat breeder, was depressed almost to the point of suicide. For a change of scenery and a chance to recover stability, perhaps sanity, he withdrew to Mexico. One day in July Hayes visited Norm's fields at Chapingo. As they strolled along the rows, he idly asked: "Where did you grow the last generation?"

"Up in Sonora in the winter season."

"Hell, I don't know anything about Mexico . . . where's Sonora?"

"Well, we're now at about 18 degrees [latitude] and 7000 feet [elevation]. These were last planted at 28 degrees and near sea level."

So blasé an admission of ineptitude visibly shocked the old man. "My God, Borlaug," he ejaculated, sticking out his bull neck. "Didn't you ever learn the first lesson in crop breeding? What you're doing will get you nowhere . . . you'll just take one step forward and one step backward!"

Norm met all this with magnificent unconcern:

> H.K. was very strong-willed and under a lot of personal stress, so there was no point in arguing the matter. I just let it rest.

Calmly confident of his course and only too happy to let others hew their own, Norm happily contravened crop-breeding's most basic tenet. Saving years of delay was his preeminent priority. After all, if the new wheats weren't soon available the republic would fall either into famine or financial ruin, and he'd be packed off home to live forever in disgrace.

Yet there was a second power behind his perseverance: Wheat is the best teacher about wheat, and it was telling him he was doing okay. Indeed, his green charges were beginning to thrive.

It was the first secret shared between the species.

In the latter half of ultramodern 1947 Borlaug's plants certainly *seemed* to be thriving. The Tarpaper Shack was now swaddled in a golden wrap of grain fields and breeding nurseries.

Some of the 50,000 short rows involved gene mixes that were nothing more than blue-sky bingo; most, however, reflected refinements to an existing line. To battle-harden the plants he uses a method that would help certain other species: piling in more genes *from just one parent*. This so-called backcrossing demands care, concentration and above all luck. Without all three, it musses up rather than mobilizes the seminal qualities already coded in the genome.

Beyond tweaking and battle-testing bloodlines, Norm also made hundreds more plants from scratch. In fact, although only two years have passed since pollinating his first wheat flower, he's now following 1500 separate crosses, a figure merely hinting at the operation's size. You see, the first cross produced sixty seeds and *each of those* produced a hundred more. After that, sowing any seed produces a hundred new ones. And each of those in turn produces a hundred more. Not many sowings need pass before a million plants clamor for consideration.

Thank goodness he's now master of this domain. April in the north and October in the south provide the Judgment Days for millions of plants. At season's end he moves through the plots, his mind imbibing each plant's features, and his hands reacting with neither restraint nor regret over trashing hundreds of thousands of plants.

Despite ruthlessly removing every specimen failing to measure up, he's still surrounded by enough complexity to short-circuit the broadest brain stem. And with cross-breeding operations proceeding season by season, the notebooks were critical to understanding from whence he's come. By now the office sports whole shelves of screw-bound binders identifying not only which male had satisfied which female but the subsequent generations' histories and performances as sons and daughters, sires and dams.

Norm and Joe approached these Judgment Days for 1947's summer season in a buoyant spirit. They'd never felt closer or more energized. Back in May they'd begun the season by venturing into unmapped territory. Now in October they'd discovered a wild and wonderful new landscape on the face of the unknown.

For Norm, this is the first affirmation of all he's attempting. High points in the genetic topography include at least four of his first personal creations. Fashioned from various combinations between Newthatch,

Marroqui, Mentana and Kenya, this new quartet of stellar performers are becoming uniform. Next year they might supplant his Foundation Foursome.

With all that on their minds it's understandable that the rebellious research partners were in high feather when, late one Thursday afternoon they dropped by the office in Viena #26. Their goal: to file the field notes and grab their mail before heading home for a good night's rest. But as the secretary handed over their piles of letters she let slip six fateful words: "Doctor Harrar wants to see you."

Better let him tell his own terrible tale:

> I dropped the mail on the corner of the secretary's desk and followed Joe into the director's office. George was behind his desk as usual. But I was surprised to see Stakman lounging on the sofa along the right-hand wall, pipe gripped between his teeth and tobacco tin tight in his hand. Although retired from the University of Minnesota, he came down a couple of times a year to see how we were getting on.
>
> After we'd exchanged greetings, George dropped his bombshell with his standard suddenness. "Funds are running short," he said, "so we want you to abandon the Yaqui Valley. Sorry Norm but you've got to do this. Sonora is too isolated; it's costing too much. From now on, focus your work on the Bajío."
>
> In a long life containing many shocks this was maybe my greatest. His words fell heavy as an axe. We were being instructed to ignore the very place that was the key to getting the country fed. To think we'd not be going back was almost unbearable.
>
> At that point, sad to relate, I began losing self-control. "You gave me the responsibility to make Mexico self-sufficient in wheat." The words came out far too loud for that tiny office. "Now you're tying one arm behind my back, and ensuring I can't succeed. The Bajío can't meet the country's needs. Only Sonora can do that. In the Bajío there's not enough water or land, and the holdings are too small."
>
> Then I completely lost my composure. "If this is a firm decision," I yelled down at Harrar behind his desk, "you'd better find someone else because I'm leaving!"
>
> A second thought occurred: "I'll stay until you find a replacement. If Joe takes over the program I'll leave tomorrow." And I swung on my heels and headed for the door.
>
> Before I got halfway I noticed Joe beside me: "That goes for me too!" he shouted over his shoulder.
>
> And we stalked out side-by-side.

In refusing to abandon Sonora or shuttle breeding Norm showed he'd rather resign than retreat from his professional convictions. But the story then took an even weirder twist:

> Back in the secretary's office I grabbed my pile of letters and then flung them down in disgust. What was the use of checking the mail?
>
> Then in the spread of scattered envelopes Aureliano Campoy's return address stared up. Intrigued, I opened the envelope to find a blind carbon copy of a letter the old farmer had laboriously typed out in English: "Dr. Harrar," it began, "I want to congratulate the Rockefeller Foundation. For the first time in the history of Mexico someone is helping the farmers. I admire what you're doing, and it will have a big effect here in Sonora."
>
> But the kicker came at the end: "Why don't you help your own staff? Why don't you give them the things they need? Borlaug and Rupert are living and working under terrible conditions. Why is that? Why do you treat your people so badly?"
>
> Pinned to my copy was a handwritten note: "It is time somebody was helping you," it said.
>
> I handed the missive to Joe. I was convinced that I'd just let our friend down by quitting. "Hell," I said, "this is the worst possible time for a letter like this!" and stalked out of the building feeling worse than ever.
>
> In truth, we should have gone straight home. Instead we went to a cantina and drowned our sorrows. I've seldom been intoxicated but this was one unforgettable time. Midnight was long gone before we got back to the apartment. Margaret was so angry we'd skipped her dinner and were obviously the worse for wear she wouldn't let us in.
>
> She and I got into a shouting match through the front door.
>
> It was like some comic-opera farce.
>
> It was also the final straw: my career was over; my marriage too.

Impartial observers might not believe how all this turned out: the aggrieved party behind the locked door actually relented. Despite every provocation, she admitted the worthless miscreants.

Nonetheless, next morning both scuttled away before dawn, too wretched in mind and body to endure another flurry of feminine fury.

They planned to devote their last day on the job to a final wrap-up. Letting their hard-won results go unrecorded and their stellar seed go to waste would have been a crime against humanity. Before abandoning all hope for helping the hungry they wanted to see just how far they'd gotten. Moreover, they'd leave behind the top seed as well as a tidy record for those who might follow.

First, though, they needed to retrieve the field notebooks. As they entered the Viena #26 administrative center a voice called from Harrar's office, and Borlaug received yet another shock: Stakman was sitting on the sofa, puffing his pipe and holding the tobacco tin tight as before. This was truly historic since it was 6:30 and, as far as Norm knew, no one had ever seen Stak at work before 10:00.

The crafty professor looked straight through his protégé. "You're acting like a child!" he said in the tones that cut students into pieces like a knife.

Norm was by now past the point where such words and the faraway look were effective. Instead, Stakman's stiletto sounds merely severed the cords restraining his emotions. "What the hell do you mean?" he yelled. "Dutch is making it impossible to solve Mexico's wheat problem. It's that simple!"

Stakman now stared at him exactly as he did exceptionally wayward undergrads but this time he could see he was getting nowhere. "Calm yourself, calm yourself," he said at last. "You and Harrar are too much alike . . . ornery as hell. Let me see what I can do."

For Joe and Norm that Friday disappeared in despondency even as they recorded astounding yield figures. Afterwards, the disconsolate pair returned to Viena #26 to pick up their final mail, surrender their notebooks and conclude their careers.

Pinned to the mailbox, was a note instructing them to report to the director's office. On entering, the mystified hunger warriors found both Harrar and Stakman waiting. The moment was taut with tension. A breathless silence hung in the room. Norm concluded he'd now reached the absolute end of all his aspirations. He was about to be fired!

Then George Harrar's staccato voice delivered an even greater shock: "Forget what I said, Norm. Go on working in Sonora. We'll find some way to support you."

This revelation was nearly as unnerving as its forerunner. Harrar never reversed a professional decision. Stakman surely used his personal influence. But the letter probably clinched the issue. The Sonora farmer who—whilst himself living hardscrabble—was reaching out to better the lot of those who'd come to help would have touched Harrar's heart.

Here again the fragile chain of circumstance received a new and improbable link. Aureliano Campoy's feat of friendship connected the succession of earlier coincidences in Borlaug's serpentine career to the many unforeseen and improbable links yet ahead.

Had the continuum parted here in the fall of '47 there's no telling what might have transpired during the later course of human affairs. And it is especially noteworthy that the golden shackle holding together the full saga of how the world got fed was fashioned by the first of what would in time become millions of grateful dirt farmers. All in all, Aureliano

TECHNICAL PROGRESS, 1947

By the close of Round 5 in November '47, following three seasons in Central Mexico and two in Sonora, Norm is a year ahead of schedule. Without his doubled-up dedication he'd not have reach this level of advance until 1948.

On the upside 1947 has brought advances:

- The scene around his research facilities now reflects an abstract landscape. The core parents—Frontera, Supremo, Kenya Red, Kenya White, Mentana, Marroqui and Newthatch—limn the background whilst the mayhem and mischance of chromosomal re-assortment imprints an ever-brightening foreground as the few progeny proving most productive, most uniform or merely most intriguing get re-sown. Eventually one or two may achieve immortality. The rest are toast. Literally.
- Those fields also expose the long-sought uniform F5 lines of his first personal creations. And some of the Kenya-Mentana crosses and various blends turbocharged by Marroqui are projecting star quality.

In the cross-breeding fields he's now dealing with graduates to freshmen:

- F5 seeds—the sole remnants of his summer 1945 inaugural operations, his most advanced lines have segregated and a few quality performers are settling into stability;
- F4 seeds—gathered from the fourth generation of descendents from the winter 45/46 matings, these are already exhibiting particularized personality;
- F3 seeds—chromosomal combos laid down During the summer of 46 (three plantings back), are beginning to segregate and expose individuality;
- F2 seeds—descendents from crosses made during the winter of 46/47. Their genes are still knotted; none offers any hint of promise;
- F1 seeds—collected from this summer's cross-pollinations. These need time to unwind—years of replanting will pass before any talents emerge.

In two years this greenhorn gold-digger had panned considerable nuggets from a very shallow gene stream. His spirit has risen from the dungeon of despair and with customary zeal he's making up for lost time. Of course he's produced no botanical wealth; Mexican wheat production hasn't budged.

All in all, the campaign is on track. To parts unknown. And wheat's resistance to friendship is weakening.

Campoy earned the honor of Career Saver #17 for personally saving Borlaug's bacon.

After completing the work at Chapingo, Norm drove to Toluca to help Dick Spurlock gather the hundred-acre harvest. His hopes, however, were rebuffed by a cloudbank rolling in from the wide Pacific. After waiting a few days for the land to dry he tried again but as if on cue the clouds rolled back. Subsequently, this action-and-reaction repeated itself until the bottom dropped out of Spurlock's fields. Though the wheat was ripe for picking, no machine could move across 40 acres

CAREER SAVER #18

Fate's 18th facilitator, Richard Spurlock. This Wyoming cowboy bulked up Borlaug's seed to make enough for farmers to plant. Norm had no way of doing that. For years to come Spurlock would contribute time and energy to Borlaug's cause . . . wholly without pay, contract, funding or demands. Because of Spurlock's contribution Mexican wheats got carried past the challenging realm of research and into the even more challenging realm of reality. Photo shows the second multiplication Spurlock grew in 1948 on this ranch in Toluca.

that had become little more than marsh.

To wheat farmers water is a fickle friend. Early in the season there's no greater ally; at harvest time no greater foe. Dampened grain attracts mold and may even sprout before leaving the parent plant. Either way, the crop is rendered worse than worthless.

For that reason the multiplication that would empower Mexico's wheat farmers now teetered on the brink of disaster. And with the forecast predicting more storms marching forward in echelon from the South Seas, Norm was about to lose a year, if not his whole venture. You see, he'd committed all his available seed to the multiplication. Willful weather was about to make him look as addled as adobe.

In desperation, he grabbed Joe Rupert and hauled him out to Toluca. Slaving like Caesar's serfs, the lookalikes sickled several hundred thousand plants and bound them into what old timers called sheaves. Spurlock provided peons for the even bigger task of hauling all those bundles through the marshy mud to shelter.

Finally, having endured a week slogging in soupy slop—hair sodden, clothes filthy and boots like mud footballs—they could admire the several thousand bundles safely stacked in the big barn. Later, Spurlock's workers methodically turned the sheaves to ensure the heads dried without molding or sprouting.

Beyond being far-fetched, this exploit produced a fantastic 2800 pounds an acre—at least four times Mexico's average that year. Despite Mother Nature, they'd reaped 50 tons of grain *by hand*.

"You know what this means, Dick?" Borlaug gushed. "We're on our way! Another planting will give us 5000 tons. Next year maybe we'll have all the seed the farmers can use!"

1948

Breakout

Before leaving for Season 6 Norm and Joe packed 200lb of Kenya Red and Kenya White that are to be multiplied specifically for use by Sonora farmers. They of course also packed Round 5's research winners for the trip north.

This time Harrar relents and releases to their care a small tractor and *two* pickup trucks. One is the old green Ford with the government logo, the other a brand new long-body Chevrolet with a screened-in top. Harrar stipulates, however, that both be returned once the supplies have been delivered.

Norm drives the smaller vehicle, with Oscar Nery Sosa, a Guatemalan student, as his passenger. Joe Rupert follows in the fancy new Chevy, accompanied by Teodoro Enciso and Alfredo Campos, now fulltime co-workers. Norm's truck carried the Kenya seed as well as a camping stove and the cache of emergency food; Joe's totes the tractor as well as miscellaneous supplies and equipment. With his mind still shadowed by the hassle in El Paso, Norm decides to risk a new route being cut right through the Sierra Madre directly connecting the states of Chihuahua and Sinaloa.

When the convoy set out the mid-November morning was bright and clear, and the 800-mile run to the city of Chihuahua proved uneventful. After a night in a downtown (and downscale) hotel they headed out on the main road west. This morning was also fair. However, toward noon, just as they began bending up the eastern wall of the mountain massif the sky turned leaden. Indeed, both road and weather deteriorated in tandem, an especially unwelcome pairing since the Sierra Madre Occidental isn't nicknamed Devil's Backbone (*Espina del Diablo*) for nothing.

Still they pressed forward, and on arriving at the section of road newly cut through the Devil's seemingly invulnerable vertebrae they discovered a single lane carved from the perpendicular rock comprising the south wall of the Copper Canyon (Barranca del Cobre).

Though this was still the dry season, the midday sky hung low, shading the canyon's stark profile with cloud-strands that dangled like bangs from the brows of heaven. Then, just as the quaint convoy entered the giant gash through the mountain barrier, the sooty sky let loose. What began as drizzle later morphed into downpour. Water cascaded down the cliff, skittered across the fresh dirt roadbed and disappeared into the emptiness beside the wheels, plummeting like a wide waterfall into seemingly endless space.

Peering through the waltzing wipers Borlaug saw the road surface turning greasy. Still he kept on until after just rounding a blind bend he had to brake to avoid hitting the back of a large truck that loomed out of the murk before his bumper. He and Enciso sloshed forward to discover that the road ahead of the truck merged into a tumbled mass of earth. The canyon wall had collapsed.

Norm then sloshed back around the blind bend, hoping to find a way out of the impasse but as he approached there came a rumble, and the ground commenced shaking as an avalanche of rock and earth collapsed the section of ledge beyond the bend.

They were now in peril: should the central portion of this newly carved cliff face loosen they too would be cast into the void.

A fourth vehicle, a pickup truck, had pulled in behind Joe's just in the nick of time. It happened to carry the engineer in charge of building the road. He'd come because his workers had struck columnar rock. Indeed, the hard outcropping had proven so recalcitrant Mexico had reached across the seas to the Soviet Union for help. Moscow, in turn, had dispatched a renowned specialist to personally oversee the placement of the explosives. He was right there in the engineer's pickup. The bulky truck in Norm's windshield carried the dynamite.

To Borlaug the Russian's presence seemed fortuitous. The authorities might not bestir themselves for agriculturists but they'd move mountains to rescue this famous foreigner who probably reported to Premier Stalin.

Thankfully the rain let up, and as evening came on Norm set up his camp stove and retrieved the emergency rations. Those few cans of meat, peas, peaches and coffee as well as bags of dried beans and rice provided the sole sustenance for eight souls wedged on a ledge higher than the Grand Canyon.

He recalls the scene with a laugh:

Neither Joe nor I minded doing the cooking and sharing our food but the Soviet engineer was perhaps the most offensive individual I've ever met—and I've certainly met my share. Somehow Joe's former tour of duty in North Africa came out, and even while eating our food the Russian sneered about Rommel whipping the whole U.S. Army. He made the point not once but endlessly. Amazingly, Joe stayed cool, calm and civil. To this day I can't believe he didn't tip that guy over the edge!

Tension remained high until the second afternoon That's when the food ran out. Then they heard the clank of a bulldozer echoing off the rock walls up ahead. An hour or so later the machine itself emerged into view, pushing tons of liquefied spoil off the ledge, whence it surged with a sucking squelch into a 7000 foot free fall.

The operator next hooked a chain to the front of the big truck, told Borlaug to attach his towrope to the back, and began hauling both vehicles over the still-oozing surface. This was scary, since either the big truck or the little pickup might fishtail over the lip. Alternatively, the dynamite might do the job.

But the outcome proved an anticlimax. They negotiated the danger zone. Then Joe got the Chevrolet across. And they cautiously descended the long and winding road down the Sierra Madre sodden western wall. And with heartfelt joy the little party crossed Sinaloa's flooded flats to reach the town of Los Mochis as night fell.

Having paid for rooms in a hotel, Norm and Joe retired to the bar to try to rebuild their shattered spirits. Settling back into the comforts of a highball, they observed the communist engineer saunter in and look around. They kept their heads down, and under his breath Joe expressed a rather coarse comment explaining just where the man from Moscow might go. The unwelcome presence, however, sauntered over and sat down, acting with seeming genuine friendship. Following a Cuba Libre, conversation blossomed and all three got on like old comrades in arms. Absent the tension, a day on the wall of death seemed almost a lark.

With the coastal highway washed out, the trucks couldn't make Sonora. So Borlaug made a crucial decision: He and Joe hustled Enciso and Campos to the train station, packed the seed and the small tractor aboard the "flyer" to Sonora, and told the pair to get everything out to the old experiment station and *plant the damn seed!*

Then, being duty bound to return the pickups to George Harrar, the three remaining members—Norm, Joe and the young Guatemalan trainee—headed southward. Again they undertook the direct descent down the coast. This time their nerve ends wouldn't escape a workout.

The incident began when they reached the Santiago River. It was a Saturday afternoon and Borlaug still drove the boxy Ford with Oscar Nery as his passenger. Joe was behind them in the long-bed Chevrolet. Rain from the Sierra Madre cloudburst was by then barreling out of nearby Lake Chapala in a heaving, hurrying, bubbling brown tide. Indeed, the river was so swollen it seemed to be draining half the nation, which in a sense it was since Lake Chapala is like an inland sea and the Santiago is its major outlet.

Let him take over the tale:

At the river crossing a couple of women were washing clothes by the water's edge. They told us a truck had gone across earlier. The other bank was just 150 yards away, and we could see a road-worker camp. I decided to go ahead despite the oncoming darkness and the swollen torrent.

After removing the fanbelt to stop the blades throwing water over the wiring, I attached a piece of rubber hose to the exhaust pipe and tied it so that the end stood up like a snorkel. Those were common procedures when driving in Mexico in the 1940s.

Then, following the imprint of the previous tire tracks, I drove that little pickup down into the flow. The view ahead was not comforting; the river writhed between its banks and the current seemed to have raised the middle. And right there, in the highest part of this surging chocolate tide, the engine stalled.

At first I wasn't concerned but the engine refused to start and water was spurting in through cracks around the door. Oscar was clearly scared and as the cab began filling he let on that he couldn't swim. I had to do something. So I yanked off my boots, yelled I was going get help, climbed out the window, and started walking toward the road-building camp.

Although the water was only waist deep, the bottom was stony and sharp and cut my feet as I pushed against the current to keep upright. Then, all of a sudden, one foot slipped, and I went tumbling into the deeps below the ford. In that powerful tide there was no chance of swimming. The turbulence sent me rolling and tossing into the dark depths. I could feel consciousness passing away. It seemed like the end.

Luckily for me, instinct stayed sharp, and on sensing the clutch of the current slackening I kicked my way to the surface. The river had curved, and the water churning around the bend was depositing me toward the inner side, which happened to be the far bank.

Hope rushed back, and willing my body to move I struggled into the backwash and dragged myself out onto a rocky shoal. I'd made it across. I was sodden, gasping like whooping cough, my whole body shaking from shock.

There was no time for musing about myself . . . Oscar needed help. Somehow I managed to stumble the 200 yards to the road-building camp. To my horror, the crew was standing around staring at the truck stranded in mid-river . . . awaiting the inevitable. Water had filled the cab and Oscar was standing on top pleading for help. Yet despite his cries, no one was doing anything.

Even I was out of ideas. Then I noticed the Caterpillar grader. I strode to the man who appeared to be the foreman and told him to start it up. He said it was out of fuel. When I pointed to a tanker trailer nearby he explained that only the engineer had a key, and he'd gone off to the next village for the Saturday night movie. Then he shrugged; nothing could be done.

Grabbing a stick, I stuck it in the grader's tank. It was empty all right but dregs of diesel remained. The sight of that brown stain on the tip of the stick won over the foreman, and he started the grader and drove it to the ford.

Luckily, it was fitted with a winch wound with steel cable. I grabbed the sturdy hook on the end and waded out along the ford to stretch that lifeline out to our little truck. Five of the road crew came behind, holding up the cable as it unwound. We were all very scared; darkness was descending, the speeding water was ripping at our bodies, our hold on the cable was precarious. Also my legs weren't too steady and the sharp stones were again cutting my feet.

On reaching the pickup I found that there was no place to attach the cable. The current had scoured out so much soil from beneath the tires the front bumper was resting on the bottom.

But something had to be done, so ducking under the bubbling tide, I scraped away rocks and gravel, and managed to loop the hook under the bumper and back onto the cable. Then I waved to the grader driver on the shore. As the cable took the strain I felt sure our boxy green pickup would flip over and toss Oscar into the deeps downstream but with all six of us hanging onto the upper side, it slowly slid forward, grinding on the rocks as it went.

The moment when it finally emerged in the shallows and slid up the bank was one to remember. That old Ford looked like some sea creature yanked from its natural habitat. Brown fluids spurted from every pore.

By then, night had fallen and getting the second pickup across was impossible. Next morning, however, the waters had receded enough for Joe to drive over. Even so we couldn't proceed. Getting the drowned government vehicle back in running order took all day. To our amazement, the crankcase was empty. Even now, that seems hard to believe; the water must have pushed out the oil.

In the upshot the adventure turned out okay. The bulk of the seed was in Joe's pickup, and remained undamaged. Nonetheless, we dared not mention the incident to George Harrar. It took about a year to pluck up the courage to show him Joe's photograph of the scene—just the top half of the OEE's precious pickup sticking above the raging waters and the young student who'd come from Guatemala to learn how to be a scientist standing on top in terror for his very life!

On arrival at the Lomas apartment Borlaug was in bad shape, and Margaret demanded he seek help. But after long soaks in the bath he retired to bed. When he awoke 10 hours later she called the neighborhood doctor, who dressed the cut and swollen feet and ordered a week of bedrest. "Impossible," Norm retorted. "The season is already passing and our whole program depends on that seed in Sonora."

Within 48 hours he was landing at Cajeme airfield. Anxiety had his heart racing as he was driven toward the unprepossessing experiment station out in the arid emptiness. But when the taxi turned in through the concrete pillars the worry turned to wonder as he noted the rows of seedlings emerging from the damp earth, stretching the tips of green and graceful cotyledons toward the desert sun.

Teodoro Enciso and Alfredo Campos had done their job.

The program was back on track.

That winter campaign involved assaults on multiple fronts. Of the different plantings the largest entailed the 200lb portion of the harvest salvaged from Spurlock's bottomless bog. Those Kenya Red and Kenya White multiplications demanded bigger operations than any previously attempted at the derelict old station. Norm wanted several tons of seed for Sonora farmers to test.

Moreover that season, he also instituted a wholly new form of endeavor: demonstration plots. These involve pairs of tiny plantings carefully arranged alongside a path that cut across the fields. Each set is designed to showcase the powers of a particular plant line or cultivation practice. Each carries a plaque handwritten in bold Spanish script. By season's end, they'll expose the best seed and the best way to realize its potential. At least that's what he hopes they'll expose five months hence.

Coming on top of the normal research operations, these demands brought an unexpected difficulty: manpower. That winter he had but one helper. The students were back in the capital doing their designated duties. Joe Rupert had retreated to the University of West Virginia to complete his PhD. Oscar Nery Sosa had gone home to start wheat

TECHNICAL CHALLENGES, 1948

Round 6 (Nov. 1947-April 1948). Third stint in Sonora. In March he turns 34.

Prime focus this winter season is on:

MULTIPLICATION. He needs to multiply 200lb of the four Generation-1 survivors for advanced-placement with a few friendly farmers in Sonora.

STEM-RUST RESISTANCE. He must advance a massive array of plants that are in different stages of refinement. The "Borlaug Finishing School for Wheat" now has a middle school containing a dozen separate half-acres of the latest descendents of the '45 and '46 couplings. Like all "sophomores" they have identity crises to resolve. The freshmen—seed of the summer past—are in a separate area where over the summer they'll get new gene infusions. A few cross-pollinations will combine Kenya Red's rust resistance with that from Frontera and Supremo.

DEMONSTRATION DAY #1. A special planting will highlight the new varieties and the ways to elicit their best performance. By season's end he hopes this will excite the interest of Sonora farmers.

Round 7 (May-October, 1948). Fourth stint in Central Mexico.

Prime focus at Chapingo during the summer is:

STEM-RUST RESISTANCE. That season's product will be his 7th Generation in his stem rust research. It will add yet more complexity.

MULTIPLICATION. At Toluca this season Spurlock will multiply the 50 tons of the four Generation-1 champs to create 5000 tons of seed for planting nationwide.

research in Guatemala. The bird-boy brothers remained bound by their family to the far-away village. And Alfredo Campos had returned to the agriculture college at Chapingo for a Masters degree.

Norm now faced five months caring for hundreds of thousands of individual plants with only Teodoro Enciso to help. Wonderment still refracts off the mirror of memory:

> Even now I can't believe that we were out there alone. The amount of work we faced was inhuman!

Wonderment was justified. The future course of history depended on whatever this lone pair lost in a virtual vacuum could achieve from the masses of plant life stretching all around them, absorbing the desert sun.

Moreover his partner was not among the ardent strivers whom the OEE had chosen for their mastery of the college curriculum. Barely into his 20s, Enciso was both proud and prickly. Content to slide over the surface of life, he was unassuming, sometimes withdrawn, and bounded by a seemingly eggshell thin psyche:

> Enciso was so sensitive you could not avoid upsetting him. He balked at the very hint of criticism . . . even when I merely asked how his day had gone he seemed to consider it a slur.

Luckily Enciso came from a farming background and knew his job. Norm delegated him full responsibility for running the nurseries. It was a risk because the nurseries were the key to future successes. But left alone with his responsibility the temperamental trainee proved both qualified and capable. He ran the nurseries well.

After the normal Christmas break with the family, Norm left Margaret, Jeanie and baby Billy and returned north late in January 1948.

When the fields began flowering in February, both he and Enciso worked as if the weight of the world rested on their shoulders, which it did, though neither would know that for years to come.

During the three-week wheat-mating period the lone rangers in the desert set up and satisfied tens of thousands of stigmas. It required an all-consuming preoccupation as each struggled to complete every cross possible with four hands, two heads and 12 hours of midwinter daylight. During those feverish days—before mindless nature nixed the plant's power to pollinate—the pair was lost to view, head-down dawn to dark, fully focused on the day's burden.

Among many hundreds of crosses, a handful involved pollinating Kenya Red with Frontera and Supremo and vice versa. For this, there was no apparent practical need; he was just double-charging the chromosomes with Kenya *and* Hope resistance as a kind of umbrella policy. Redundancy was being built in just in case the unthinkable should happen somewhere down the line. Of course the unthinkable could never be that cruel.

At the experiment station the living was easier. Much of the muddle, chaos, clutter and mess had been cleared away; a few windows had been restored; and the rats had been run out. Norm and Enciso each appropriated a staff house, uncoiled a bedroll and dossed down on the stone floor. Heaven!

Despite the classy lodgings, life remained low. For one thing, the duo was basically marooned. Although just 12 miles from town, the old station was commonly cut off from the rest of mankind. They'd then be prisoners of the desert void. The last 7 miles of the access road—a dirt track squeezed between a drainage channel and the main Yaqui Valley irrigation canal—often turned impassable and sometimes impossible. For one thing, winter rainstorms rolling in from the nearby Pacific could convert the roadbed into a seven-mile mud hole incapable of supporting feet, let alone wheels.

For another, the onset of spring sent the temperatures soaring over 105°F. Then the mud seemed to sublime: A thick brown cloud literally ascended from the slime to levitate on the afternoon winds. Among other things, that flying dust carpet made the seven-mile approach not just unbearable but un-breathable. It is recalled with a shudder:

Sometimes we almost choked getting in and out of the old station.

Nevertheless, travel discomforts affected him less than might be imagined. You see, OEE vehicles were still banned in the north. During the winter stints of '45, '46, '47, and '48 he had to rely on Mrs Jones not just for food but for bare necessities.

Fortunately, another local volunteer now stepped forward. A small, bright bundle of mental energy, Rafael Angel Fierros was different: Not only technically trained, he was perhaps the only Sonora farmer still wedded to wheat. On hearing a weirdo was working at the worthless station across the valley curiosity transcended native caution and he drove over to study the newcomer's science . . . nay sanity.

This short and sharp-eyed stranger, his face fronted by droopy mustache and topped by stylish straw hat arrived unannounced, giving no hint of his identity. Borlaug nevertheless spoke frankly, forcefully and philosophically about his program and plans. The visitor could see that this gringo wasn't as goofy as he expected. Eventually, Fierros became entranced enough to offer to host duplicate plantings on his own fields.

That for Norm was a gift beyond measure since a replicate testbed can uncover flaws hiding within the most reliable looking research-station plants. He instantly agreed. He'd share his best seed. They'd begin when he returned in November.

L ate in April, Judgment Day arrived. Time for the plants to meet their maker.

With the experiment station lacking so much as a balance Norm had to cadge lifts and carry thousands of samples to Cajeme just to determine how much grain his winning plants had produced. During those several weeks he toted his notebook and pile of paper bags to the Hotel La Colonial, the flea-bitten hostelry from which he'd often tried to phone home. The place was crumbling and crawling with critters but it possessed the one thing he needed. Commandeering the far end of the check-in counter, he spent hours weighing his seed samples on the scales the clerks used when posting letters.

Should no vehicle capable of carrying a stack of paper sacks be heading back to the station—a common enough occurrence—he'd stay over in that rundown establishment where nights were very long, very sweaty, very smelly and sometimes very itchy.

On such occasions the safety of certain star-studded samples caused high anxiety. "These seeds are precious," he once told the manager. "Have you got a safe?"

The face behind the counter shot him a quizzical look; a thumb was jerked toward the faded-yellow wall at his back; and a strongbox was mentioned. "But I'm afraid it's full," the clerk said

Borlaug then went beyond the point of rudeness. "Take the cash out, please; lock it in a drawer. These are worth much more!"

At the time he seemed to have lost all sense of proportion . . . even propriety. Experience, however, would confirm his prescience. Eventually his seeds will prove priceless and many will get stolen.

A lso late that April he organized his first Farmer Field Day. By then, the tiny plots really did present a fairground of the future. Any casual observer need but stroll the path slicing across the fields to see the best seed to plant and the best way to plant it. The side-by-side plots demonstrated good and bad; old and new. Among other things, they displayed the importance of weed control, watering at the right time, and sowing on the right date, with the right spacing and right depth. The differences were, for the most part, dramatic. Properly sown and properly supervised, top performers such as Kenya Red produced twice what Sonora farmers were then getting.

Trouble was, no one evinced the slightest interest:

In the spring of 1948 I attempted to drum up interest in our first Demonstration Day. I visited radio stations, newspapers and government offices. I paid for advertisements and put up flyers in town and along the roads. In big letters the flyers said: FARMERS FIELD DAY—FREE BEER AND BARBECUE.

Still, not a single soul would commit to coming. Then on the street in Cajeme I chanced to meet Reza Rivera, an economist working for the Banco de Mexico. "Leave it to me," he said, "and don't worry . . . you'll have an audience."

When the Saturday arrived, Enciso and I were ready. We'd

rehearsed our talks and printed a pile of handouts. We had small bags of seed to hand out as gifts. Aureliano Campoy had found a flatbed truck from which I could address a throng. Mrs Jones had supplied trestles and tabletops for the beer and barbecue.

Our problem was a lack of audience. Through the morning Teodoro and I sat on the back of Campoy's borrowed truck, waiting for the crowd to arrive. Above all, we wanted the big farmers whose word carried weight in the community.

By midday the attendance had built to 25. Accountants, secretaries and clerks from Reza Rivera's office made up 20. Five more were farmers. One of those was our neighbor Aureliano Campoy, who already knew everything. Three more had come for the beer. Only one person out of the whole audience genuinely wanted to learn.

Putting aside our disappointment, Enciso and I showed off the new wheats and how they should be grown. We didn't do too well. And it was not just my poor Spanish; a couple of farmers loudly challenged every statement I made.

I replied with equal frankness and considered I'd put across a good case. But their harsh words, which mainly reflected ignorance and prejudice against Americans, undermined the audience's confidence. At the end when I called for questions no one spoke up. Not one of the 25 wanted any of the seed packages, either . . . they just wanted to get to the beer and barbecue.

This seemed the utter collapse of his schemes and dreams. Clearly, the locals didn't want help. Maybe didn't deserve it.

Nonetheless, some subterranean signal must have wormed across the valley because during the following week a dozen different farmers showed up at the station—arriving in pairs as if not wanting to be alone with a gringo. They explained their sudden presence with statements like: "We've heard that interesting things are going on out here."

Borlaug escorted each pair through the demonstration plots, giving them the full explanation. This ate into his days. Before he knew it his regular chores had fallen far enough behind to threaten the whole venture. By then he should have been heading for the central region, where the sowing season was already nigh.

Frustration still flares in flashback. But from then on relations with the locals began to rally. Though it took him a long time to realize it, the disastrous demonstration day actually constituted the first step toward earning Sonora's trust.

During that Farmer Field Day Norm had noticed a young man standing silent but attentive in the background. This was the single participant who'd genuinely come to learn about wheat.

After all the others were engaged with the beer and barbecue he sidled up and introduced himself: Roberto Maurer.

Pablo's brother proved of median height and modest manner. Aged in his late twenties, he was handsome in an understated way, with serious dark eyes and the romantic sagging mustache Mexicans equated with manliness. His manner was courteous, his attitude reticent, and his English flowed in slow, pleasant, modulated tones, each word loosed with care. Borlaug liked him at once.

Later it transpired that Roberto had been nine years old when the squatters overran the Maurer estate. They'd shot his father from ambush and seized all the land, other than the corner housing a flourmill. Not willing to risk more lives, the family had fled.

Although murder and misappropriation were high crimes even under Mexico's constitution, government indifference, as we've indicated, effectively condoned farmland grabs. Not until 1936 were the Maurers compensated with the swatch of Sonora desert. Young Roberto—then barely 18—had come north, cleared away the cactus and mesquite and erected a tin shack for shelter. Later Teresa, his teenage wife, joined him. Then, when the irrigation department's new reservoir supplied water, they tried sowing wheat.

Given their inexperience, success proved elusive. By 1938 they were cultivating just 10 acres. But through that winter they took heart: the wheat crop promised a generous harvest. Of course it proved a mirage. As the season advanced into its final six weeks, rust rode in on the north wind, took up residence, and rotted Roberto and Teresa's hopes into matted messes.

Given the awful depths to which they'd descended from their sylvan existence in the serene central uplands, this was hard to bear. Teresa shed bitter tears. The couple seemed at the end of their string. Their dream had died.

By 1948, the year of the first Demonstration Day, that contagion lay quiescent but the Maurers still suffered. "I've never really learned how to grow wheat well," Roberto explained. "Will you come out and show me what to do?"

Norm recalls the scene:

> A week later, I took a morning off from the end-of-season chores and dashed off to the Maurer's place. These were the days before herbicides took the heartbreak and back-break out of weed control, and the Maurer fields were strangled.
>
> "Roberto," I said. "Never plant wheat without first preparing the

land. The soil around here contains too many weed seeds. You must irrigate and get those to germinate. Then you cultivate. Only after that do you sow wheat. Next year we'll take 50 acres and do that. And I'll also share our best seeds and all we've learned."

So ended his third session in Sonora. Once the plantings on the tumbledown experiment station had been harvested, the seed sorted, sacked, stacked and stored, and the yield data recorded he was ready to head south. His only overt success had been the multiplication field. He'd turned 200 pounds of Kenya Red into 2 tons.

Before leaving, he decided to donate the lot to local farmers, together with samples of the four still-unnamed breakout varieties he'd made from scratch back in 1945. Doing the rounds, he called on the biggest Sonora wheat growers. All evinced disinterest:

> They made no bones about it. Their indifference was clear. Each said something like: "Thanks but I've already got the best seed." Not even my friends Aureliano Campoy and Rafael Fierros showed enthusiasm.

This was errant foolishness on the part of farmers who needed the best seed they could get. Still, he made no comment or judgment and merely piled the sacks in a corner of an abandoned staff house. Time to head home; he'd pry open the iron minds when he returned in the fall.

That May of 1948 sees the start of Year 4; Norm's already put in 6 seasons of nonstop research. Yet as he approaches the summer's genetic jousting at Chapingo most observers, including his superiors, regard his labors with distrust, not to mention dismay. All that immense effort and not-inconsiderable expense have produced little to brag about. His successes, though critical, have all been cerebral.

Taken all round, Norm is confident the plants he's readying for release will baffle rust's malign designs. They'll be shock absorbers for the food supply. They may not add much but they'll stop rust from subtracting any. And that, after all, had been the campaign's key objective.

First up, the Foundation Foursome needs multiplication. Norm drove to Spurlock's upscale spot under the skydome over Toluca and within two days the planting that'll produce enough Frontera, Supremo, Kenya Red and Kenya White to fill the national need for seed was safely sequestered in the sandy loam. This was the first summer wheat in Mexican history.

BORLAUG GROWS . . .

April, 1948. At the Yaqui Experiment Station Borlaug gets ready to harvest the multiplication of Kenya Red. This is where the 200lb of seed got turned into 2 tons.

Then at Spurlock's suggestion they took a sack of Supremo seed and a sack of fertilizer and called on an impoverished farm a tad past the village of San Juan del Río. The gifts seemed to delight the farmer. Holding out the sacks containing the keys to a fine future, Norm told the campesino to apply fertilizer to the planting site, which at the time simulated scorched earth. With his arm outstretched to receive the gift, the man froze. "Señor," he said, looking terrified and almost shaking with fear, "that is *venemo*! It will poison me . . . and my family."

That was an unshakeable superstition and neither Borlaug nor Spurlock could be bothered arguing the point. Taking back the prospect of prosperity, they drove farther along to a larger landowner named Carlos Rodríguez. Having passed over the seed sack, Spurlock

. . . A GIFT FOR FRIENDS

What Norm doesn't yet know is that no local farmer will take the seed. And when he offers it to his friends Campoy and Fierros both will turn him down.

hauled the bag of fertilizer from his pickup, mimicked the act of broadcasting it by hand, and placed it at the man's feet so there'd be less chance of a refusal. Though the farmer seemed dumbstruck at the risk he was being conned into taking, he made no move. The two Americans left him standing rigid by his field, the bags of seed and fertilizer side-by-side beside his shoes; a look of perplexity plastering his face like a mask.

Driving back to the city, Borlaug worried aloud. "We're on the right track, Dick. But we're never going to get seed out to farmers this way."

At Chapingo, Norm gathered up the winter's winners and dashed headlong into his seventh campaign season.

This was, of course, long before the understanding of

deoxyribonucleic acid began demystifying the process, so there was no way to slice and dice DNA or fit genes together like puzzle pieces. With the genome still *terra incognita*, crop breeders relied on chance reshufflings of two sets of what we now know are 25,000 individual genes. Those odds generated unimaginable numbers of possibilities, and the resulting chromosomal sweepstakes offered only the slimmest chance of ever plucking out a winning combination. Great varieties were not unlike Lotto winners: aberrations, accidents, rare mathematical miracles. Given the near impossibility of ever getting anything useful, forced matings had to be made by the thousands. At the very least.

"If you're a plant breeder, you pay your dues," explains Garrison Wilkes of the University of Massachusetts, who's paid his several times over with corn. "Any plant breeder has to be dumb, because it doesn't take much in the way of brains to sit on a stool in the sun for hours on end and pollinate a few hundred, or a few thousand, plants. But it sure does take a cool hand."

By now, the coolest hands belonged to Reyes Vega. The boy who'd formerly chased birds for five pesos a week now had earned the professionals' trust. Though sadly lacking in schooling he'd proved a star at wheat breeding. Soon, he was emasculating and pollinating twice as fast as Borlaug, who prided himself on his blinding speed.

And that was far from the kid's last contribution. In a single day he revolutionized the whole procedure. This extreme makeover began when he pointed to the minute horseshoe-shaped structures in the wheat flower and asked, "What are those things?" Norm explained that they were the glumes that covered and protected the ovary and pistil.

Reyes Vega then slipped his imagination into top gear. Clipping the glumes off with small scissors he exposed the whole interior, and saw that all the pollen sacs could be pulled out in a single motion.

To Norm this mass-deflowering was an amazing spectacle and a big boost to his efforts.

> Reyes Vega's discovery saved us man-years of effort. Before, we'd picked out each of the male parts one by one with tweezers; now, we yanked them out all together.

The boy with the bright eyes and deft digits soon found yet another shortcut. Taking a flower head from the plant selected as the pollen source, he similarly clipped the end off its glumes, and then stuck the stem in the ground. Under the sun's severe gaze the pollen sacs all burst open within five minutes. That was a special sight: the head blossoming into a bright yellow ball and shedding pollen like a Roman candle.

This discovery saved time and secured a bigger and more reliable pollen supply. When researchers spun the yellow-crowned heads between their fingers, male dust doused all the female parts.

The boy's new technique underpinned all that would transpire. It lifted efficiency, saved time and money, boosted the success rate, and generated many more cross-pollinations per season. Elsewhere, wheat breeders might cross a few hundred flower heads a year. But thanks to the boy's insight Borlaug's group crossed thousands twice a year.

Moreover, this watershed year would deliver yet more advances. That summer Norm's insight and intuition became powerful enough to understand wheat's workings. From here on, the plant's silent patois began telling him many happy things. Each specimen's appearance, feel, manner and movement, bared private mysteries. The distinguishing traits included the height, length, thickness and angle of the leaves, the awns on the heads, the hairiness and shape of the "shoulders" on the glumes, the color and glint of the leaves, and the stiffness of the stems as they bent before the breeze:

> In a strange way the plants explained themselves . . . not by sound but by look, color, feel; the height and angle of their leaves; the shine and hue on the surface; the size, appearance and weight of the seeds; and the spread and depth of their roots.

Indeed, in the patterns of leaf, flower, stem, seed and root he was able to sense personality traits. Some plants were bold and brassy, others weak and wan. At a glance, he could detect the almost ineffable subtleties that made a winner. Sometimes, he couldn't explain why he chose one over another . . . the flicker of sunlight and shadow across the plot was all he needed to surmise the plant's inherent quality.

During that fall of '48 he could see that the four made-from-scratch elites were acing their final exams. Thus, he accorded them the ultimate accolade: formal names.

Christening a variety is not unlike awarding the diploma at the commencement ceremony; Borlaug released these four finalists into the mainstream of mankind as: Yaqui, Nazas, Chapingo (all from Marroqui-Newthatch crosses) and Kentana (from the Kenya-Mentana cross). They became his second quartet—the Follow-Up Foursome.

These fresh new brooms—his first personal creations—matured a couple of weeks earlier than his Foundation Foursome. With them,

Central Mexico's farmers could rest easy during the last fortnight of the season. Furthermore, all four could produce over 2000 pounds of grain an acre. Above everything, though, they possessed the exquisitely rare—almost mystical—ability to deny stem rust access to their cellular temples.

Every stem-rust race then known in Mexico, that is.

A round this time he recognized that commerce held the crop at its mercy. The disturbing fact was that wheat growers, especially the poorest, were beholden to grain merchants who paid as close to a pittance as possible. That reality crushed all prospect of progress. Without financial incentive, why should any grower chance his family's existence on a new variety, regardless of performance?

Once more Norm had hit the wall separating warm heart from cold commerce. Scientists are supposed to stop right there and relegate the rest to society or serendipity. Again he abandoned his researcher's reserve, leaped the professional divide, and plunged into direct action.

Collaring George Harrar, he poured out his concern. "Our new varieties have good yield potential and good disease resistance," he explained that afternoon. "But there's a practical problem we'd better solve right away."

"What's the problem?"

"Well, it's the pitiful payments the farmers get. You see, at the time of harvest the millers send their buyers out with a cash offer amounting to only half the world price. Naturally, the growers request more. The buyers argue that the bakers won't buy bad flour, and then go straight to Texas and buy whatever they need. A few months later they return to the farmers, who by then are so squeezed by their creditors they accept the original or an even more miserable offer. With that going on no one will ever try new varieties, and we'll get nowhere."

"Oh hell," Harrar said: "We'd better go downtown and fix this."

A couple of days later the two visited the Ministry of Agriculture and called on Subsecretary Alfonso González Gallardo. Formerly a sugarcane specialist and professor at the Chapingo agriculture school, this kindly, soft-spoken administrator had helped Harrar set up the OEE. Both Gallardo and Harrar were wise beyond their years; both were scientists; both were sympathetic to the plight of farmers; each trusted the other.

But at the time it didn't seem that way to Norm. The official heard Harrar out and responded by saying nothing whatever. He occupied his

TECHNICAL PROGRESS, 1948

By the close of Round 7 in November '48, following four seasons in Central Mexico and three in Sonora, he's a year and a half ahead of schedule. Without his three and a half years of nonstop research he'd not have gotten this far until the first year of the following decade.

1948 is his breakout year:

- Four varieties are being released to farmers. They are from crosses made in 1945, and none is perfect or permanent, but each surpasses anything Mexican farmers have ever sown.
- He's now preparing Yaqui, Nazas, Chapingo and Kentana as his second quartet of named varieties—the Follow-Up Foursome.
- Government rules now favor Mexican production over imports;
- Borlaug and Spurlock produce Mexico's first ever commercial wheat crop to be grown during summer.
- Seed is being bulked up in both Sonora and Central Mexico.
- The first Farmer Field Day has been held, though all but one participant came only for the beer and the barbecue.

Borlaug finds his second basic principle: the social and political system should support improved food production.

By now the uncertainty in his mind is clearing like morning mist. The plant is showing signs of friendliness, perhaps even a willingness to expose a secret. He's becoming a wheat whisperer.

In the 4 years since his arrival, the number of mouths in Mexico has risen by 2.5 million, or 11 percent, to 24.5 million.

large ornate desk, lost in thought, sucking his pipe. The silence that enmeshed all three continued long enough to turn unsettling. Tension permeated the air like gravity. Something about the tableau convinced Borlaug the official was figuring how best to rid himself of the meddlesome foreigners.

Then, instead of dismissing the pushy pair or advancing dead-end delays, the Subsecretary slowly began nodding. "Well," he grunted at last, "what should I do?"

By then Harrar had worked out the answer. "Look," he said. "Go to the Ministry of Industry and Commerce and tell it not to issue import permits *until the grain merchants have bought up Mexico's own wheat*. The merchants will then have to pay the farmers promptly and also pay them fairly *before* trooping to Texas.

"The low quality is definitely a concern," Harrar added, "and no merchant should be forced to pay top peso for poor grain. Give the merchants the option of demanding a discount. That will give the farmers an incentive to upgrade the quality of all they produce."

The administrator continued serenely puffing his pipe. Borlaug was more than certain the man was seeking a way out. But after a couple more awkward minutes there emerged the fateful declaration: "I'll do it."

From that moment onward, Mexico's own farmers stood first in line for the harvest payments, a feature that quickly earned wheat unprecedented levels of trust. This single, obvious, unexpectedly powerful national policy swept away the fear, suspicion and misguided mental deadweights that had burdened the resource in the rural mind. It lifted wheat to a place in farmers' hearts. It also lifted the frown from the brows of the future.

■ LESSON TWO: Policy Matters

This surprising and hard-earned revelation would in time morph into his second principle for building an embracing and enduring food supply. *Government policy should be sensible, supportive, and never hinder the farmer's will to produce more.*

1949
Crossroads

As Round 8 of his research begins farmers have adopted not a single Borlaug product. Sonora still relies on Barigon, whose grain is too bad for bread. Central Mexico still relies on scrub wheats hearkening back to Conquistador bequests almost three centuries before Austrian monk Gregor Mendel pioneered plant breeding.

Those dark-age holdovers were particularly prevalent in the Bajío, and in 1948 the summer across those six upland states happened to favor the fungus.

Having heard the traditional fields were faring poorly, Norm swung by in November 1948 on his way north to Sonora. With him was Teodoro Enciso, and on first sighting the Bajío it was clear that stem rust had run riot across the republic's breadbasket. As far as the eye could see scrub wheats were succumbing. Rust had had a field day. The area smelled like sour milk. Those sights and smells foreshadowed the misfortune he'd long feared for Mexico.

At one point they stopped the seed-laden pickup truck and climbed down for a close up. Then out of nowhere an old man appeared, his face on fire. "What," he yelled in Spanish, "are you doing on my land?"

Borlaug fumbled among the alien phrases muddling his mind; then looked desperately to Enciso. A torrent of syrup flowed as the young student explained that this was a great man who worked for an American foundation and the truck was carrying seed of experimental wheats.

The farmer remained sullen and suspicious until the moment Enciso mentioned the new wheats resisted this very disease and that the American was headed for Sonora to produce more seed and give it to farmers. As the implication sank in the eyes blazed up again, and the man grabbed Norm's arm. "You must give me some. Please!"

TECHNICAL CHALLENGES, 1949

Round 8 (Nov. '47-April 1948). Fourth stint in Sonora. In March he turns 35.

Besides the normal crush of stem-rust resistance work, that winter he'll oversee:

MULTIPLICATIONS. Fields to produce hundreds of tons of seed of his Follow-Up Foursome. He's now named them: Kentana, Yaqui, Mayo and Nazas.

DEMONSTRATION DAY #2. Although only a single needy farmer attended last year's demonstration day, he'll put in a new set of plantings that come April will show how to get great wheat yields in the Yaqui Valley. The focus now is fertilizer.

Round 9 (May-October, 1949). Fifth stint in Central Mexico.

Besides the normal crush of stem-rust resistance work, this summer he'll carry forward a project aimed at raising Yaqui's resistance to leaf rust.

The scientist hesitated. Every grain on the truck would soon be multiplied a hundred fold, and thus was vital for supplying *all* the farmers quickly. But this man was near to tears. "I've lost so much," he said, nodding toward his fields.

Unable to resist the pain behind the appeal, Norm wrenched his arm free, stuffed handfuls of several seed types into paper bags and passed them over.

Doffing his sombrero, the farmer stooped, bent his head, gripped the scientist's hand . . . and kissed it.

Upon arrival in Sonora he recovers the sacks containing the seed of the two promising new lines (Kentana and Yaqui) from the abandoned staff house.

This time, Aureliano Campoy and Rafael Fierros accept the gifts with good grace. Over the summer, both have rethought their reluctance and decided they should at least show a visitor politeness.

Although neither knew it, they'd been given the opportunity of a lifetime: seed enough to plant 60 acres with the varieties about to eclipse all others. In part, Norm regarded it as fair recompense for the equipment and land they'd shared. In the main, though, he wanted to see how his creations survived a dirt-farmer's fingers and fancies.

Finally he visited Roberto Maurer, bearing enough Yaqui to plant the 50 acres they'd discussed. Maurer had already irrigated that field, and the foolish weeds were exposing themselves to the sunlight and the hoe of destruction. Norm explained how to sow the new seeds and recommended adding nitrogen at the rate of 40 pounds an acre.

Having discharged his duty to his friends, he set about installing the winter experiments, which included an amazing array of plantings:

- Multiplication plots—scaled to produce hundreds of tons of seed of Kentana, Yaqui, Chapingo and Nazas.
- Tens of acres of segregating plants, among whom several seem likely future food-suppliers.
- A substantial crossing block wherein, come flowering time, he hopes to wrest more out of the wheat genome, and render all the foregoing models obsolete—just like General Motors.
- A planting aimed at raising resistance to leaf rust by crossing Yaqui with a variety known to resist this distinct and different fungus. This was just a preemptive move; should the disease that infects leaves rather than stems ever invade Mexico he'd be prepared.

Given the traction gained in the world of wheat, it's unsurprising that a sense of mastery was creeping into Norm's mind. He now can decipher signals radiating from his pals of the plant realm. It was certainly agreeable to walk among these friends of the fields and feel the positive vibes emanating from all sides.

Yet it was a lonely sensation. No human was interested. Not a single Sonoran farmer had asked for seed. Stem rust's ravages had freighted the crop with a reputation so evil it would take more than a gringo to counter it. Half the growers had switched to flax; more were following year by year. Even his friends and benefactors Campoy and Fierros seemed suspicious of the seeds he'd foisted on them.

Realizing that a gringo was never going to be believed, Norm tried to win over a few farm leaders. Buttonholing each in turn, he managed to create only collective curiosity. None agreed to try his seeds.

To surmount that antipathy he needed Rodolfo Calles [KY-es]. Without this leader's endorsement no local wheat grower would do anything as repugnant as abandon the seeds everyone else sowed.

Towering above all others in prominence, Calles was the former governor who'd built the Yaqui Valley Experiment Station almost two decades back. Now, however, the place had him strangely spooked. Norm invited him to tour the research plots and offered the latest seeds. It was all in vain: the invite was declined, the offer refused. The rejections were gracious but left Norm gritting his teeth in frustration.

Tall, handsome, proudly mustachioed, Rodolfo Calles was in his early 50s. Like Harrar, his bearing and manner exuded distinction and authority. He too had the power to energize a room just by entering.

Polished, even cosmopolitan, he spoke English almost as if born to it. In this rural backwater that would normally arouse deep suspicion but he'd legitimately inherited his accent from history. Rodolfo, you see, was the son of a revolutionary who'd risen from poverty in Sonora to become presidente and founder of Mexico's main political party, the PRI (Institutional Revolutionary Party).

Groomed from boyhood to follow his parent, Rodolfo had not only been governor, he'd been elected to the national legislature and had himself run for presidente. However, on the night of April 10, 1936 Lázaro Cárdenas rousted the father from the sanctity of his bedroom and hustled him across the border and into banishment in San Diego (horrors!). Rodolfo awoke to find he'd fallen from political destiny to political poison. He then chose to withdraw from public service and go wheat farming in El Yaqui, hoping to eke out a full life beyond the eagle-eyes now pulling the drawstrings in Mexico City.

His most sensitive spot was the experiment station. Beyond providing the funds, building the facilities and connecting the fields to the life-giving Yaqui Canal, he'd personally selected the best seeds, the best fruit tree stock, and the best stud animals from research stations in Texas and Arizona. He'd taken special pride in the pillared entrance, built to symbolize the station's significance. And he'd had the pleasant stone houses crafted to attract the finest faculty and students.

On surrendering the governorship in 1934 Calles had left his brainchild picture perfect. Thus his soul was stricken when Sonora's new brooms first slashed the budget and later palmed the place off to the unfeeling Federales across the mountain wall. Yet who could blame his replacement? Could a small research station stuck in the middle of the desert *really* drive a state's prosperity up and out of dust and destitution?

The resulting desolation constituted a personal hurt. Roldolfo Calles had by then lost both his political legacy and his place in history. Heartache explains why, a decade onward, he remains spooked. Despite eagerly waylaying Norm on the streets downtown, the former governor never ventured anywhere near his abused offspring. Whenever they met, the two would gab at great length as Rodolfo extracted every detail of the experimental findings. But the thought of seeing the actual workplace aroused sensations too searing to stomach.

As the winter season progressed Campoy and Fierros became desperately unhappy. Each had lost faith. Their fields seemed so mediocre they felt duped by their foreign friend.

Indeed, Borlaug's plants *were* underwhelming. Yaqui had a wan look, its seedheads small and awnless. Appearances were, however, deceiving since its spikelets produced three grains instead of the normal two. Put another way, an acre of Yaqui produced *half as much again* as any acre hereabouts. Kentana looked more impressive, with long awns and large seedheads. But it too was a plain-Jane plant. In appearance, that is.

Unaware of the veiled details, Campoy and Fierros scanned their underwhelming prospects and plumbed the bottom stratum of despair. They'd squandered a year's profits; they faced financial defeat; they'd been gulled by a gringo. This one was a scientist who'd seemed sound but had proved as air-headed as the rest.

Yet for all the manifestations of mistrust, deep down in Yaqui Valley consciousness something strange was stirring: open-mindedness. That became apparent in April when he arranged his second Farmer Field Day and found he no longer needed to cajole an audience. Without flyers, advertising, barbecue or beer there were almost 200 attendees. Moreover, most were farmers keen to capitalize on the experience. And they treated him with respect and asked good questions.

Speaking through a megaphone from the bed of a pickup truck, Norm issued his welcome and launched into his spiel. As before, he'd laid out something like a fairground of the future with plantings arranged so that differences were visible at a glance. Some highlighted up-and-coming varieties. Others showed how to wheedle the best performance from the new wheats. A few disclosed his very latest discovery: that the land was malnourished.

Neither rust nor genes limited the growth of the new high-octane plants. Soil was the chief check; the republic's farmland is too worn out to sustain the performance he's plaited into these chromosomes.
To illustrate this truth he'd laid out side-by-side squares that had been treated with different fertilizers in different amounts and at different points during wheat's growing cycle: Nitrogenous fertilizer applied in the right amount and at the right time generated 60 percent more grain than even the finest farmers attained hereabouts.

Other plant foods showed no effect. The Yaqui Valley, he boomed through the megaphone, needed nothing more than 40lb of nitrogen to make *each acre* produce 480lb more grain.

Actually, he used metric units and his Spanish now spun out in smooth sentences, so he believed he'd explained things clearly. Having finished with a flourish, he asked: "Are there any questions?"

FARMER FIELD DAY

Sonora, 1949. the key Farmer Demonstration Day. Norm addresses the crowd of 200 farmers who'd come with serious intent to learn. This is where he showed that the land was exhausted and needed fertilizer.

Naturally he anticipated howls of interest and inquiry. Heck, for a few pesos worth of plant food he'd virtually promised a 60 percent raise! Yet, only stares emerged; all 200 faces gazed upward. He thought he'd bombed or perhaps mistakenly employed a Spanish word so vulgar he'd shocked everyone into silence.

Jorge Parada and Eduardo Vargas—two of the rural leaders he hoped to win over—stood in the front, deadpan like the rest . . . not even scowling. Then Parada stepped forward and seemed to speak for all when he said: "Doctor Borlaug, I'd prefer not to say this because you might misunderstand." The Spanish was formal, the diction exquisite, the wording polite. "We appreciate your work on breeding wheats and we see that it could become very helpful. But the soil in this valley *needs no fertilizer*. Yes, you're getting an effect; we can see that. However, this experiment station has been mismanaged for years; the land here is the poorest around. Any good farmer will tell you that you'll get no response on his place."

"I'm sorry," Borlaug replied in Spanish. "This is what we've found, and I'm so convinced nitrogen will generate greater production that next fall I'm going to hire an agronomist and send him out to establish fertilizer trials on different farms."

Jorge Parada immediately spoke up. "Well, I want to participate," he said. "Use my place for one of your tests."

A week or so later, Norm took a morning off. Roberto Maurer's specially treated 50-acres proved stunning to the eye. The rest, however, remained a weedy wreck. "Why didn't you make me plant the whole farm like this?" Roberto said with a smile so plaintive it suggested resentment at his advisor's professional oversight. "Well," Borlaug said, letting out more of the truth than was good for his reputation, "I really didn't know it was going to turn out *this* good!"

From that point on the Maurers—Roberto, Teresa and their twin daughters—joined Mrs Jones, Aureliano Campoy and Rafael Fierros as colleagues and close friends. They too threw in their fate and fortune to help the loner who'd brought their dead dream back to life.

When it came time to harvest his crop Aureliano Campoy left until last the field he'd so foolishly sacrificed to Borlaug's worthless seed. He couldn't bear to face the reality of ruin. Finally, though, he had no choice and sent in the combine harvester.

Then, as he later explained, came the biggest surprise of his long life: "A huge stream of grain was pouring out. I hadn't anticipated so much. I told the foreman to go back and bring more sacks. He returned with two or three and I took one look and said: 'Hell, go back and get twenty or thirty!'"

So much grain spilling from so small an area left Campoy dazed. Even though both varieties were comparable, Kentana most touched his heart. Still in shock, he drove across the valley to confer with Fierros. Upon arrival, though, he saw his friend's crop still standing, and the sight kept him from blurting out the news. For a time, he turned the talk to this and to that, and then he slipped in an innocent sounding question: "What are those wheats you've got there? They look pretty poor."

"Oh, they're just experimental things Borlaug gave me," Fierros said: "Neither is any good."

That gave the visitor an idea: "Tell you what," he said, "You give me the harvest from your Kentana and I'll give you my Yaqui in return. Neither of us will have to handle *two* bad seeds."

Thus the two farmers struck up a seemingly pointless bargain.

For Norm, that winter's research provided a taste of the future. Here's where his first-born wheats fully expose the genescape his first fumbling attempts had fashioned four years back. In the spring of 1949 Kentana and Yaqui proved not only early-maturing and rust-resisting but also capable of generating 2800lbs an acre.

Compared to the 750lbs Mexico's finest growers achieved, the newcomers—given a fillip from fertilizer—added a ton or more an acre. For farmers (who by constitutional law were permitted no more than 250 acres) and for the Yaqui Valley (which had a million acres) this represented a tripling of food and income. Moreover, the built-in disease resistance rendered rural life more reliable and secure.

Beyond all that, Kentana and Yaqui were far from the only stars in the new firmament. By the end of April the Chapingo and Nazas seed-multiplication plots were yielding amounts approaching *3600lbs an acre*. Should such performance hold up in the real world of mischief and malice, Mexican farmers—most of whom had never topped half a ton and only a lucky few with irrigation had ever seen one ton—might approach two tons an acre.

May of 1949 sees the start of Year 5; he's already put in 8 seasons nonstop. Nowadays he operates like an automaton, seamlessly blending high-speed science and ice-cool intelligence. He's also a juggler with half a dozen clubs in the air—each perpetually poised to fall.

Although functioning in this nerveless state, he nonetheless found mental respite during interludes in the central zone. Indeed, these May-October home-stays had turned into treats every family member anticipated with high excitement. This is when they got their balance back and functioned by the divine plan.

In addition, the Rockefeller Foundation funded six weeks of "Home Leave" every two years. In those, he takes the family to scenic spots across the U.S.A. "We hit all of the national parks—Yellowstone, Tetons, Redwoods, Sequoia, Grand Canyon, etc," recalls Jeanie. "We always went to Wichita, Kansas to visit my Mom's sister and family. And we always ended up in Iowa and Minnesota."

None enjoyed these treats more than Margaret. Life for her was rough. Most days she faced not only a foreign language, a foreign neighborhood and foreign friends, but also a nearly foreign husband.

Obviously, she tolerated more than a wife should. Down the years, though, neither she nor the children expressed annoyance at their separations from the so-called head of the house. "He's never been home a lot," she once told a reporter. "We just live with it."

That matter-of-fact acceptance is remarkable. It's worth remembering, too, that by "just living with it" Margaret and the children made possible all that is about to transpire.

Actually, their sacrifice was shared. The long absences disturbed Norm just as much. Behind his mask of dedication there hides a homebody. He lived with a perpetual pang of guilt and fear he was becoming something of a cipher to his children despite all attempts at breaking through their reserve—playing ball with Billy, for example, and talking with Jeanie in Spanish, which was their secret code.

For all that, he couldn't resist slipping in a little work. Jeanie remembers summertime picnics taken in the wheatfields where she got the "thrill" of covering wheat flowers with long paper spills. By now she's growing up fast. Having mastered herself and Mexico, she gave neither parent a single worry. Blonde and blossoming, this six-year-old-going-on-sixteen functioned with an easy grace, coping effortlessly with the differences between the cultures. While attending school with local children she'd discovered a natural ability for language and, much to her father's amazement, spoke Spanish with a flawless Mexico City accent.

By contrast, Billy was a trial. Now entering the "Terrible Twos," he's not only rambunctious but also subject to frightening bouts of asthma as well as allergies severe enough to spread alarm. His father, the cool, calm composed scientist was alarm's easiest touch. Billy merely had to murmur in the night and he'd be by the bedside, wheezing too.

Toward the end of May 1949 he prepared the fields for his ninth campaign. His fifth summer planting was notable for the first graduating class of his own creations. Members of the Follow-Up Foursome were here prepared for public duty, which is why he'd trucked so much seed from Sonora. Those several tons of botanical booty were about to be launched toward the greatest of all unknown quantities, consumers.

Actually, bringing out Kentana, Yaqui, Nazas and Chapingo was beyond his capabilities. Scientists lack the facilities, perhaps even the faculties, for inserting food crops into commerce. Yet there was no one else. Though justly proud of its corn seed commission, the government considered wheat seed a waste of resources. And Mexican corporations deigned to deal in seed of a cereal with no future.

CAREER SAVERS #19

Billy, Margaret and Jeanie, 1949. These three formed the backup team that left Norm free to focus on hunger fighting. Jeanie and Billy contributed through their tolerance of a father who was absent much of their lives. Margaret, the rock of the family, did all the chores Norm hated, such as banking and bill paying.

Again the career saver was Dick Spurlock. First, he busied himself getting Kentana, Yaqui, Nazas and Chapingo into El Cerrillo's soil. Second, he cared for the acres of plants as they grew through the summer. Then in the fall he gathered, dried, cleaned, stored and protected the separate harvests from each of the graduates upon which rode so many prospects and prayers.

These final few steps in the process of turning seeds into national food producers may seem routine but even experts have trouble drying, cleaning, storing and properly protecting a crop's seed. Each step requires exquisite care lest the embryos, existing in a delicate state of arrested development, be damaged. The process of drying is especially tricky since dampness fosters mold and desiccation is fatal to the germ.

Yet even without a mechanical dryer to fine-tune the temperatures, Spurlock managed the process with proficiency. Later that year he proudly took his production seed—free of mold and full of life—and handed it out among his Toluca neighbors as well as acquaintances in the states of Puebla and Tlaxcala.

Thus did a Wyoming wrangler become the Johnny Appleseed of Mexican wheat. Doubtless Spurlock's spirited friends considered it strange that a cattleman should come bearing gifts of cereal seeds. But those who took the plunge reaped their reward in riches, thereby spurring irresistible desire among their neighbors.

Spurlock's enthusiasm and the Follow-Up Foursome's promise sparked an agrarian revolution across the huge farming area centered on the capital city. Kentana, Yaqui, Nazas and Chapingo delivered four times more grain than had ever been seen in this hilly zone where irrigation was rare.

Moreover, it's a rural maxim that if one farmer produces just 10 percent more than the rest, every neighbor will plant the same seed *within three years*. Spurlock exploited this force of nature. Hundreds who got his home-grown gifts inspired hundreds more, and that started Borlaug's seeds spiraling outward on a journey wherein they'll eventually gain the world.

With the harvest season imminent, Norm and Spurlock toured the Central zone and found the fungus still felling scrub wheats. The fields once more smelled like sour milk. Indeed, the panoramas of putrefaction scarified every sense, even common sense.

On the way home, the pair stopped by the place where a year earlier they'd left the bemused farmer standing rigid beside bags of seed and

Second bulk harvest, Toluca, October 1949. Spurlock's second bulk-up of Borlaug seed for distribution to farmers. This time there was no rainstorms to mess up the harvest.

fertilizer. As they admired a handsome field of Supremo, Carlos Rodríguez appeared from behind his house. With a yell the farmer raced down to the dirt path. Falling on Borlaug, he embraced him in a bear hug, his eyes unashamedly gushing liquid joy. His lips seemed to spill equal sweetness, though the words were too fast for Norm to fathom.

Other men then came running. They also embraced the scientist. Finally the women appeared, more hesitant but obviously thrilled by the great man's presence.

"What's this about, Dick?" Borlaug asked. "They hardly know me!"

Spurlock explained that the farmer had harvested three times more than his little patch had ever provided. More to the point, though, his were the only healthy plants across the whole neighborhood. His family deemed it a gift from God and Borlaug the angel of deliverance.

"They're saying thank you," Spurlock said. "It is a simple thing—a matter of having something to eat when there'd have been hunger!"

A ctually, a significant part of that farmer's success was due to the second little bag Borlaug had left.

Fertilizer's impact was magnified by the fact that Mexico's farmers had never routinely replenished their soil. Indeed, depleted soil had been second only to disease in suppressing Mexico's wheat production. Norm had suspected as much since soon after his arrival, when he helped Bill Colwell run a series of fertilizer tests across Central Mexico using corn. Those small plots—slight refinements of the one the Vo-Ag teacher had made him run 25 years earlier as a sophomore at Cresco High—demonstrated deficiencies in nitrogen and phosphorus. Millions of farmers harvesting corn for centuries had sucked the vitality from the soil.

The tests, however, had also shown that the depleted dirt was easily rejuvenated with the simplest and cheapest nutrient: A smidgen of nitrogen kicked corn yields from the age-old 10 bushels all the way up to 40 bushels; adding a fillip of phosphorus punted productivity to 45 or, in certain locations, even 60 bushels.

Though these revelations provided a simple path to rural prosperity, apathy reigned. In Mexico fertilizer was almost impossible to find because corporate leaders were indifferent, government authorities were blinded by false witness, and farmers were convinced it was either too expensive or too toxic to touch.

No matter how much Norm talked up the need to properly feed the plants, his words fell on fallow minds. Even professionals trotted out unimpeachable reasons why this passionate interloper was misguided. The agriculture ministry, for one, ballyhooed its own research confirming that fertilizer lifted corn yield only slightly. And almost every expert—domestic and foreign—staked their souls on the fantasy that fertilizer was too expensive for so poor a country.

Borlaug remains disgusted to this day:

> I got damn sick and tired of hearing that Mexico needed no fertilizer or couldn't afford fertilizer. The hell it didn't! We'd seen that nitrogen and phosphorus doubled or tripled productivity. Mexico couldn't afford *NOT* to use fertilizer.

Whereas the alien scientist proved powerless, the alien cattleman proved persuasive. Dick Spurlock talked up fertilizer among his now-trusting neighbors. He passed on Borlaug's advice to add 40lb of nitrogen to each acre of wheat and twice that much for corn. Norm had suggested those levels using nothing more than American precedent but within two years Spurlock's neighbors were adopting it with the kind of alacrity that sprang from financial gain. And despite all the critics' claims, even the poor farmers found the funds for fertilizer. No worries.

All this was made possible by the new seeds' heightened horizons. The government report on fertilized corn reflected the fact that their mediocre plants were already near their upper limit. Borlaug's astounding improvements had lifted wheat's yield ceiling skyward, leaving lots of scope for nutrients to leaven production.

And the gain was broader than might be imagined. Nitrogen and phosphorus are building blocks for all life forms: plants, microbes, invertebrates, mammals. Environmentally speaking, therefore, the effects on Mexico's worn-out land were electric. Fertilizer nourished the famished footings of the food chain and, despite the modest applications, nature responded with glee: above ground, thicker growth shaded and cooled the soil; below ground, roots and organic matter increased; worms appeared, tilth returned, water percolated downwards, and everything displayed vigor together.

■ LESSON THREE: Feed the Plants

This revelation became his third principle for building an embracing and enduring food supply: *To feed the people first feed the soils; make them capable of supporting high-production plants.*

It was about this time in 1949 that a professor from the National Polytechnic Institute approached George Harrar bearing a personal request. "One of our best students is being forced out of school," Pablo Hope [HOO-PAY] explained. "Her family is too poor. If you could provide her a part-time job she'd be able to complete her studies."

The scholarly supplicant noted that the student's father had fallen ill and her mother was behind in tuition payments. The student, he reiterated, showed exceptional promise but was being forced to abandon her studies. Maybe she'd become a seamstress.

To Harrar, such a request was irresistible, so the group expanded to include Evangelina Villegas. There being no vacancy, Eva [EH-vah], as she was called, was appointed Library Assistant, Part-Time. Slight of build and retiring of manner, she seemed as shy and self-conscious as an elf. Indeed, she slipped into the OEE family with almost no one noticing.

Assigning Eva to the library was doubly dubious since she knew no English and the books were almost all American. This came clear one particular Saturday morning when Borlaug was checking the latest journals. Suddenly, Wellhausen dashed past the library door barking as he went: "Eva, please bring me the *Who's Who!*" Having no clue as to what he wanted or even what he'd said, she stood in the small book-lined chamber, frozen with fear. Noticing her paralysis, Norm pointed to the big red volume. She seemed immensely grateful.

He had no way of knowing it then, but Eva's arrival had completed the cadre of key colleagues that will carry him far into the future.

Around this time too Richard Spurlock enticed the participation of additional volunteers to his task force in farm country. Like their predecessors, the newcomers approach from a strange angle and contribute in strange ways: They are farm-machinery salesmen. They are also father and son. And Norm will not meet them until they've been quietly assisting his program for several years.

Like so much else in this saga of science, serendipity, and Good Samaritans this involvement resulted from near-miraculous connections. Despite Mexico's poor prospects for farm machinery, the Massey Harris company had established several outlets and awarded the Capital's franchise to a middle-aged businessman named José Huerta. That dealership happened to be where Dick Spurlock had bought the machines for managing El Cerrillo's prize Holsteins just days before the government marksmen showed up with their rifles and bulldozer.

Two years later, when he sought spare parts, Spurlock casually mentioned the seeds that had opened the summer to wheat growing. Instantly intrigued, the tractor dealer introduced Spurlock to his son and namesake, José Huerta Jr., whom everyone called "Pepe." Huerta junior happened to own the Massey Harris dealership for the Bajío.

Following that casual contact the Huertas *per and fils* made it their mission to spread the Borlaug message along with their machinery. Customers who came to talk tractors in both Toluca and the six-state breadbasket region also got an earful of the new possibilities for production *and* profit.

Both salesmen were perceptive, passionate and ideally positioned to influence their clients. Theirs was an independent voice and, given their constant contact with those who'd taken the plunge, they spoke with currency as well as clout. This unique link inspired farmers by the hundreds to sample the new seeds as well as the latest recommendations for making them perform to their potential. Thus, the gospel according to Borlaug spread outwards via grassroots evangelism and the Huerta's earned the honor of Career Savers #20.

In addition to his main thrust, Norm also included efforts to ward off miscellaneous microbes that choose to live off the plant we ourselves depend on for our own lives. Thus, while building a framework of stem-rust resistant varieties he forever sought to add genetic resistance to fungal threats beyond stem rust.

Most of these were low-profile endeavors that never made the historical record, let alone the headlines or the reports to the waxworks in Manhattan. One was his attempt to raise leaf-rust resistance. It was in 1949 that he began crossing Yaqui with wheats renowned for resisting this separate, lesser, but still often fatal rust fungus that prefers using the leaf entrance to wheat's inner sanctum.

This, he was sure, would soon produce yet another support for sustaining humankind's Number 1 food crop. He wouldn't, of course, find out until after a couple more years of nonstop effort.

Sad to say, while winning the farmers' trust, Norm was fast losing the foundation's. You see, the Big Apple had finally uncovered the disgraceful state of his administrative records.

To paper-shufflers this maverick employee not only lacked professional competence and the ability to plan ahead, he never sent in proper reports. To pay someone who couldn't say—didn't seem to even know—where his work was going was more than disturbing . . . it was discombobulating. Worse still, New York had finally discovered his clandestine annual jaunts. This nettlesome novice insisted on wasting half the year a thousand miles from where he was being paid to work. Was anything more needed to demonstrate ineptitude? No question, this misplaced pathologist was way beyond his depth.

In this special sense, Norm *was* a poor team player; he placed the interests of the hungry above those of his handlers. It remains a character flaw. Recently he told a reporter:

> I like to see action. I don't know how to deal with paperwork. Neglect of paper is my worst habit.

To his credit, though, George Harrar now ignored this appalling imperfection. He'd learned to accept that the more latitude Borlaug got the more he'd accomplish.

The fiscal worms in the Big Apple were, however, paid to ensure foundation funds were expended not just properly but according to the regulations they themselves had established with exquisite precision. Soon Norm was receiving demands for written projections precise enough for checking, step by predetermined step, from 3000 miles away.

Borlaug complied with only half a heart. He had no interest in making proposals that were more akin to palmistry than planning. His program's power lay in fluidity and flexibility:

> I needed to be like a scrambling quarterback, able to dart and weave and grab each chance that showed up on the field in front of me. I couldn't know in advance what would appear, let alone how I'd respond.

Through the years in which he was fighting fungi and farmer indifference this hurtful, harmful and irksome sniping issued periodically from the shadows behind his back. From time to time the Manhattan offices buzzed with rumor, and his every move got scrutinized for bureaucratic blemish. Consultants were dispatched to evaluate his competence. Typically pencil-pushers were sent, and few provided a positive review. One described the work as, "not up to the standards of research expected in a university."

This exclusive focus on systems rather than solutions—a fundamental failing of modern research management—brought depressing outcomes: For a decade the far-away fretters who signed his paychecks were convinced they were wasting money month by month. Each April his performance came up for review, each April he anticipated a pink slip. Looking back, he's sure that George Harrar's passionate plea for just one more chance was all that saved him in April 1949.

And many more Aprils, too.

Given the negative emanations from on high, Harrar warned Norm never to talk to journalists. We may consider that peculiar for a project leader. Harrar, however, knew that the Manhattan mandarins were itching for an excuse to fire this embarrassing underling. One public error would provide grounds for dismissal.

In light of Harrar's directive, Norm stifled his inclination to tell anyone other than the farmers themselves what he was doing. So it came as a shock to learn that Aureliano Campoy—unasked and unannounced—had initiated yet a second support mission.

In October 1949 the old farmer took himself to the City of Mexico and approached a nephew who edited the leading newspaper. In heartfelt tones Campoy relayed all that Borlaug's work could mean. He urged Chaves Camacho send reporters to interview this newsworthy neighbor, currently working beyond anyone's view in the farthest back corner of the nearby ag school in Chapingo.

Accordingly, late one morning the chief editor, his writers and photographers stood around staring at the Tarpaper Shack with a disconsolate air. Clearly, they'd been misled. This dump offered nothing newsworthy.

However, as Borlaug escorted them through the plots and explained the power behind his procedures and plants, spirits began warming until the visitors were bubbling over with delight. The crop was then nearing ripeness and its golden productivity and promise were plain to even citified eyes. By afternoon, feature writers were shouting questions and photographers were shooting pictures. All remained until the moment deadlines forced them back to their copydesks.

The following morning's article splashed across the front page of the national daily *El Universal* created more than a stir . . . it created a sensation. So popular was this powerful prose piece that other papers reprinted it, carrying the great news to the land's farthest corners.

The fallout was astounding. For one thing, the national outlook brightened. For another, Borlaug and his buddies were no longer nonentities; they were Mexican heroes.

Perversely, free publicity can exact a high price, and the OEE staff remained more than a little disquieted. Indeed, their foreboding proved out. Local agricultural careerists felt resentment. This vulgar arriviste was invading their turf. It was intolerable. He had to be stopped.

Among those feeling this loss of face was Jesus Merino, the agriculture ministry's Subsecretary. A former senator from the state of Puebla, he'd opposed the Rockefeller Foundation coming to Mexico. Now, at least as Norm heard the story, he fed his powerful political boss, the Minister of Agriculture, stories built on fears and fantasy. For one thing, he declared the research subversive. It was undermining local agriculture and was structured solely to serve the interests of America. The wheat program was singled out as especially sinister. Borlaug was turning loyal citizens into Yankee lackeys, and was using them to breed wheats for his own glorification.

And that was merely the beginning of the backbiting. Soon other sourpusses piled on, circulating innuendoes impugning more and equally malign motives. Among such detractors were certain political leaders, one of whom publicly declared the Americans discriminated against their Mexican coworkers, claiming in shocked tones that they kept separate bathrooms for themselves. Borlaug is still furious about that one:

> That was a lie, and it stung. We included our co-workers as complete equals because we'd been charged with training them and *easing them into our jobs*. Besides, there were too few bathrooms to reserve one for anyone's exclusive use.

As the disinformation campaign gathered momentum, intellectually minded Mexicans began hurling abstract academic accusations. From a cozy classroom one declared the foreigners "too aggressive"—a curious claim when his country was beset by hunger.

In an article for a popular magazine another learned know-nothing said in so many words: "These Americanos are down here breeding wheat just to keep stem rust from reaching Minnesota."

In 1949 an equally embittered cretin of the college set plumbed the nadir of pessimism: "The spectacular performance of the new wheats has created enthusiasm among Mexicans," he wrote in Spanish in a professional publication, "which is almost frightening because of the danger of disillusionment."

Fortunately, George Harrar knew how to deal with such dilemmas. "Pay no attention," he told his staff. "Don't listen to any of that nonsense."

Those cautions had the desired effect. Norm explains:

> We worked all the harder; and we kept our mouths firmly shut. It wasn't easy passively accepting slurs. Deep down, though, it was

TECHNICAL PROGRESS, 1949

By the close of Round 9 in November '49, following five seasons in Central Mexico and four in Sonora, he's 2 years ahead of schedule. Without the doubled-up dedication he'd not have got this far until 1951.

On the upside the year had ended with good, though not spectacular progress:
- His Foundation Foursome [Frontera, Supremo and the Kenya pair] are maintaining Mexico's wheat in survival mode.
- His Follow-Up Foursome varieties [Kentana, Yaqui, Nazas, Chapingo] are coming on line.
- All in all, stem rust appears to be showing signs of fatigue.

On the downside:
- Public adulation for the foreigners has induced hostility among Mexico's senior scientists. Borlaug's work could be ended any day.
- Also the bosses who provide his paycheck are far from satisfied with his performance, of which they've been misinformed.

Borlaug finds his third basic principle: *To feed the people first feed the soils. Plants must be well nourished to produce their best.*

To outsiders the fields may seem monochrome but to Norm they're pointillist masterworks flashing myriad colors, textures and patterns. In those, the plant is exposing many genetic secrets to him alone.

As 1949 ends, he and stem rust are at a crossroads. The hope for hungry Mexico is that he'll take the right path and the fungus the wrong one.

terribly disappointing that our work was inducing opposition.

This was his first lesson on handling public censure, and it would come in handy during coming decades when public censure will turn into white noise in the background of daily existence. Part of his ultimate success derived from having a skull thick enough to ignore the bad things people bandied about. The skull-thickening began here in the aftermath of Farmer Campoy's generous gesture in October 1949.

1950

Counterweight

On reaching Sonora for the winter planting Norm found his credibility challenged anew. This time farmers resent his claim that their soil is worn out.

Actually, they seemed to have a point. Yaqui Valley boasted the country's best land. Compared with the Bajío's 400-year submission to the plow, this dry valley had been barely scratched. Irrigation is so new that the soil must surely be as fertile as God made it.

Thus in lecturing Borlaug at the second Farmer Field Day Jorge Parada was neither foolish nor fantasizing. And when Norm starts his promised fertility trial the locals consider it a referendum not on their soil but on science or on gringos and their weird, weird ways.

Naturally, the local money was all on Don Jorge. Who knew Sonora better? No question, the blue-eyed foreigner had overreached by daring to doubt God's gift. His naiveté, nay arrogance, will now be exposed.

Realizing he was putting his own reputation into untested hands, Norm dispatched a newly hired Chapingo graduate to establish the critical plantings on the five farms across the valley.

Luckily Raúl Mercado proved immune to beliefs and blandishments, despite dealing daily with the locals on their own turf. Fresh of face, manner and college degree, he tackled his task with the verve and integrity to build a career on. And in the upshot that's what resulted, though he never imagined how high the career would take him.

Mercado's five trials were unusual for being on working farms and for being subjected to real-world routines. Each covered five acres of regular wheatland divided into two equal sections. One half was dusted with ammonium sulfate (at a moderate rate, equivalent to 40lbs of nitrogen an acre). Borlaug's seed was then evenly sown over both halves. Finally,

TECHNICAL CHALLENGES, 1950

Round 10 (Nov. '49-April 1950). Fifth stint in Sonora. In March he turns 36.
The experimental plots now contain millions of wheat plants, some being multiplied for seed, some for roguing and stabilization, some for segregation and selection, some for the tiresome pre-segregation cycles, some for sidelines such as resistance to secondary diseases, some for general observation, and some for cross-pollination when the flowers arrive in February. Except for the immense scale and complexity that pretzels the mind, all these operations have become customary.

Whereas most of this massive effort is still aimed thwarting stem rust, that winter he'll tee up two new operations:

ON-FARM FERTILIZER TRIALS. This season soil-fertility trials will be established on five farms scattered across the Yaqui Valley.

DEMONSTRATION DAY #3. Given the second Farmer Field Day's success, he'll arrange a third fairground of the future highlighting various issues about the new varieties and the best ways to elicit their potential.

Round 11 (May-October, 1950). Sixth stint in Central Mexico.

STEM-RUST RESISTANCE. Come summer, he'll have been in Mexico six years and this will be his eleventh attempt to protect wheat from the fungal fingers. Again he'll follow the normal course: multiplying graduate plants, sorting segregating sophomores and cross-pollinating promising juveniles in hopes of inseminating generations of even greater prospect.

AN ATTEMPT TO DOWNSIZE WHEAT. He'll sow samples of every plant in the entire World Wheat Collection, 30,000 different seed types, in hopes of locating a small plant stiff enough to hold up heavy loads of grain.

the plants were left to the vagaries of fate and fortitude.

That winter of 1949/50 the pair of farmer friends who'd struck their strange bargain quietly swapped the unwanted half of their seed. Aureliano Campoy grew out Kentana; Rafael Fierros grew out Yaqui. Both were courageous acts, since the farming community remained as hostile to new wheats as to fertilizer. No one across the vast valley wanted either. They had no confidence in scientists—those hopeless dreamers who inhabit the clouds.

Although everyone else took a decade to move a promising plant from nursery plot to dinner plate Borlaug, through his efficiencies, road-tests, and clever shortcuts, has cut the gestation by more than half. Later he'd write:

In El Yaqui, La Laguna [Torreón], the Bajío, and Chapingo, the four principal wheat regions of Mexico, seed was sown for increase of the best lines that resulted from the crosses made in Chapingo in 1945.

In the summer of 1949 seed of four new varieties was increased for the second time, in order that they might be available to farmers as soon as possible.

Although he'd cut the crop-gestation time to four years, he didn't mention that now in 1950 the farmers showed no interest in planting it.

January 1950, the sixth campaign year is well underway. In this, his tenth nonstop season Borlaug still has yet to produce any additional food for the hungry. To outside viewers, everything he's attempted has proved unproductive. Though he's multiplying four plants for seed, he's fallen far short of the person who fifty years hence will, according to *Time Magazine*, rank among the 20th Century's 100 most influential.

Having spent a few weeks enjoying home comforts and helping the family welcome in Christmas, he returns to his monkish existence in the Sonora hellhole. Then, following early-February's requisite three weeks of wheat-mating madness, he several times tours the valley peeking at the fertilizer trials. By spring the five farm sites clearly show one side carrying much more grain.

With the advent of April, he advertised his third Farmer Field Day at the crummy old calamity post. Come that Sunday, 400 farmers showed up—twice as many as the previous year. Once again, all were there to learn and were respectful and bursting with good questions.

This was an affirmation that just possibly a gringo might be able to break through the reserve and energize the El Yaqui spirit—not by telling the farmers what to do but doing it under their noses where technical trickery couldn't be concealed and where they could judge the result for themselves, in their own time and on their own ground.

■ LESSON FOUR: Demonstrate, Demonstrate, Demonstrate

This revelation became his fourth principle for building an embracing and enduring food supply: Work *where everyone can see your results and judge for themselves. Farmers don't need to be told . . . but they* do *need to see.*

Also during that busy April the farmer friends who'd struck their strange bargain each recorded exceptional harvests. Their timing was terrific. The tide of popular opinion was starting to swing in favor of buying new seed to replace Barigon, whose seed was free but whose harvest was nearly worthless.

As to the valley-wide fertilizer trial, when the five farmers subsequently submitted the harvest weights, ammonium sulfate had in four cases boosted production. Two of the four farms reported the fertilized side having 60 percent more grain.

Jorge Parada, however, reported a lackluster result. His field—an awkwardly shaped tract with an irrigation ditch angling across the middle—had yielded the same amount on both sides. Here, the modern magic powder had done nothing.

There was more to this than you might think. Being among El Yaqui's leaders Jorge Parada helped codify the local wisdom. Having personally inspected the property, Norm sensed an error had occurred, so when they met he deliberately raised the issue: "Something's wrong, Don Jorge, my eye doesn't deceive me that much. Next season I'll provide more seed and fertilizer, and you try the test again."

For the moment that was the best he could hope for. Without Parada's endorsement, Yaqui farmers would reject fertilizer. He'd have to wait yet another year .

One participant, however, had no doubts about what had transpired. During that spring of 1950 the student, Raúl Mercado, asked for $500 to rent some land and grow Yaqui *with fertilizer*. Norm provided the cash, and the young man turned his back on secure employment, rented a section of local soil, and stepped forth into a dizzy dream arising from the wonders he'd just helped perform.

May 1950 sees the start of Year 6; Norm's now put in 10 seasons of nonstop science and is back on home ground where his bosses suppose him always to be. Chapingo's 160 acres are, however, getting overcrowded, and when visiting Richard Spurlock he discovered a farm for sale. It was high in a mountain valley in Toluca.

The owner was friendly and fascinated enough to low-ball the annual rent, a concession that overcame Harrar's initial opposition to research operations 40 miles from headquarters and 70 miles from Chapingo where the proper researchers worked.

Though located in the same valley, the new site was several miles from Spurlock's fancy American-owned corporate spread. It was also a world apart, being a practicing farm of the standard Mexican model. The only structure was a shed the farmer had erected. The fields were those the farmer had prepared with an ox and a wooden plow for growing his own food. Nonetheless the place fitted Norm's need. Here, there was room for many more and much larger trials; here too he was with his clientele rather than his colleagues.

The crude farm in Toluca and the decrepit station in Sonora now become the prime work sites. To professionals, this finally proves he's mad. Neither place has facilities for laboratory support, office support, staff accommodations or storage for equipment or seeds.

Moreover, the two could not be more dissimilar:

At 8,500 feet above sea level, Toluca was perhaps the world's highest wheat-breeding station. The Yaqui Valley, by contrast, was more than 1.6 miles lower. Being essentially at sea level, it was among the world's lowest wheat-breeding stations.

The latitudes clashed as well. Toluca was located at about 18° north whereas Sonora was at 28°, a latitudinal disparity of 700 miles.

Their topography and substrates diverged: Toluca was hilly with clay-loam soil; the Yaqui Valley was flat and sandy.

Their water came in different ways. Toluca depended on summer rains that arrived at nature's whim. Sonora had the government canal, so whenever the soil got thirsty you merely started up a pump.

The cropping seasons conflicted too. Toluca hosted the summertime crop, so from May through September the specimens experienced days that got shorter and steamier as they matured during the onset of fall. By contrast, the generation at the northern end grew as a wintertime crop experiencing days that first got longer and cooler as February's flowering season approached and then got dryer and hotter until by the April harvest the plants were blasted by sand carried by desiccating desert winds.

Although he knew he was ignoring precedent, Norm was initially unaware of how inspired this choice of sites would prove to be. Here's where "shuttle breeding" took shape. Now when the winning plants from the winter planting in the north were carried south and planted in Toluca they got exposed to the opposite conditions from those they'd just conquered. Then the winners from that summer's challenge got carried back north for another season in the alternate winter world. The plants were thus wrenched this way and that twice a year, and only a few— those most successful at *both* ends—moved forward into history.

In time, this in-built adaptability would prove critical, not to mention legendary. Indeed, Borlaug varieties will prove the greatest producers under the greatest range of conditions any wheat had ever faced.

Adaptability becomes the second pillar of power behind Borlaug wheats. His Cornucopia Combo now has two pillars that make the top food-producing plant fast maturing and extremely adaptable.

MOUNTAIN HIGH

Toluca. In 1950 Norm moved his Central-Mexico research to this valley high above the City of Mexico. Here's where the ultimate wheat-breeding system took form. From now on his plants must succeed here in the mountains as well as in the distant desert at the top end of the country. Winners from each site get immediately replanted in the other. And the cycle proceeds twice a year.

Thanks to this so-called shuttle breeding Borlaug-bred seeds will work in almost every wheatland worldwide. At the time he just wanted to get away to Toluca and Sonora where he could work among the farmers and not the fretters. But the resulting adaptability will see his plants perform miracles on the far side of the world and in the face of imminent famine when there's no time for research or delay.

Despite its subtropical latitude, Toluca is cool. Due to the altitude (8,793ft), this is central Mexico's temperate zone. On winter nights temperatures can drop well below freezing; summer days rarely exceed 81°F (27°C). For Norm added joys came from the near-absence of insects and the generally reliable summer rains.

Beyond the two primary experimentation sites he also established a formal presence roughly half way between Toluca and Sonora. Here, at La Piedad in the state of Michoacán, his tests occupied a corner of a Ministry of Agriculture experiment station. The spot came to be called Campo La Cal Grande, and its importance lay in the fact that it was centered in the Bajío, so results could be moved directly into the republic's breadbasket stretching outwards a hundred miles all around.

However, La Piedad posed a practical problem: Without an ag school or farm-service facility, no one had the skills to care for, let alone breed, wheat.

This is when he devised a plan daring enough to yet again scandalize cereal science: he initiated a dozen of the largely unlettered bird boys into the secret art of controlled cross-pollination.

This group—most of them barely into their teens—quickly developed a sort of mutual reverence. All bubbled with delight at the chance to grab the golden ring and make something of themselves. He drove them by his own example and they responded by matching his maniacal zeal. And like Reyes Vega 200 miles away in Mexico City, the Bajío backwoods boys possessed cool hands.

Emasculating wheat flowers requires steady finger work not just because wheat's male organs are tiny but also because each can spray hundreds of pollen grains, which ruins the research. Borlaug had to ensure that every last pollen sac got removed. Put another way, he had to make sure his young partners were disciplined and precise, and performed each step correctly, completely and efficiently *every time.*

To this end he first divided the group into crews of five and then devised a simple game: Anytime anyone (including himself) finished preparing the all-female head they initialed and dated the cylindrical envelope before slipping it over as protection against stray pollen. Three days later, when it was time to consummate the mating, that particular plant was assigned to another crew.

Wheat pollen hits the eye like Day-Glo, so when the envelope was opened any yellow radiance confirmed the guilt of whomever had initialed the paper cover. For the ultimate infamy of not removing *every* pollen sac the bungler's crew was required to buy a bottle of Coca-Cola for each member of the finder's crew. "One of two things is going to happen," Borlaug explained: "You're going to learn to do it right or you're going to pay the price. Hopefully, you won't be spending all your pay on soft drinks."

The boys quickly caught on. The daily Coca-Cola contest neatly balanced competitiveness with camaraderie and stimulated youthful juices. To them, though, the best part was the free treat after ten hour's toiling, broiling and building thirst.

In a surprisingly short time these under-schooled novices mastered processes previously performed by over-schooled professors. Indeed, they crossbred wheat with more will and skill than probably any scientist before (and maybe since).

Although Norm appreciated that education sometimes must kneel before the needs of survival, the idea of employing school dropouts remained disturbing. For that reason he and the other researchers established an education fund. Operated by the poorly paid scientists, not their rich employer, this was an unofficial contribution to the unlettered youths who'd become so integral to their success and satisfaction, not to mention professional survival.

From the start, Eva Villegas was treasurer. In the year since being lost in the library the barrio waif had come far. She now speaks halting English and, though still taking courses for her BS degree in biochemistry, she's worked herself into a permanent place on the research staff. The talents and tenacity her professor had foretold were slowly emerging. Indeed, the mettle lurking behind the elfin appearance, dark liquid eyes and reserved manner revealed itself in the bid to help youngsters who'd surrendered their childhood too early. Whenever the fund's monies ran low she'd buttonhole the illustrious PhDs. "Come on, come on," she'd prod, "put some pesos in."

More mature than her 26 years, this evangelist for bird-boy education knew what a peso meant to an impoverished kid and never hesitated to hit up her seniors. Thanks to that zeal the bird boys got their schooling. In return, OEE got a potent technical team. Fashioned from flotsam, it included no superstars, no geniuses, no academic elites . . . just energetic acolytes committed to serving the *patrón* to the uttermost limits of their ability.

That fall of 1950 chilling news arrived from Minnesota and Manitoba: In places across the northern Great Plains and the Prairie provinces a new stem-rust race had taken up residence, and in those locales every major spring-wheat variety was succumbing.

For the moment the outbreaks remained small, scattered and very scary because no wheat in North America had the right gene shield to blunt this pathogenic spear.

Rust epidemics typically build slowly, biding their time before whipping off the gloves to expose the full fungal fingers of mass destruction. But in this case, for the first time in history, a new and particularly penetrating crop epidemic was rendered visible in real time for all to see and fear.

Once more, this insight was thanks to Stakman. Each summer from about 1920 onwards he'd received hundreds of fat envelopes mailed in from as far away as Texas and Canada. Inside were black, red, yellow and orange stems and leaves. Not to mention anger and alarm.

It is hard to overstate the difficulty of determining rust races in those days before DNA was deciphered, let alone differentiated. Stakman attacked the race problem obliquely using a standard cluster of a dozen wheat varieties. Any given wheat is immune to some rust races, moderately susceptible to others, killed by the rest. His standard cluster's pattern of responses—resistant, intermediate or susceptible—crudely distinguished the strain.

Each spring, Stak's students sowed the standard cluster in hundreds of separate blocks. Then, on the appropriate late-summer day they showered each envelope's rust spores onto its own separate block. Six weeks later the speckles disfiguring the block's dozen different plants were coded against those of known rust strains.

For about four decades these mind-numbing operations engaged U of M grad students and greenhouses. Yet this was not some federally funded intervention for securing a healthy food supply, just an academic and his apprentices figuring out a fungus's immunologic foibles.

As with his other stem-rust research, Stakman revealed a previously unseen new world. By about 1950, he'd "fingerprinted" *more than 300* strains and mapped their fluctuations across the precious wheatlands. Stem rust turned out to be an evolving muddle of races that each winter congregated in northern Mexico. Then in summer it sent the mass of newly mixed malevolence surging up the country in a vast wave.

Of all rust races, the most obscure appeared in 1938. A variant of the 15th they'd identified, it came from a single plant from New York State. Too rare to worry about, stem-rust 15B merited interest mainly because it killed all twelve wheats in Stakman's standard block. No major variety could stop 15B spores penetrating its personal tissues. This was an observation filled with menace but for years the fear flitted only in the shadows in the mind of Stakman, who worried this deadly agent might in some mysterious manner multiply and move on out. Then, should the weather bend in its favor, 15B would rise up like some pre-positioned terror cell and bring down America's food supply in a single, invisible, seemingly coordinated, insurgent strike.

LODGING

The problem of lodging. By 1950 Borlaug wheats were out-growing their own bodies. The stems were too weak to hold up the load of grain his plants and methods had made possible. Winds during the harvest season blew the plants flat, rendering them worthless because the grain couldn't be harvested.

The chilling missive Borlaug received from his northern colleagues in October 1950 explained that this is what had happened. Over the summer rust-race 15B detonated beneath North America's food supply. Back in 1949 only one diseased stem from Stakman's mail carried 15B (again from New York State). Now a year later at least one in every four of the fat envelopes contained that race. Most of those envelopes were postmarked from the Upper-Midwest and Canada.

For Stakman this must have been a terrifying moment. Clearly, 15B had embedded itself in the fabric of the northern farmscape, and each fall from then onward trillions of its spores would fly south, refresh themselves along the border, and storm back the following spring energized and eager for mayhem. The consequences were plain: Fields of opportunity stretched north a thousand miles encompassing hundreds of millions of acres, all the way into the heart of Canada's north woods.

TECHNICAL PROGRESS, 1950

By the close of Round 11 in November '50, following six seasons in Central Mexico and five in Sonora, he's 2.5 years ahead of schedule.

On the upside 1950 has brought advances:

- Practical progress can finally be seen: The national average yield has risen 50 percent to 900 lb per acre—thanks to his first quartet of varieties;
- He moves to Toluca. Though some nurseries are still grown in Chapingo, the main Central-Mexico research is high on the mountain west of the city. Here's where his shuttle system solidified;
- He's produced 4500 tons of seed—enough to sow 110,000 acres, roughly eight percent of Mexico's wheat area.

On the downside this year:

- Things look mighty ominous because a terrifying new race of rust has broken out north of the border;
- Yaqui Valley fertilizer trials still show a good response but the key farmer still insists fertilizer does nothing on his place;
- The area under wheat is still stuck at 1.5 million acres and the overall production remains 400,000 tons.

Borlaug finds his fourth basic principle: *What counts is what you do, not what you say.* People committing to big change risk their lives; they need and deserve the physical evidence of how it will lift them up.

From here on he systematically builds into his plants the cornucopia combo's second pillar: adaptability to extreme conditions. By now he needs a full-sized truck to carry seed between the sites. And wheat is sharing some of its secret capabilities.

In the 6 years since his arrival, the number of mouths in Mexico has risen by 4.3 million, or 19.5 percent, to reach 26.3 million.

And every plant therein was defenseless.

From the beginning, word of nature's new-sprung menace flashed fear through the plant pathology profession. Heightening the distress was the knowledge that a different, equally virulent, stem rust race was decimating Argentina's wheat. Should that race reach North America and 15B reach South America, wheat might be finished in the New World, if not the whole world.

To top all that, it was about this time that Norm began to suspect that the stems on his plants were too weak to bear the grain load the plant was telling him was possible. Growing up to 5 or even 6 feet, the plants became top heavy as the yield rose year by year. This was evidenced by the ease with which late-season breezes blew them over. "Lodging," as it is called threatened disaster because crimped stalks cannot feed the juvenile grains waiting at the top to be fed. Any bend in the stem blocks the juices bearing starch, protein, vitamins and minerals, leaving the young grains starving, stunted, shriveled and worthless to man or beast.

The only feasible way to get stronger stems seemed to be through shrinking the plants. None of his own was short enough so he dashed off a letter to the U.S. Department of Agriculture asking for a few seeds of every sample in the World Wheat Collection. He'll grow them out in Mexico in hopes of uncovering undersized wheats strong enough to uphold heavy loads of grain.

This was a big ask. The World Wheat Collection had seeds of 30,000 different plants.

The research roundup that spring, however, ended his casting call for strong-stemmed wheats. Naturally, he'd hoped that out of the vast World Wheat Collection at least one shorty would show up. Sadly, that hope was now dashed. Although a smattering of small specimens appeared, none possessed stems sturdy enough to heft a heavy head of grain. Despite 30,000 possibilities, the wheat world had no shrunken stars to strut the boards. The few promising pint-sized specimens all fell over when fertilized.

Imagine his frustration. The plant clearly could yield even more than 3600lb an acre except for a quirk of nature that made its head too big for its body. And there was nothing he could do to correct such monumental ineptness. No spring wheat possessed any aptitude for weightlifting.

The gene pool, so it seemed, was more like a gene puddle. And wheat would forever be limited by its own flawed architecture.

1951
Smackdown

As Borlaug heads north for Round 12 and his sixth desert campaign in Sonora, he stops by La Piedad, Torreón, and Saltillo, to sow a new set of multi-location tests as well as numerous nursery plots. These are places where North America's rust races congregate for a winter on the wild side. Thus, while calmly establishing his plots and breeding nurseries, he knows that 15B will come a-calling. And his plants are as vulnerable as those above the border.

This, though, is no moment for panic. The doomsday clock may be ticking but the alarm bell has yet to ring. In time, 15B will teach him if any of his millions of specimens possess any aptitude for resistance.

In Sonora he finds the desert air rife with change. His seeds are finally attracting farmer interest. For one thing, Campoy and Fierros have been besieged with orders.

As first in a long line of farmers to profit by peddling Borlaug seed among their peers, Campoy and Fierros set a terrific precedent. He chuckles about it:

> In the beginning they hadn't wanted to take the seed. Then they were turned off by the look of the plants. But after they'd harvested their fields I'll be damned if they didn't pull off the best bargain I've ever seen. Both made a killing!

In Norm's view this was great. His friends were welcome to their pesos. More important was the fact that wheat growers scattered across the million-acre valley were getting their hands on Kentana and Yaqui. And those early adopters would surely strive to make the most out of their investment. After that the seeds would sell themselves; raw envy

TECHNICAL CHALLENGES, 1951

Round 12 (Nov. '50-April 1951). Sixth stint in Sonora. In March he turns 37.

That winter he'll undertake at least five concurrent lines of research:

STEM-RUST RESISTANCE. It's imperative he find plants capable of withstanding 15B stem rust.

DEMONSTRATION DAY #4. His fairgrounds of the future are getting evermore popular and are becoming the prime means of disseminating his research results.

NURSERIES. Again he'll harvest the multi-location road-tests and nursery plots in Saltillo, Torreón, and finally La Piedad. The road-tests have become a sort of finishing school; the nurseries are like childcare centers where he can observe behavior traits.

ON-FARM FERTILIZER TRIALS. Amid the press of his myriad chores that fall, Norm found time to drive across the Yaqui Valley carrying new seed and another bag of fertilizer to Jorge Parada, so the soil-fertility trial could be repeated.

Round 13 (May-October, 1951). Seventh stint in Central Mexico.

At Chapingo this summer he'll be focusing on:

STEM-RUST RESISTANCE. The search for plants capable of withstanding 15B stem rust will continue.

DOWNSIZING THE WHEAT PLANT. He'll plant the World Wheat Collection to see if any known wheat is short enough to hold all the grain the species can yield.

would spur the neighbors to get on the gravy train.

Thus, thanks to those gifts to farmer friends, his creations were both moving out and developing the trust to take them spiraling onward to that expansive *mañana* Mexico needed.

Another change in the desert air was the acceptance of soil shortcomings. During that winter a dozen Sonoran wheat growers plunged into progress by indulging in the most unorthodox of all acts: fertilizing their fields.

Most did it very tentatively, as if toying with trouble. A few, however, tossed caution aside. Thus it was no surprise that when Norm visited the Maurer farm to discuss the imminent plantings, Roberto casually mentioned that Rodolfo Calles and two others had *each* contracted with a visiting Connecticut salesman to buy *20 tons* of fertilizer.

"Well, that's good," Norm beamed. "What kind did they buy?"

"I don't know; I'll find out."

Next day Roberto reported the formula as 2-18-18.

To us this sounds banal; to Norm it spelled big trouble. With just two percent nitrogen, this formulation would do nothing for wheat in the Yaqui Valley. Worse, the 18 percent phosphorus and 18 percent potassium, both of which were very expensive, were unneeded and would provide no benefit. The bellwether farmers thus were squandering big bucks for nothing.

Norm feared his research was about to be discredited:

> There wasn't just a matter of wasting cash. After six months, when the production levels failed to rise, every farmer would be told that fertilizer didn't pay for itself and that my advice could not be trusted. I was sure our effort was about to be set back a decade.

In his concern, the scientist caught a ride to town and arranged to meet the fertilizer salesman at nine the following Saturday morning. But when he showed up for that appointment the secretary shook her head: "I'm very sorry Dr. Borlaug," she said, "but yesterday we got an urgent call from the Mexico [City] office. He had to leave by the midnight train."

Norm nowadays smiles at the recollection:

> That was a dead give away . . . the man was a shyster who feared exposure. I guess he figured farmers who'd never used fertilizer wouldn't know any better than to buy the most expensive type. By the time they found they'd been defrauded, he'd be long gone and with a fat wad of pesos in his pocket.

Yet a third surprise occurred that same November: Rodolfo Calles plunged into change by sowing his first Borlaug variety, Kentana. The former governor nonetheless devoted most of his planting to a new variety from Texas. He'd just returned from visiting Edgar McFadden, who'd provided a sack of his very latest creation. Norm quickly learned of it:

> Early that season we happened to meet on the main street. Rodolfo was bubbling with enthusiasm for McFadden's latest. He kept saying how productive the plants looked and how great was their potential. "Austin," he declared, "is the future for our country."
> I wasn't so sure about that. The variety was derived from Hope, and the embedded emmer genes could give it a weak neck. "Yeah, it's pretty impressive," I said, "but we gave up on its sisters [Frontera and Supremo] a couple of years back. The necks broke. Sonora's too hot. You'd better harvest your field on time or you'll lose the whole crop."

Despite the warning, Rodolfo Calles remained excited by his discovery. Austin was soon the talk of the town. That put Norm's reputation on the line yet again and on yet another kind of charge.

Having enjoyed a few weeks helping the family welcome in Christmas, he's still not a happy camper. Although practical progress is finally in train, every genetic combination he's created is edged around with nagging threads that could quickly unravel. On top of that 15B is heading his way. Like a tidal wave.

Back in Sonora, he spends February 1951 making evermore cross-pollinations. By now all this is quite routine and the warming April weather brings the myriad rows to sudden ripeness. Thousands of plant lines in the massive experimental plantings need to be assessed all at once. Then the winners must be harvested, documented, threshed as well as packaged, labeled and trucked south. Beyond all that he must harvest the multiplication fields and organize the fourth Farmer Field Day.

That particular demonstration day in April 1951 attracted a crowd of 800—almost too many for a lone scientist and a handful of helpers to control, especially given the visitors' newfound exuberance and endless questions.

Despite that relentless press of end-of-season responsibilities, he found time for two seemingly tangential topics.

First, he dropped by the Parada place to check on the second run of the valley-wide fertilizer trial. The planting occupied the same cockeyed field. Although a few weeks short of maturity, the specimens on the fertilized side of the slanting divide again carried a grain load Norm judged to be twice that on the other side.

Nonetheless, some weeks later when Jorge Parada submitted his final figures both sides had produced the same amount. No change.

More than frustrating, this was maddening. There'd be *yet another* year of delay before the truth could get out.

The second tangential topic related to Rodolfo Calles' infatuation with McFadden's Hope-based variety. Since their discussion on the dusty main drag Norm had given this no further thought. Then one afternoon in mid-April the issue suddenly sprang back to life:

> That Saturday Enciso and I were driving to the airport to ship part of the harvest back to Mexico City. As we neared Don Rodolfo's place, we noticed activity in the fields and hastily turned down the side road.
>
> Several small combines were going flat out, harvesting 25 acres of what looked like a great crop. The plants were magnificent, with heavy heads and obvious rust resistance.
>
> Nevertheless, Rodolfo was running around like a crazy man,

waving his big white hat and screaming to his two foremen and their gangs to work harder.

Seeing me standing by the fence he strode over. "When I was here yesterday this field was beautiful," he yelled. "Now look!"

The boiling afternoon had turned windy, and as I watched, gusts of hot air broke the tops off the plants in waves that ran across the field like sickles. The whole crop was in the process of losing its head. Rodolfo's harvest was falling onto the dirt.

This proved to be the break Norm had hoped for. You see, that blustery afternoon a conversion occurred beside the road to the airport. Rodolfo Calles finally got religion and from then on stuck with Borlaug's counsel and creations like a disciple.

The Yaqui Valley's most influential voice had won *himself* over. From this point onward the former president's son would lead his compadres in following the recommendations arising from the research done right there on their own doorstep. Whatever was done in Texas or anywhere else no longer seemed important.

Though this outcome was as good as any Norm could have conceived, the next steps would have to wait. For the moment he must head home for his "official" duties. Within days, he's packed up his top picks' seeds and is moving southward, harvesting successively the multi-location road-tests and nursery plots in Saltillo, Torreón, and finally La Piedad.

At this last stop the routine got rudely disrupted. During a face-to-face inspection of the Yaqui multiplication he spied a patch of plants bearing more grain than he'd ever seen.

A casual observer might dismiss this as a mere quirk of soil or season, which had been notably mild. The patch was only a few square feet out of a 10-acre planting and it was hiding in a far corner where few ever ventured. The sight, however, proved so astounding Norm became like one possessed. No wheat in Mexico had yielded so much. The sight was surreal. What could be the cause?

Wellhausen also happened to be on hand, harvesting corn trials. Suddenly he found himself yanked to the back of the station. "Just have a look at that, Ed!" Borlaug yelled. "What do you make of it?"

The mellow maize man was intrigued, then suspicious. He'd just arrived himself and had already endured heartache. During an earlier visit he'd told his work crew exactly how to harvest a special field producing hybrid-corn seed. Now, three months later the field manager, so much smarter than any gringo, beamed with pride. Neither birds nor rats, he explained, had gotten a single seed. The whole crop was right there in the sacks!

Wellhausen's response was far from what the beaming employee expected. The agronomist exploded with such rage he could scarcely contain himself from doing violence!

For that he had good cause. You see, although physically speaking nothing had been lost . . . scientifically speaking everything was gone. In those sacks the male-parent seed was mixed with the female-parent seed, and this unique line of work, which promised to mirror for Mexico the uplift Henry Wallace had provided America a decade earlier, was ended.

Still smarting from that fiasco, the normally stoic Wellhausen strode back to the Campo La Cal Grande office and rousted out the field manager who'd fertilized the wheat during the growing season. "Just tell us," he demanded, "exactly what you did."

Extracting the truth took time. The man was too scared to talk, having disregarded the strict instruction to refill the bins at scattered locations. Instead, he'd stopped at that inconspicuous corner to discreetly fill the bin on the back of the tractor. The sacks were heavy and hard to handle, and he'd piled them there. All the spillage had accumulated on that single patch of soil. Eventually, the scientists estimated that those few square feet had received two, and most probably three, times more than the rest.

The man's disobedience nonetheless was of historic import. The nutrient overdose—equivalent to 80 or perhaps 120lbs of fertilizer per acre—had obviously done the plants a power of good. Clearly, for peak performance, Borlaug's high-test wheat needed twice the nitrogen and phosphorus in the Bajío as the American wheats in the textbooks. Perhaps three times.

This misadventure—unforeseen, unplanned, unprofessional and quite unscientific—raised the perception of possibilities. Thanks to a technician's disregard of orders yet another and much higher horizon defined itself out of the scientific shadows.

On returning to the capital at the end of April, however, he suffers a series of shocks:

The first struck when he visited Chapingo to see a modern research facility arising on the land he'd leveled with a rebuilt bulldozer nearly seven years back. Instead of the Tarpaper Shack there now stood long low-slung buildings of concrete and glass, replete with laboratories, offices, seed-handling facilities, greenhouse, machine shop and field-equipment storage.

OEE's professional staff had surged as well. Among recent arrivals were potato specialist John Niederhauser, entomologist John McKelvey, and agronomist John Pino, who'd fought Nazis and was now preparing to fight famine with an infantryman's zeal. Borlaug's own group had expanded too. Ignacio Narvaez, who'd so providentially soothed the souls following a sodden night on a Coahuila mountainside two years before, now put in long days in Borlaug's Chapingo wheat plots while also pursuing a Masters degree at the nearby agricultural college.

This transformation of the decrepit facility with a shack for shelter was thanks to the commander in chief's potent powers of persuasion. George Harrar had convinced the Rockefeller Foundation trustees and administrators of the value of a unified school of hunger fighting. The focus, he said, should be corn and wheat, and the work should encompass every need, from soil to seed handling.

This direct assault, with all guns blazing against whatever was keeping corn and wheat from their ultimate potential was a majestic, even magnificent, vision. Despite the age-old horror of endemic human hunger, nothing like it had been tried before.

The second shock struck when Norm discovered that over the years weevils had worked their way inside the adobe lean-to. When Wellhausen's structure was torn down, the contents comprised hollowed-out seeds and lively, fat, exceptionally happy, insects. The 8500 seed lots gleaned at such effort six years before had perished. Their genes had reverted to nature.

The third shock hit when Eva blurted she was quitting. Her mother's continuing poverty meant she could no longer work where pay was never lavish and half pay was close to pathetic.

Norm and Wellhausen then provided some pesos so Eva could take extra classes, learn English, and advance her career prospects.

Both later declared it their best investment, ever.

May 1951 sees the start of Year 7; Norm's now put in 12 seasons of nonstop research. Viewed in retrospect, this year was notable for being the first in which his varieties measurably lifted Mexico's food supply. The country's overall output that year jumped from 400,000 to 750,000 tons. Moreover, the average national yield, which had been stuck at around 750 pounds an acre soared to 1000. In addition, the wheat acreage soared from 1.25 to 1.8 million.

What's truly amazing is that behind his years of manic activity was the faith that eventually someone would step forward and take over from the edge where the research world ended. You see, although he could produce enough seed for a few friends, he couldn't produce enough for the nation. And Mexico itself had no way to do it. Government wasn't about to waste its time. Nor was private enterprise. Both knew wheat was a hopeless case.

For a while there seemed no possibility of our parable proceeding. Then Richard Spurlock and the improbable pair of tractor traders stepped in. They not only produced the seed, they primed the adoption process by whipping up interest across the central zone and getting friends, neighbors, acquaintances, clients by the hundreds to try Borlaug's products.

This spontaneous, truly grass-roots initiative spread seed so well it left observers in awe. And the amateurs behind it were all working for free!

Their efforts were of course facilitated by the fact that Borlaug seeds provided a ticket out of poverty. Like Henry Wallace's hybrid corn they exuded the alluring attraction of wealth. Prosperity is the ultimate contagion, and its effect on Mexico's campesinos was no less magical than on Iowa corn growers a decade earlier. Those who sowed Borlaug seed could double their output and double their income. And when that news began circulating millions climbed the ladder and took the plunge from the high board.

Accordingly, in that summer of 1951 Central Mexico's wheat crop suddenly expanded as if by a physical force. By fall the Huerta showrooms had become the de facto distribution centers for high-performance seed as well as tractors. Spurlock and the Huertas thereby unleashed the genie of prosperity across the traditional breadbasket.

■ LESSON FIVE: Make a Profit

The revelation stemming from this voluntary support provided his fifth principle for building an embracing and enduring food supply: *When something makes a profit people will adopt change. To succeed on a grand scale a plant should be profitable enough to double the family income. That is true among the hungry, and especially among the poor.*

During that summer in Central Mexico the previous winter's valley-wide fertilizer trial in Sonora continued to perplex the mind. His seeds possessed the magical magnetism of moneymaking but nitrogen helped elicit the most pesos.

That's why in May he was puzzled when Jorge Parada appeared in the doorway of his office at Chapingo's new edifice. Seeing this farmer a thousand miles from his roots was strange. And his hasty outburst made the scene surreal: "Dr. Borlaug," he said, "I owe you a great apology."

"What for, Don Jorge?"

"My foreman repeatedly assured me that both sides of that field were of equal size. But after writing you that second note I got a tape measure and went out and checked for myself." He paused, looking distinctly uncomfortable: "The truth is that the unfertilized side is almost twice as big as the fertilized one. So, what you've been saying all along is absolutely true."

Then he added another signal shock: "My mistake is especially embarrassing because I've just come from the Shell Company . . . I've signed an agreement . . . I'm now the Yaqui Valley distributor for ammonia and urea!"

All this was great news. From here on, Jorge Parada, like Rodolfo Calles, could be trusted to lead his compatriots marching toward the next horizon.

Like racing greyhounds, researchers continually chase elusive quarry. Each discovery opens new enticements. Thus, even as Mexico embraced his wheats Norm was absorbed in countering the invisible enemy that was heading his way. Although 2000 miles south of the Upper Midwest where 15B had been detected, Mexico was the winter gathering grounds, so he'd likely be the first to experience the full scope of its wrath.

No one thereabouts had any inkling of the threat. For almost a decade Mexico's fungal rust swarms had lain low but in the fall of 1950 the north winds carried the new mutant below the border and in a few places it lucked into luscious wheats and enjoyed a salubrious winter.

Normally, that would have been hardly more than the rumble of a distant thunderstorm. However, the summer of '51 proved wet enough to turn Mexico into a Petri dish. As the season progressed, red, yellow and orange spots began dotting his plantings in Sonora, Saltillo, Torreón, the Bajío and Toluca. The occurrences were small, scattered, seemingly minor but their significance was actually immense: this fungal race was feasting on the Borlaug-built beauties.

Thus did Mother Nature finally show her hand, and send him reeling back all the way to his beginnings. In his fields he could see the varieties

TECHNICAL PROGRESS, 1951

By the close of season 13 in November '51, following seven seasons in Central Mexico and six in Sonora, he is 3 years ahead of schedule. Without the doubled-up dedication he'd not have reach this level of advance until 1954.

On the upside 1951 has brought great changes:

- Kentana and Yaqui 48 are spreading to a world of their own making.
- Mexico's wheat production has jumped from 400,000 tons to 750,000 tons.
- The average yield has soared from 750 to 1000 pounds an acre.
- The area under wheat rose from 1.25 million acres to 1.8 million acres.
- The fourth Farmer Field Day is so popular the crowd can barely be controlled.
- The new plants have so much unfilled potential that doubling or tripling fertilizer (to 80 or 120 pounds per acre) lifts yields to the stratosphere.
- The "squire" of Yaqui Valley, Rodolfo Calles, comes on board at last.

On the downside as 1951 comes to a close:

- Stem rust is ready to deliver the ultimate smackdown. It has mutated and is beginning to maul *every plant* he's released—13 seasons of immense dedication have gone for naught;
- Lodging is becoming widespread. The plants are too tall, and there's nothing he can do about that. Out of the World Wheat Collection, no plant is short enough to hold all the grain the species can yield.

Borlaug finds his fifth basic principle: *varieties will fly by themselves if they double a farmer's income.*

carrying the faith of millions, if not the whole country, starting to collapse. Across this already hungry land 15B was on the loose; once again the controlling force behind food production was the fungal fingers of mass destruction. Any return of warm damp weather would likely fell the nationwide crop like a scythe.

1952
Restart

As Mexico's only wheat specialist, Norm's only option is to start again. Yesterday he'd been on the edge of tomorrow; now he's at the back of beyond as if he'd never started.

Moreover, he's in a race against time; within perhaps two years the malicious microbe is likely to overwhelm all the republic's wheats. During that two-year easement he must fashion replacements capable of resisting the small and deadly thing that has its fungal finger on the wheat genome's soft spot.

The massiveness of his response can be judged from the fact that during that summer of 1952 his nurseries contained more than 40,000 distinct wheat lines. And his quest for genetic advances that year included a staggering 6,000 individual crossings between separate wheat heads. Nothing on such a scale had been attempted before.

For this fresh campaign, his major prospects lay with 60,000 different wheat types from his own collection as well as 6000 more from the U.S. Department of Agriculture. The latter included the duplicates he'd deposited in 1945 as a professional courtesy, now returned to perhaps his own rescue.

To the untutored eye that giant planting at Sonora didn't look like much but everything rode on those fields. This was the last chance to deflect disaster by deploying the plant's own genes.

To further complicate things, it was also in 1952 that Norm decided to initiate a breeding program to downsize the wheat plant. His current plants are structurally flawed, and cannot support the heavy grain load he can get them to produce.

Fertilizer worsened this phenomenon. Though most farmers applied

TECHNICAL CHALLENGES, 1952

Round 14 (Nov. '51-April '52). Seventh stint in Sonora. In March he turns 38.
That winter he has a big agenda:

STEM-RUST RESISTANCE. He must prevent Race 15B taking out Mexico's wheat. Unless he can do that nothing else will matter.

DEMONSTRATION DAY #5. The Farmer Field Day has become a major operation as well as the main means for distributing seed and advice to farmers.

STUD FARMS. The specific nurseries have now morphed into germplasm banks, wherein he grows wheats showing unusual qualities of any kind.

ON-FARM FERTILIZER TRIALS. Amid the press of his myriad chores that fall, Norm will carry new seed and another bag of fertilizer to Jorge Parada, so the soil-fertility trial can be repeated.

Round 15 (May-Oct., 1951). Seventh stint in Central Mexico. First at Toluca.

As he starts his eighth year of relentless campaign that May, he needs to improve the Kentana/Yaqui 48 cross to build a barrier against 15B. This season's new initiative is:

BETTER BREAD, Round 1. This is the first season that includes consideration of the eating quality of the grains he's developing. It's a whole new kind of challenge—one that involves consumer preference rather than biology.

DOWNSIZING WHEAT, Round 1. On top of the 15B rust and everything else that was descending on him, the issue of plant architecture demands attention. He needs plants that stand at attention even when fertilizer fills their heads to near bursting. Wheat is too tall for its own good. Shorter, stiffer plants might achieve a plane of production surpassing all expectations.

hardly half the recommended amount and many used none whatsoever, lodging became widespread in 1952. Wind was now enemy number one. In certain fields the fury of a late-season blast crumpled whole fields of Borlaug's spindly-legged beauties. The grain yield then tumbled below that of Mexico's woeful traditional types.

There was only one way to solve this problem: shrink the plant. His varieties averaged out at shoulder height; if he could just make them hip-high they'd likely prove sturdy enough to defy the wind.

But how to achieve that? He's of course already grown out the 30,000 different specimens in the Department of Agriculture's World Wheat Collection, hoping to uncover undersized wheats. In addition, he'd grabbed heads off every undersized individual that appeared among the millions of segregating specimens arising amid his arranged marriages. Moreover, he's sown thousands of short candidates in the special "stud farms" wherein unusual gene lines as well as seeds from as far away as Argentina, Brazil, and Chile could be inspected for rare qualities.

These genetic supply depots at Chapingo, Toluca, La Piedad, Torreón, Saltillo and Sonora were favorite places that displayed an amazing array of wheats. He enjoyed showing them off. "These," he'd explain to visitors, a gleam in his eye, "are our 'new bulls.'" The phrase always raised a laugh but also conveyed the message that biodiversity is as important to crops as to cows.

Those stud farms were exceptionally well stocked with talent. Yet for all the "spare parts" stashed therein no specimen had ever demonstrated genuine dwarfism. They all fell over when fertilized.

This was immensely galling. Bringing the stems down a peg would bust wheat through its age-old ceiling. But genes for the job did not exist.

For over a year frustration flourished, finally to flirt with obsession. It's thus hardly surprising that on seeing Burton Bayles in 1952 he exposed his most heartfelt hope. "Burt," he said, "Where can I find shorter straw? I grew out the World Wheat Collection but the promising ones all lodged when we fertilized. Is there any other source?"

A wheat breeder of unparalleled experience, Bayles worked in the Department of Agriculture's Washington, DC headquarters. He and Borlaug were touring South America to report on the rust race then assaulting Argentina and Brazil for the third year running. What they found was a calamity of unprecedented magnitude. Norm explains:

> Argentineans take great pride in their bread. For the good life they neither want nor need anything more than bread, beef and wine. But in 1952 stem rust took out Klein Rindadora, the country's best wheat variety. There wasn't enough flour left in the country to make all the bread. That year, by god, we ate bread concocted out of dough containing sorghum flour.

One evening in the Argentinean capital while relaxing over a cocktail Burt Bayles at last addressed Norm's plaintive query. A few years earlier, he said, a co-worker had stumbled upon some *really* short, strong-stalked wheats—ones that were true dwarfs.

This revelation sent Norm's soul soaring. Unfortunately for him, though, they were the wrong kind of wheat for Mexico. They'd been found a world away, in Japan. And they were new and not looking good.

This conversation over a beer in Buenos Aires will prove another defining moment in the saga of how an over-populated planet avoided mass starvation. Bayles' tantalizing tidbit will in the fullness of time transform Borlaug's operations. Thus, its origins are

CAREER SAVER #21

Fate's 21st facilitator, Burton Bayles (on left, in hat). Here at Chapingo in 1953 he confers with John Gibler (standing in cap, who will feature later in the book) and with Ralph Caldwell (one of America's top wheat breeders, who on the book's opening page indicated that for every cross-pollination he made in Purdue University Borlaug made at least a thousand). Bayles was the USDA scientist who put Borlaug onto the dwarf wheats from Japan, which will play a pivotal part as the Borlaug saga unwinds into the future.

worth a sidelong glance. They provide a lesson from Japan.

As with the other varieties we've highlighted, a precarious chain of chance and circumstance lay behind the unexpected discovery of tiny wheats on the Pacific's nether shore. For one thing, they might never have been seen had not Douglas MacArthur focused his gimlet gaze on restoring Japan's food production after World War II.

In a long and jagged career the general had frequently misdirected his gaze but from the minute of Japan's formal surrender in August 1945 this quintessential man of war focused his prodigious leadership talents on waging peace. The hardboiled brass hat who 12 years earlier had positioned machine gun nests along Pennsylvania Avenue to protect the newly inaugurated FDR from decorated dogfaces down on their luck now walked unconcerned, unarmed and unguarded amid his sometime enemies, including fanatics incensed by the indignity of defeat and with Samurai swords beneath their bed rolls.

But combat no longer concerned MacArthur, who was consumed by the challenge of fashioning a modern democracy from a feudal social order. His initial concern was the national spirit. "Never in history," he wrote, "had a nation and its people been more completely crushed. It was not merely the overthrow of military might—it was the collapse of a faith, it was the disintegration of everything they believed in and lived by and fought for. It left a complete vacuum, morally, mentally, and physically."

That malaise was anchored in hopelessness. The Japanese had been cast back into a much older, cruel, primitive, brutal world whose every tomorrow was a struggle with, among other things, disease and hunger. Members of this once-proud society now had nothing: Nothing to treat disease; nothing to eat; nothing to do; nothing to wear. Paper clothing served for a while but created concern because it could dissolve in the rain. Having exchanged their last kimonos for a bag of rice, women mostly hid their nakedness by remaining indoors; whole families were reduced to going out singly, swapping off the same cotton unisex robe, the yukata, before emerging into society's glare.

Despite not having been home for nearly a decade, MacArthur immersed himself in Japan's recovery for five more years. That was vital: Local leaders, by and large, were dead or detained for war crimes. And with the society *in extremis* many big things needed doing together.

Creating a civil society from scratch brought out MacArthur's best. He gathered about him aides of vigor, talent and honesty, requiring that each produce results not rhetoric. Then, following the example of his sometime nemesis FDR, he demanded his hand-picked helpers get out and find things to found the future on. Finally, he set a brilliant opening order of nation-building priorities that may be summarized as:

- Get the people fed,
- Get the people healthy,
- Get the agriculture healthy,
- Get the economy healthy, and
- Educate everyone but above all women.

To get the people fed, MacArthur erected thousands of Army kitchens across the devastated land and cabled Washington for *3.5 million tons* of food to be sent *immediately*. At such an outrageous demand the Pentagon dithered, the State Department dawdled; vital forms had not been filled out, officials had not been consulted, diplomatic channels must be explored. The infuriated general cabled back: "Give me bread or give me bullets!"

Attitudes like that are contagious, and they infected his associates. The one designated to get the people healthy was Colonel Crawford F. Sams, who had been a neuroanatomy expert, public-health specialist, parachutist, and veteran of half a dozen World War II campaigns. Bestselling journalist John Gunther described him as: "A compact decisive man, tough-minded, studious, he is, like many people of the top rank in SCAP [MacArthur's outfit], an idealist of realism."

That he was. And just as well, too. Health was rushing headlong into the dark ages as millions were wracked by malnutrition and disease. Released from exile in history, ancient plagues displayed an amazing command of modernity, with 80 million Japanese to provide them play and social subsidence to smooth the way.

Sams never flinched. Before his time Japan had had a total of two sanitary engineers. The colonel quickly recruited *60,000 six-man teams* and dispatched them to every corner of the land, wherein they went home-by-home checking water supplies, combating mosquitoes, demonstrating sanitation methods, teaching preventive medicine, dispensing advice on nutrition and looking for trouble

Then the can-do colonel hired a further *80,000* Japanese and organized them into 800 district health centers, through which the invisible munitions of immunology could be targeted against the half-dozen major killers then leagued against this shaky society. In his gunsight were:

Tuberculosis. Having long hounded the land of the rising sun, TB was on a new killing spree. Sams vaccinated over 35 *million* Japanese, and dropped the death rate 40 percent in four years.

Cholera. When this dreaded bacterium broke out in 1945 Sams' teams cleaned up the water supply and vaccinated almost 35 million people *in a couple of months*. In August there'd been 1200 cases; four months later there were none. MacArthur declared it "our greatest triumph."

Smallpox. Springing from nowhere to over 17,000 cases in 1946, this much-feared virus threatened chaos. Sams launched preventive vaccinations on a national scale and by 1948 the cases had fallen to 124.

Typhus. This mass killer, carried by body lice, broke out in 1945 among Korean slave laborers in the southern ports. Sams stopped the virus-like microbe by dusting DDT onto the groins and armpits of *50 million* Japanese, not excluding the survivors in Hiroshima and Nagasaki, which are both southern ports. (This huge human exposure, by the way, caused none of the consequences Western worry warts would later invoke to get DDT banned from the face of Planet Earth; indeed, that generation of Japanese would go on to have the longest average lifespan ever recorded.)

Others. Typhoid and paratyphoid were reduced 90 percent, dysentery 79 percent, and diphtheria 86 percent . . . all in three years.

Crushing so many diseases so swiftly and so sweepingly was a high point in public health history. Yet it was no great international endeavor with a bureaucracy and billion-dollar budget—just one man with a clear mind, a clear mission, and behind him the god named MacArthur.

Despite the dysfunctional society and local indifference, Sams' crews rousted out and vaccinated each person—80 million in total—at least *twice*. And by 1949 modern health had returned from forced retirement in the past. "If a character like Sams were discovered by some journalist in Iceland, say, or Libya, books would be written about him," Gunther wrote in 1950. "But he is an American working all but anonymously in Japan and not one American in ten million has ever heard his name."

The amazing uplift in morale was of course vital, but it was MacArthur's order to get the agriculture healthy that nudged the nation toward prosperity. For centuries Japan's food had been produced on estates owned by industrialists and government associations who knew nothing about farming and whose shoes seldom got soiled. Land was a closed and class-ridden commodity, unavailable to mere mortals.

The idea that farmers were born to be tenants disturbed MacArthur, who soon got parliament to pass laws that opened land to all and protected it from repossession by the power elites. The new owners transformed food production. The rice crop was soon ramping upward. Vegetables, hogs and chickens came pouring from the hands of grateful growers. And fruits appeared in abundance from orchards in the hills.

The effects of this were so far reaching as to affect even MacArthur. This political conservative (who'd soon throw his hat all the way across the Pacific and into the ring for the 1948 Republican presidential primary) fell so far into heresy as to promote unionism. He'd come to understand that rural stability was the key to lasting peace, and helped the freshly enfranchised farmers establish self-help operations in almost

THE GREATEST MEDIC

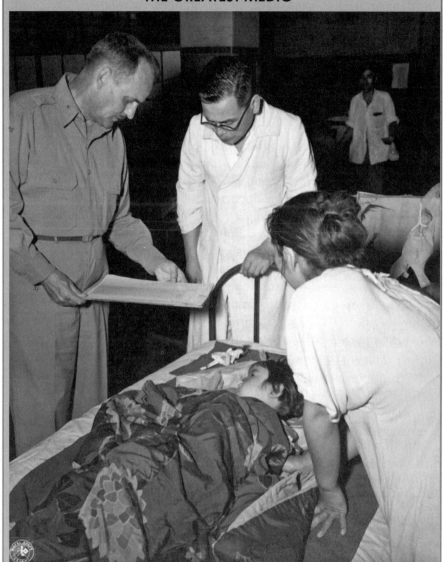

Crawford Sams overseeing care of a child stricken with encephalitis. In the chaos following World War II Sams suppressed a dozen concurrent epidemics by mobilizing 60,000 six-man teams to go home-by-home in every corner of Japan. This brought stability to a suspicious and shattered society that had feared and resisted the occupiers who'd so recently been enemies. Sams was 43 years old when he took up the challenge of ridding Japan of tuberculosis, cholera, smallpox, typhus, typhoid, dysentery, diphtheria and other scourges. And in five years he won more than lives . . . he won hearts, raised a stricken nation's morale, and swayed social support toward all things American.

every village and town. Within three years there were over 33,000 "democratically constituted" farmer-cooperatives, with a total membership of 8.2 million.

From the imperial heights MacArthur declared in December 1949. "The farmers of Japan have carried through an organizational task perhaps unsurpassed in the history of the world cooperative movement. In so doing they have demonstrated their growing capacity to handle the tools of democracy."

The thriving fields did more than get the farms going . . . they got Japan going. National progress marched from the hinterland, leading the way to freedom from want. In turn, Peace marched forth from the prefectures. And Hunger and Strife, both of which had been taking an all-too-intimate look at the opportunities in Japan, went off to check out China. It was as good a Hunger Fighting lesson as you'll find.

A mong other specialists helping steer rural Nippon from feudalism to freedom was a wheat specialist whom MacArthur charged with restarting rice and wheat production.

Samuel Salmon naturally inspected the country's farthest corners, and one day in 1949 300 miles north of Tokyo he stumbled across a line of wheats that piqued his interest. Notwithstanding the highly fertilized soil, they remained upright, stiff and strong. Most intriguing of all, they were tiny. "In spite of these very favorable conditions for vegetative growth," he wrote, "the plants were [only] about 24 inches high but stood erect."

These so-called Norin varieties—ten in all—had been bred at the Morioka Branch Experiment Station. To shorten the stems their creator, Gonjiro Inazuka, had used a single knee-high plant whose origin remains lost in mystery. Borlaug suspects a local farmer who was ladling on "night soil" (human waste) spotted this tiny plant standing straight amid taller ones that had toppled like tired drunks. Thankfully, he saved the seeds and eventually some reached the knowing hands of Inazuka, who employed their pollen to create the Norin line.

Although Japanese farmers had ignored these home-grown creations (and in fact would never adopt them), Salmon was captivated. Of all the people then alive, he was among a handful who understood their uniqueness and potential. On mailing the seeds back to his colleagues in Washington he spilled his excitement onto the accompanying note: The plants, he wrote, are "so damn short, they're pretty much underground!"

The few seeds from his package were grown under quarantine in Arizona. Once the petite progeny were confirmed disease free, an envelope

CAREER SAVER #22

Fate's 22nd facilitator, Gonjiro Inazuka. Wheat was shoulder high until Inazuka bred the Norin wheats that were knee high. These rare plants existed only in his small research plots in northern Japan. Fewer than 100 of Inazuka's seeds reached Borlaug in 1952. A dozen years later Borlaug wheats will provide the universal joint in leveraging the global food supply upward. Genes from the Norin wheats not only strengthen the joint, they make it work. Norm credits his Japanese colleague with providing the key that made possible a better-fed world.

containing 100 seeds was sent to Orville Vogel in Washington state. All this was pretty much what Burt Bayles had related that night in Argentina, just three years after the envelope had reached Vogel. Norm had never met this Pacific Northwest wheat breeder, and as they were parting that night in Buenos Aires, Burt Bayles urged him to work fast, since Vogel wasn't going to be around for long. Twice already, his USDA bosses in Washington DC had mailed missives suggesting he seek other employment. The stubborn recipient had ignored them. Now his future was clear: Bayles let slip the fact that the department's top brass were even then preparing to sever Vogel from government service.

CAREER SAVER #23

Fate's 23rd facilitator, Samuel C. Salmon. In the aftermath of World War II Salmon was in Japan helping resurrect food production. During a trip to a remote research station he spotted Inazuka's quarter-sized wheat plants. The seeds he picked up that day provided the genes in all Borlaug's later high-yield varieties. By one estimate half the world's population goes to bed every night after consuming food made from one of those varieties. Today, though, not even the history books know the names of Inazuka or Salmon.

You may wonder what transgression could produce to such a reaction. Rest assured it was truly terrible. You see, Orville Vogel's career was about to perish for a lack of published literature!

Knowing that such a sin was mortal, Norm immediately dashed off a letter asking if a few seeds might be spared for testing below the border.

May 1952 sees the start of Year 8; Norm's already put in 14 seasons of nonstop research. He's now handling more than 40,000 distinct wheat lines each season. In addition, that July he made 6,000 individual cross-pollinations.

Rust race 15B remains the main target. Word trickling down from the center of the universe atop Mexico was truly disquieting. In just two years 15B had gripped the heartland. Fields in the upper Great Plains and Canadian prairies bring to mind the Red Sea. That fall, the scarlet tide misappropriated 75 percent of pasta wheats and 35 percent of bread wheats.

That fall, too, farmers wrote off millions of acres by plowing their crop under. To them it seemed like the sky was falling. And it was. Early in June 1952 Stakman's greasy glass slides indicated that 4000 tons of rust spores landed on 4 million acres of wheat in just 16 counties of northern Oklahoma and south-central Kansas. Given that there are 150 billion spores to a pound, that modest area received 600 trillion infectious particles. Winds carried similar quantities on to Minnesota and the Dakotas, where 40,000 square miles received 3.5 million spores *per acre*. And the even greater generation arising therefrom got dumped onto Canada's wheat-dependent provinces.

Remember, those were raining down on wheats with no capacity to resist. Not one variety could withstand the 15B spores landing on their stems. The latest fungal phantom had rendered Stakman's creation as obsolete as Ceres (which by now was known to have fallen to rust race 56 in 1935) or Marquis (monstered by rust race 38 in 1916).

Fields that had gushed golden tides of grain for over a decade had become bloody blots on the face of the countryside.

Panic once more pervaded wheat country.

D uring 1952 an unusual possibility suddenly popped up among the myriad advanced progeny in Norm's research fields. This singular plant matured fast, yielded well and possessed the red-tinted grains Mexican millers preferred.

Norm and the wheat-breeding bird-boys had made the original blend at La Piedad. In time, he named it "Lerma 52,"after the long snaky river that ambled past Campo La Cal Grande. Although raising hopes, this rangy powerhouse had a singular fault: its grain produced bad bread.

For this reason, that summer he opened a second front with a parallel campaign aimed at ensuring all his varieties made good eating.

For the good-bread initiative's first bout he sowed plots of both Lerma 52 and Newthatch, the variety whose flour raised bakers to rapture. In July he cross-pollinated their flowers; by October he knew that that first backcross had produced a few specimens whose grain produced fair loaves. One stood out above the rest, however, and that's what he pinned his highest hopes on.

It was also in 1952 that the Rockefeller Foundation suddenly decided to replicate the Mexican operation. The first copy would be erected near Cali in Colombia. Arrangements were underway for counterparts in Chile, Brazil, Ecuador and Peru. Even India was asking for a Borlaug-type operation.

Given this global expansion, the foundation brass needed help at headquarters, and only one person fit the job description. Thus it was that George Harrar got plucked out of Mexico and made Director of Agricultural Sciences in the foundation's New York HQ.

To those left behind the decision came as a body blow. The idea of operating in Mexico without Harrar was beyond imagining. Talents for administration and diplomacy had made him irreplaceable. The project was essentially his personal creation. He held the institutional memory. He'd initiated the political and scientific contacts, and was trusted. Indeed, Mexican officials, foundation administrators, local hires, and the researchers above all, regarded him with near reverence.

This universal appreciation was not because Harrar was a nice guy (few ever thought that) but because he was both practical and visionary and understood when to be the one and when the other. In addition, this man of magnificent presence possessed enough courage and understanding of the technical issues to release his researchers to act upon their own design with complete freedom. Taken all round, Harrar's competence, calmness and confidence kept the miasmic enterprise from turning to mush.

Sadly no like-minded leader could be found. Thus, by default Wellhausen was designated to fill the big shoes. Ed had the necessary technical understandings but lacked the outsize personality and the aura of authority that had served Harrar so well.

Indeed, this quiet stoic to whom corn plants uniquely exposed their secrets had no earthly interest in indoor servitude. Corn had by then turned garrulous and was letting him into crucial secrets never before exposed. One was the mystery of why the all-American corn varieties had failed in '45. Corn had shown Wellhausen that it came in two climatically restricted cousins: one was acclimatized to the temperate zone, the other to the tropical zone. The American All-Star corn plants had performed poorly because Mexico lay beyond their comfort zone.

This insight helped Ed develop so-called "tropical corns" that came to feed most of Latin America and much of Africa. Indeed, his corns had become so expressive that Barbara McClintock, who in time would win

CAREER SAVER #24

Fate's 24th facilitator, Ed Wellhausen. Ed was a master at making crops—above all corn—produce to their uttermost potential. He understood their wants and needs as if sharing them himself. Their botanical secrets he learned face to face. "Put the old eye to your plant," he told Borlaug at the beginning; "look close. Form a picture of how it lives. Get to know its nutritional requirements, its diseases and pest problems. Then it will tell you all its requirements." That pretty much sums up his future research.

Though initially skeptical of Borlaug's work, Wellhausen would later help keep it going. Mainly, he ran interference for his friend. After being forced to become OEE's director, Wellhausen forwent his fondest desires and in the interests of the team took over the leadership. In that capacity he several times saved Borlaug's bacon.

the Nobel Prize for the secrets corn genes whispered, came down each year to listen to Ed's plants. And to Ed too.

Although his progress with corn had paralleled Borlaug's with wheat, Wellhausen had to ditch his one true love and direct the OEE.

At first Ed tried running research on the side. Cruel fate, however, would not let him off so lightly. Within weeks, militant students invaded the ancient edifice in the suburb of San Jacinto—the one housing the OEE's main office. That government structure, the students declared, must be gifted to the university and renovated as a dormitory for themselves. This issue was so vital they barricaded the site, screamed anti-American slogans and threatened to burn the whole place down unless the government and the gringos got out.

To the soft of heart (or of head), student demands can seem almost democratic but Wellhausen understood that this was in reality extortion. Rather than let the OEE fall prey to firebrands' fancies, the new director sought a quieter locale, settling on a small complex in the business area called Londres. Both the English- and Spanish-speaking secretariats quickly took up residence together in the heart of the huge city.

From that downtown center the Master Plantsman would waste his capacity to converse with corn. Of more significance to us, however, he remained true to Borlaug and down the years devoted months, emotions and mental anguish running interference for his contrarian friend who always seemed at odds with everybody.

In helping the wheat specialist, who so maddeningly and mindlessly failed to follow proper procedures, Ed gave up more than anyone has realized. And Norm is grateful:

> Ed Wellhausen was well on his way to lifting corn yields as much we lifted wheat yields. In fact, he was ahead of us in those days. But thank god he took the time to protect the wheat program. We might never have made it otherwise.

Later that year the Rockefeller Foundation hired a new president. Dean Rusk, a big shot emanating from the thin-air zone of the State Department, was destined for fame as a Vietnam War advocate. But he lacked any understanding of hunger fighting. In his view Borlaug's was to complete the research and let the Mexicans carry it onwards and upwards. From 1952, at roughly annual intervals, the new president needled Norm to wrap up and retreat. From the perspective of his perch atop the richest charity in the world's richest city, the time to declare victory was long past. If Mexicans wouldn't pick up the mantle that was proof positive Borlaug was neither needed nor wanted.

It is a sad fact that can-do projects demand managers with the mojo to move through the smog caused by setbacks, uncertainty and surprises without falling prey to panic or paranoia. Harrar could; Rusk couldn't. The man who'd helped direct the world and the war from the White House epitomizes those executives who prefer scientist underlings to be

TECHNICAL PROGRESS, 1952

By the close of season 15 in November '52, following eight seasons in Central Mexico and seven in Sonora, he's 3.5 years ahead of schedule.

In his eighth year of hunger fighting Norm seems to have made a good restart:

- Mexico's wheat production is rising;
- Stakman and McFadden's gifts are the reason. Borlaug's own haven't yet kicked in. So the future will be even brighter;

On the downside though:

- The battle with Black Stem Rust is beginning all over again. It's a surreal moment—everyone thinks that everything is going great but he knows otherwise. He's got to develop backups, and fast. Or disaster will strike and he'll be packed off as an impractical charlatan.
- His great yielding Lerma Rojo makes bad bread.

Here again we see the galvanizing power of a seed. Those four special wheats are starting to fashion the fabric of society as a surf of golden grain surges from the wheatlands and uplifts the whole economy. And in their freshly oxygenated air farm folk sense possibilities for even greater things. The crazy gringo has provided them not just seeds but stability, financial strength and hope for a better future.

Wheat is firmly leading him onwards now, and making him an elemental force in hungry Mexico. But there's still far to go.

In the 8 years since his arrival, the number of mouths in Mexico has risen by 5.8 million, or 26.4 percent, to reach 27.8 million.

brainy bureaucrats. He wanted the work scripted, even to write the script.

Unlike his nominal boss, Borlaug knew the danger of fixed opinions or prearranged plans. In his fields of genetic chance *mañana* would unfold in mysterious ways. For one thing, Mother Nature would someday exact retribution, and her arrows would arrive unannounced. His success therefore demanded rapid reaction. Above all else, he must outmaneuver surprise itself.

For the time being, though, the top man's attitude seemed logical. In 1952 Mexico's wheat production rose. Never before had it ever topped 400,000 tons; now it touched 500,000 tons. Furthermore, the average national yield jumped by half to the unprecedented level of 1000lbs an acre. And the acreage under wheat increased 3 percent, a not insignificant amount considering that, ever-so-recently it had been shrinking.

1953

Fightback

Upon arriving at the old Sonora experiment station for the opening season of 1953 Norm sensed social change in the air. The farming community seemed more secure, more serene. The tide hadn't fully turned in wheat's favor but considering how strongly the ebb had previously run even slack water signified progress.

That fall, Aureliano Campoy, Rafael Angel Fierros, Roberto Maurer and other Yaqui Valley farmers planted Kentana and Yaqui—not for tentative testing but for personal profit. Amid the vastness of the Yaqui Valley these initial plantings contributed little but their significance was beyond measure: These were the first of dozens of Borlaug-bred wheats that will contribute to commerce and consumers.

To Norm personally, this waypoint was of little note. He knew that in reality Mexican wheat was on the verge of collapse.

With farm country now reliant on his plants, the issue was what to do. When the stalks no longer stood golden in the sunlight but were spotted and blackened and wizened and bent, hundreds of farm families would tremble over their plight. And by then it would be too late:

There'd be financial loss.

There'd be hunger.

There'd be suffering.

And recriminations too.

To stave off that disaster the country's sole wheat researcher needed to solve a disquieting dilemma: what replacement to recommend. His wheats were the best Mexico had ever seen . . . or ever dreamed of seeing. But 15B was about to end their reigns, and each new sowing raised the risk.

The time had come to hit the kill switch. So, during the early days of

TECHNICAL CHALLENGES, 1953

Round 16 (Nov. '52-April 1953). Eighth stint in Sonora. In March he turns 39.

His greatest challenge is stopping farmers from growing all 8 of his previous recommendations, which are about to die. Only Kentana is safe from 15B.
That winter he'll establish the by-now standard operations.

STEM-RUST RESISTANCE. His prime goal is still to prevent Race 15B from devastating Mexico.

DEMONSTRATION DAY #6. He'll organize several dozen contrasting plots for the Farmer Field Day which will take place during the season's final weeks in April.

ON-FARM FERTILIZER TRIALS. That fall, Norm found time to drive across the Yaqui Valley carrying new seed and another bag of fertilizer to Jorge Parada, so the soil-fertility trial could be repeated for the second time.

Round 17 (May-Oct., 1953). Seventh stint in Central Mexico. First at Toluca.

Here he starts his eighth year of relentless two-a-year campaigning. Though he's tasted success it means nothing now that stem rust has mutated.

STEM-RUST RESISTANCE. He must refocus his research specifically on the prevention of Race 15B.

BETTER BREAD, Round 2. In addition to the crossing block, he'll sow enough Lerma Rojo to provide flour to bake test loaves. If this second backcross at Toluca proves successful the improved Lerma Rojo will be ready for the big time next year.

1953, with signature audacity, he set out to quash the very varieties he'd developed with painstaking care through eight years of endless toil. He distributed alerts and issued radio announcements. In the upcoming season none of the current wheats should be sown. A new scourge had its sights set on those widely planted varieties [Frontera, Supremo, Yaqui, Nazas and Chapingo]. Only Kentana was safe. Farmers must shift to Kentana. Now!

What would result come planting time in May he couldn't say. At bottom, farming is faith based, and switching seed is akin to a religious conversion. Farmers commit to a seed and resist alternatives as if Satanic. Moreover, righteous reluctance soars when told to ignore free seed in their own storage bin and spend money buying someone else's.

This call would be the litmus test of the gringo guru's credibility among his growing group of believers.

Americans in that era obtained up to 40 percent of their calories from the 15 billion pounds of breadstuffs the national wheat crop provided. Although in 1953 the silos and food stores still held goodly stocks of grain and flour, 15B threatened to make those the last for all time.

It was the kind of situation that nowadays gets splashed across the national news morning to night. But those were woefully backward days, before scientists learned to become headline heroes. Researchers then considered it criminal to terrify the public with their uttermost fears. Wheat breeders during this crisis never dreamed of going public, let alone leveraging popular concern into personal publicity or extra research dollars. To the contrary, they felt a dulling sense of duty, nay shame that this condition had arisen on their watch.

Urbanites were thus so shielded from the sound or sight of the faultline opening beneath their lives that not even history took note of the seismic event. Americans and Canadians continued eating bread, cookies, crackers, cakes, pastries, pancakes, doughnuts, breakfast cereals, rolls, bagels and enjoying peace of mind while the specialists stared at the food supply's failing foundation without seeing how to stop the crack from widening until it swallowed civilization.

Desperate for any idea on what to do, wheat specialists from throughout North America convened a council of war during January 1953—converging on Winnipeg in hopes their collective wisdom might uncover some magical means for breaking the fungal stranglehold. About 40 wheat breeders and plant pathologists attended, among them Harrar, Stakman and Borlaug.

From the outset panic pervaded the prairie air and the participants' morale verged on the pathological. And as the deliberations proceeded the mood plunged. The USDA's chief cereal pathologist got caught in the downdraft. "By god, Norm," Herman Rodenheiser said during a quiet moment on the first afternoon, his face pallid and stricken: "I think we're running out of genes . . . there's no resistance for this thing, anywhere!"

"Rody" Rodenheiser, however, had been peering into his own mind and as the discussions waffled on without end he proposed collecting every wheat that carried any smidgen of stem-rust resistance and growing them side-by-side in different parts of North America using a uniform protocol. This would be an all-volunteer exercise; local wheat scientists would sow the seed, maintain the plots, record the results, harvest the healthiest specimens, and return those seeds to the central organizers for consolidation into a new pool for a subsequent round of plantings the following year.

This selfless collaboration would, he explained, expose and concentrate 15B-resisting genes. It was a shot in the dark and would take time and patience but might possibly save the situation. Moreover, seeds of the surviving plants would be in the hands of wheat breeders who could seize the chance to apply their own talents. He called his conception the "International Stem Rust Nursery."

So novel a notion had never been tried, for two reasons: One, it was the thinnest of reeds for salvaging a crop in mortal danger; two, sharing professional secrets went against human nature. Nevertheless some impulse was needed to break the deadlock, so the conferees approved the idea. Aiding their decision was the fact that Rodenheiser had prearranged USDA sponsorship.

Then companies dealing with milling, baking, farm implements, grain exports, and so forth then set up a parallel program—more for partnership than for partisanship. Fearing for their future, they prayed that either organization would unveil a botanical redeemer. Their operation was called the Rust Prevention Association.

Beyond this nothing more seemed possible. The world's Number 1 food crop had reached the end of its string. For wheat there was just this final prayer-filled possibility of divine rescue.

During the Winnipeg council of war Norm casually informed both Rodenheiser and the corporate representative that he'd gladly grow their special seeds during the winter, thereby squeezing in an extra round of plantings while northern soils were snowbound. As long as the seeds reached Mexico City before November, he'd carry them north to Sonora, sow them in separate plots, and maintain the plants alongside his own. In April the separate groups could send a staff member to harvest and record the results and haul home seeds of any survivors in time for the northern planting.

The idea met with general approval and George Harrar allowed Norm to add it to his duties. This new venture, however, could neither be publicized nor formally incorporated into the OEE, whose agreement with the government strictly limited its help to Mexican interests. Thus Borlaug's involvement in the International Stem Rust Nursery was hushed up and became another off-the-books sideline he shouldered personally, without compensation and without the big bosses in New York knowing.

On April 25, while Norm was occupied with the harvest in Sonora, James Watson and Francis Crick of Cambridge University announced the discovery of the structure of DNA.

The template by which living things copy themselves, so they declared, looks like two delicate springs wound together in molecular embrace. Each strand had a chemical weakness running down its length allowing it to unzip into separate complimentary halves. This neatly explained how chromosomes copied themselves as cells reproduced and perpetuated life through time and space.

Exposing the mystery at the core of life may have launched the modern age but it made no difference to Norm. Knowing he was directing a double spiral of DNA didn't help convert gene pairs into food.

Not for decades could the hand of man parse the chromosomal alphabet into sentient sentences. Therefore, throughout his career Norm operated in the genetic dark ages, fertilizing one plant with another's pollen, then groping through the chromosomal chaos hoping the random couplings of 25,000 jiving genes might have spun off a "keeper."

Compared to white-lab coats like Watson and Crick who occupied the intellectual high ground and got the glory and great prizes he was blue-collar laborer, striving to solve practical rather than theoretical problems.

Actually, Watson and Crick were a breed apart from their own peers. They operated in a sphere more like a circus than science. Knowing almost nothing about chemistry or deoxyribonucleic acid, they developed no data. Instead, they quizzed their colleagues and rivals and cobbled together—using cardboard, clamps and chutzpah—a model linking the insights they'd gleaned, much of it from a purloined photograph. Following a couple of embarrassingly bad guesses, they hit the jackpot. Then, *zut alors*, they broke the scientist's code of honor and went public not just with their findings but their finaglings.

This was the point when the science of issue lost out to the science of image and the greatest of all disciplines began the descent from the Ivory Tower. Watson, a 23-year-old Chicagoan, confessed all in a book that became a runaway bestseller and made the pair the darlings of the age. Watson and Crick became household names, their work breathlessly reported in publications all the way down to high-school textbooks and tomes for serious-minded children.

This precedent established celebrity as a goal even scientists might aspire to. Borlaug, however, remained a defiant No Name below the bottom of the professional heap. Only those close to him knew or cared about his mission. Struggling against all the odds in the wild wastes of misbegotten Mexico he was using DNA to foil a fungus and help the hungry.

And he was happy.

May 1953 sees the start of Year 9; Norm's now put in 16 seasons of nonstop research. His wheat babies are finally growing up and showing prospects bright enough to turn even diehard skeptics into dedicated supporters. Indeed, across the countryside change is churning many formerly fixed beliefs: soils are being fertilized; yields are rising; flax growers are returning to their first love. In the Bajío, where winter coolth once constituted the sole protection against rust, commercial wheat is now being grown during the sizzle of summer. In Coahuila and La Laguna production is also expanding. Indeed, all Mexico's wheatlands are blossoming. And of the billions of plants, more than two-thirds are Borlaug products.

Beyond the persistent pressure on the rust front, a cluster of concerns in the central zone made this a summer like none before. These amounted to at least eight separate sidelights:

One. At Toluca that May he tackled Round 2 in his struggle to perfect varieties that produced good yield and good bread. Certain plants selected from the second backcross between Lerma Rojo and Newthatch already met the need, so Norm felt excited as he planted ten modest multiplication plots. These would provide the starting seed that would eventually take them into full production.

Two. To switch Mexico's farmers away from the disaster-prone varieties, he needed Kentana seed by the ton. Dick Spurlock offered to produce it, and rented 250 acres of bottomland near the town of Irapuato [eer-a-PWA-toe] in the Bajío. Here there was irrigation, something unusual in that mostly hilly central region, and he could maximize both production and the probability of success.

Then, just when the planting time arrived in May, the Wyoming cowpoke had to dash off to the Mayo Clinic for his life. Before leaving, he asked Borlaug to take over.

Pleased by the possibility, Norm remained in his research plots until darkness fell Friday nights, and then headed for Irapuato. From Toluca the drive took so long he was lucky to arrive by midnight. Even from La Piedad—just 50 miles distant—it could involve three harrowing hours fighting blackness and bad roads. Then, he and Spurlock's crew labored through Saturday, Sunday and oftentimes also through the night between, to sow the Kentana upon which swung Mexico's stability.

Although Spurlock returned in six weeks, he soon had to scuttle back to Minnesota. The problem was both simple and severe: To combat chronic diarrhea, he'd swallowed sulfa drugs for months at a stretch. Later, that was found to destroy the stomach's normal complement of bacteria, rendering digestion impossible. People died before anyone realized this downside to the wondrous new antibiotics.

Norm then offered to devote the necessary weekends to supervise the planting until Spurlock's return.

Three. In midsummer, a singular difficulty arose in the Toluca area when Spurlock's farmer friends complained bitterly about fertilizer. It was worthless, they said; it was doing no good; they'd wasted their money; the gringo scientist couldn't be trusted!

When Borlaug visited, he could see what they meant:

> The plants were droopy, yellowish, and clearly out of sorts. On quizzing the farmers, I learned they'd applied nitrogen at a rate of 40 pounds an acre. That should have made a big difference.
>
> I was both worried and puzzled because there seemed no explanation for so tepid a response. At Irapuato, the same plants were flush with good health.
>
> This mystery quietly festered in my mind. And the technical issue wasn't the prime one. At this tricky moment in the transition away from tradition, any setback could turn the farmers off high-yield wheat. Alternately, Spurlock could lose confidence. Either way, we might never recover the momentum.

Four. That befuddled year of '53 delivered a family concern. This is when fears over his son's physical condition climaxed. Six years old now, Billy was in worsening health. Asthma and allergies had become serious. Something needed to be done.

One night, Margaret suggested the possibility of physical exercise. Thinking back to his own boyhood, Norm agreed. Athletics might help. Next day, he mentioned the matter to John Niederhauser.

Intrigued, this breezy good humored OEE colleague liked the idea. With six rambunctious sons Niederhauser needed ways to keep overly healthy boys from falling into mischief. Almost casually, he suggested Little League, a new but increasingly popular sport he'd heard about back in his home state of California.

Next day they wrote to Little League headquarters in Williamsport, Pennsylvania.

Five. During the summer of 1953 a fat envelope arrived from the state of Washington. Enclosed were 60 seeds of the original Japanese Norin

10 as well as a few seeds from Vogel's crosses between it and three standard wheats in Washington State. In total, there were 80 seeds.

Norm put them together with the other items he'd haul north for the next Sonora season, still months away.

Six. In Toluca one morning late that summer he heard the dismaying words that a certain research plot had been damaged. With trepidation he tramped out to find a large patch grazed to the ground. Pressed into the mud between the stubble were the unmistakable imprints of hooves. Obviously a local farmer had seized the chance of free feed. Hustling his donkeys in for a night of feasting, he'd hustled them home before the light of day. The loss was gut-wrenching:

> This was perhaps the most sickening sight of my career. Those burros ate every last F1 plant in the third backcross we'd made in our attempt to improve Yaqui's leaf-rust resistance. Each plant was distinct; its exact genetic combination could never be recreated. The scene that morning signified the complete waste of five years of effort.

So ended the program to immunize wheat against leaf-rust. Though the project had been on the verge of victory over the disease that was second only to stem rust, Norm had to abandon the mission. From here on, that leaf-loving fungal invader could not be denied access to Mexico's wheat crop . . . as the country would later learn to its sorrow.

Seven. During that summer enthusiasm for the second backcross between Lerma Rojo and Newthatch mounted. Some of the segregating specimens combined traits for high production *and* quality bread. As the harvest season approached he toured the ten modest multiplication plots. Everything seemed fine; the plants were heavy with grain. Clearly, some possessed the wherewithal to make farmers, bakers *and* bread-lovers ecstatic. It was a new kind of breakthrough.

The happiness lasted a mere mini-minute. By this point OEE was using Orville Vogel's small combines to gather each plot's production. A sack containing the few pounds of seed from each row was unhooked from the machine, labeled and left in the field for later pickup. On this occasion thunderheads built high in the afternoon sky and with desperate haste, the researchers rushed the sacks through the downpour to shelter under a patio roof, covering them with straw to ward off wayward drops.

The mystery arose next morning: The patio was empty. The seed had disappeared. No one knew where it could possibly have gone.

The cause of season's second gut-wrenching loss remains a mystery. Whether the sack was stolen or accidentally tossed out with the straw is unknown. For a year he periodically searched farm fields throughout the area, hoping to spot the familiar sight of Lerma Rojo. All in vain. The gene combo that meant so much would never be recovered.

Lerma Rojo would live on but in lesser versions. The best probably ended up as chicken feed. If so, those grains were the costliest a chicken ever consumed.

I n October, the results of the seventeenth time he and the fungus have battled were visible in the giant planting of wheat types from his own collection as well as from the U.S. Department of Agriculture. Now he saw that his major chance for deflecting the onrush of 15B stem rust dashed. Almost every plot in that nursery was black or brown and wilted beyond recovery. This gargantuan survey of a total of 66,000 wheat types produced only six survivors. They were the only ones showing any capacity to withstand the new rain of terror. Amazingly, all six were his own creations: Kentana, Lerma, Kenya Red, Kenya White and two half-perfected lines, later named Chapingo 52 and Chapingo 53.

Those hardy half-dozen had one common ingredient: the Kenya-type resistance. Thus, at that crucial instant, with history holding its breath, the plants with the genes Gerald Burton had teased out of pasta wheat decades before in distant East Africa provided the only hope for wheat's future. Chromosomes that had been miraculously rescued from a laboratory fire on the far side of the world were all that stood in the path of 15B and the possible extinction of North America's Number Two food crop.

O wing to Spurlock's continued absence at the Mayo Clinic, Norm supervised the 350-acre planting at Irapuato right through to the end.

Managing my own creations was good experience. I found how my recommendations worked in practice—including some that didn't. And keeping the books taught me how much each step cost.

Dick returned in time for the harvest, and was delighted with the result. We got over 2500lbs an acre—a record for that time."

Initially, however, it wasn't clear Kentana seed would be needed. Throughout most of 1953 his plea to the nation's farmers hung in the

TECHNICAL PROGRESS, 1953

By the close of season 17 in November '53, following nine seasons in Central Mexico and eight in Sonora, he's 4 years ahead of schedule. Without his doubled-up dedication he'd not have gotten this far until 1957.

As 1953 comes to an end, he's begun his fightback:
- National wheat production rose to 670,000 tons;
- The crop is now grown on 1,358,500 acres;
- Maximum yield was 3239lb per acre.
- Despite those fabulous numbers from the old varieties, he's got the farmers to switch to Kentana. He's even provided the seed they'll need.

When he quit Sonora that spring and wended his way southward he was more than satisfied with the progress on real farms as well as in the research fields.

On the downside this year:
- The 15B microbial monsoon is headed toward Mexico, so the immediate future will create challenges.
- That stem rust mutation has made obsolete every plant he's released to farmers.
- His campaign against leaf rust was ended by a neighbor's donkeys.
- His leading candidate for quality bread is lost, probably to a neighbor's chickens.

balance. No one would commit to change when their fields looked so great. In the upshot, though, the farmers did switch varieties. The foreign scientist clearly *had* earned their trust.

Spurlock's seed thus proved vital. It moved Kentana from understudy to center stage. And in Mexico's wheat fields it would in time prove a star performer, both in grain production and in disease protection.

Behind all this was a second miracle: Thanks to the rapid adoption of that variety, 15B attained only a minor presence in Mexico.

The bullet had been dodged. But the cost had been high. All the previous plants, created so painstakingly over 16 seasons and 8 years of nonstop dedication got shuffled off the board. For good.

Now he had to proceed with a new and much smaller deck.

11

1954

Friendly Fire

B y the time Norm returns to Sonora OEE's center of intellectual gravity has shifted. Everyone, even the fiscal pharisees in faraway New York, now realize that working sequentially at two different latitudes is neither heretical nor wasteful of money. Indeed, the desert behind the distant mountains has metamorphosed from an uppity junior's indulgence into the prime research locale.

With OEE turned on its head, even Ed Wellhausen now puts in a winter corn crop in the north. He and Norm ride together, leading a convoy of three pickup trucks loaded with thousands of packages of seed wheat and seed corn—several tons in total.

These days the support staff and field crews also spend the winter a thousand miles from their families. The living quarters at the old experiment station, while still crude, have been renovated and raise few complaints. By now, Borlaug and the former bird boys have developed perfect chemistry. Through much of the days each works on his own designated task, never needing to say anything to anyone.

During those months Norm hustles from plot to plot sunup to sundown, handling plants that in their immature state all look alike but that require individualized care depending on their stage of selection and their role in the order of things. This provokes mental gyrations knotty enough to perplex a polymath. At each instant, though, Norm didn't consciously see the whole plant . . . just the bits that mattered. That eased his task.

During this season, the eighteenth without interruption, he and the boys sow not just their own seeds but the several hundred "thimbles" mailed by Rody Rodenheiser as well as several dozen more mailed by the Rust Prevention Association. Nestling inside all those finger-sized

TECHNICAL CHALLENGES, 1954

Rounds 18 & 19. His ninth season in Sonora, tenth in Central Mexico. That March, he turns 40.

Norm is now operating on an expanded stage. This is primarily because his field activities are accreting ever more layers of complication. There's:
- The steady, methodical research endeavors to fight rust;
- The effort to convert his best lines into great bread-makers; and
- Demonstration Day #7 to prepare.

However, *two* novel thrusts are also launched that winter.

DOWNSIZING WHEAT, Round 1. The attempt to strengthen wheat's spine by cutting the plant down a peg will begin here when he plants the 80 seeds from the envelope from Washington State.

INTERNATIONAL STEM-RUST NURSERY #1. That winter in Sonora he oversees the 15B-resistance test plantings sent by spring-wheat breeders far away over the northern horizon, most of whom he's never met.

metal canisters are seeds submitted by wheat breeders in university, government and private industry across the Upper Midwest and Canada. Getting those into the Sonora soil kicked off Round 1 in his contribution to the International Stem Rust Nursery, upon which rest the hopes and even prayers of North America's wheat-based industry, not to mention the world's biggest economy and Americans' inalienable right to daily bread.

In addition, he puts in demonstration plots. In five months time, following winter's demise, he hopes they'll present another fairground of the future and expose even more farmers to the latest progress. He's also slips in a few "teasers" to give them a glimpse of the super-charged wheats still under development.

Finally he sows the contents of the envelope postmarked Pullman, Washington. As these seeds, like McFadden's, will influence all that eventuates, it's worth yet another detour of indebtedness to yet another wheat-gene genius.

Seven years Norm's senior, Orville Alvin Vogel was born in 1907 and raised on a farm near the northeast Nebraska village of Pilger (population, 100 families). Until he turned five and entered elementary school, German was his tongue. Due to the parent's divorce and the horrors of subsistence farming, his early years were unhappy. Indeed, they stirred an irrepressible passion to escape his designated life.

Eventually he found Freedom's gate key: a teaching certificate earned at Yankton College in South Dakota. With a sense of release, the budding educator scuttled off to bury himself in an even smaller northeast Nebraska village: Wynot (population, 50 families). In its tiny high school, well beyond Destiny's gaze, he taught math and science.

Thank goodness Destiny was far-sighted: After several years Vogel gave up resisting any attachment with agriculture. By investing the meager savings from his teacher's paycheck, he enrolled in an agronomy program at the University of Nebraska. Although no great scholar, he earned both Bachelors and Masters degrees.

By a fortunate twist of fate his graduation coincided with an opening for a junior agronomist in the Pacific Northwest. That was in the fall of 1931 and the USDA recruiter who stopped by the university in Lincoln was so impressed he hired the 23-year-old grad on the spot.

At first that decision seemed to have been not only impetuous but imprudent. To his contemporaries at Washington State University the Nebraskan proved a strange and unsettling creature. Among students and close colleagues he was warmhearted, kind, thoughtful and respectful of individual perspectives. Outside that circle, though, he could be arrogant, argumentative, stubborn and dismissive of alternative views. Even while still a junior agronomist—the lowliest of the low who might possibly be seen but certainly never heard—he clashed with his superiors over the best wheat-breeding strategy for the Pacific Northwest (and was overruled, though time would prove him right).

Such conceit in a junior was so indecorous as to reflect some genetic failing. Indeed, something of a quarrelsome sheen shines through from the depths of old photographs. Despite thick-rimmed eyeglasses, Vogel's profile is not that of a bookworm; it suggests instead a sodbuster; tanned and tough with a large nose, flat mouth and grumpy stare.

Rough cast from the same rural mold as Borlaug, Vogel just wanted to improve the productivity of the nation's top crop. His bosses, however, held him to a more exacting standard: the quantity of technical articles in refereed journals. In this, the grandest arena of academic endeavor, Vogel was a dunce. His shocking dearth of documentation was, you'll recall, why he'd twice been served letters suggesting he seek other employment.

During that auspicious evening in Buenos Aires when this unfortunate series of events came up, Burt Bayles was visibly upset. He liked and respected Vogel and knew that Department of Agriculture administrators were even then preparing the walking papers. Bayles himself was trying to delay their dispatch. Fortunately for history, he seems to have succeeded, and the prickly professor helped his own cause by taking time out to write just enough papers to puff up a minimally respectable list. He later proclaimed that the public lost more than it gained. "I've never been a scientist," he'd say, "just a dumb wheat breeder."

In truth, Vogel was much more. For one thing, he had an inborn talent that others likened to mechanical genius. During a long career he invented more than a dozen machines of a type never before seen. Wielding a mean welding torch, he turned out devices that helped in tending tiny research plots. His planters, threshers and combines were portable, precise and practical for processing grain by the pound and plants by the square yard.

Naturally, the USDA disapproved of paying a plant breeder to amuse himself with a welding torch. This wasn't, after all, listed in his job description. So the creative engineer did his inventing incognito, off campus, without approval, or his superiors' knowing.

This caused problems. Warren Kronstad, recalled his professor spending the mornings in his research fields and afternoons at Bill's Welding, a machine shop on South Grand in Pullman. "People would come to the campus to see Vogel, and we [graduate students] developed a routine for coping with his absence. One would take the visitor out to look at the latest wheat, while another raced downtown to Bill's. Orville would be working amid a great shower of sparks. He'd have to shed his overalls and steel hood and climb back into his office clothes. He was usually still pretty steamed when he got back to the lab."

By Borlaug's time, wheat and barley researchers the world over relied on the devices Vogel whipped up at Bill's Welding. Though they didn't look like much, they transformed food production by simplifying and speeding cereal-crop improvement. With these portable devices, undreamed of numbers of plants and plots could be handled, and results derived with both pace and precision. Indeed, it was these backyard gadgets that allowed Borlaug to cross so many wheats and create so many lines. The Vogel-designed individual-plant thrasher and nursery thrasher were Norm's most vital tools. Those were what the El Paso customs officer objected to. The combines resembling obese lawn tractors were Vogel creations as well.

Whereas these gearwheel gadgets helped boost food production to unprecedented heights, dwarf wheat is what begot Vogel fame. As early as the summer of 1948 Burt Bayles supplied about 100 of Samuel Salmon's (now certified disease-free) Norin 10 seeds, which Vogel sowed later that year. Then when the flowers appeared in the spring of

1949 he crossed the Norin 10 plants with his own best varieties, Brevor and Baart. To his chagrin, however, the grain he reaped that April was too shriveled to charm even a chicken.

When Bayles related the saga of Vogel's seeds, the future of short wheats looked more than doubtful. And they were doubly doubtful for Mexico because they were the wrong kind of wheat. Bayles had explained the problem: "Norm," he'd said; "those Japanese lines are winter wheats. You'll have to vernalize them."

Winter wheats, we need note here, are physiological variants that are sown in fall. Though this may seem the height of folly, in a climate that is just right—not too hot, not too cold—the seedlings enjoy the residual soil warmth of fall and then snooze away the winter under a protective comforter of snowpack. Following a three-month siesta in the chiller they waken to the welcoming warmth and soft showers of spring. Then those well-refreshed juveniles thrust stems skyward, followed by flowers, and heads of grain.

Seen in worldwide perspective, winter wheats occupy only a small area because hibernation is ingrained in their makeup. Without a freeze, they merely lounge around like hopeful hockey jocks at a Minnesota lake in August. Vernalization is the process of applying artificial means to get them past this curious need to freeze.

Norm knew all this but after arrival in Sonora in November 1953 he disregarded Bayles' admonition, marched the Vogel seeds right out into the plots at the old station, and planted them *without pretreatment*.

It would prove his most shameful blunder.

That spring while Norm was away in the north a new kind of disaster descended from an entirely unexpected quarter. The government suddenly wants Borlaug out of Mexico.

The Minister of Agriculture, Gilberto Flores Muñoz, a former general in the Mexican army, was renowned for ending the careers of civil servants and contract workers with one-word dismissals sent without a scintilla of compassion let alone explanation. Now he chose to fire all his ministry's workers who'd worked with Borlaug. It was a national priority: they were traitors who were secretly working for the glory of the gringos.

Norm was appalled:

> They were good people whose sole "crime" was their association with me. One was Benjamín Ortega, who'd been among my first

ORVILLE VOGEL . . .

Fate's 25th facilitator, Orville Vogel. A maverick like Borlaug, he pioneered dwarfness in wheat. Borlaug is beholden to him for sharing his best seeds with the dwarfing gene. Vogel worked with winter wheat, a type restricted to snowy lands. Otherwise, Norm thinks Vogel would have achieved everything he did, including winning the Nobel Prize.

. . . CAREER SAVER #25

In a parallel career Vogel became a skilled welder and produced a range of machines scaled to the needs of researchers. They were a fundamental reason why the world suddenly fed 3 billion extra mouths in the latter half of the 20th Century. Borlaug relied on Vogel thrashers like the one at left. The one the U.S. border guard objected to in 1946 was like this.

Vogel also created mini-combine harvesters. Looking like obese lawn tractors, the machines were amazingly effective at separating grain from chaff in the harvest taken from plots as tiny as a single row.

LEFT: Bill Hartman, who taught Orville Vogel welding, with one of the first thrashers designed specifically for wheat and barley breeders.

BELOW: Vogel driving one of his small combines.

and most capable students. He'd risen to become director of agricultural development for much of Mexico's northern region and was among the country's most capable scientific administrators. One day at his office in Torreón he received a telegram:

Cesado [dismissed].
Flores Muñoz.

Benjamín was devastated, as were we in the OEE. He himself went to Mexico City and confronted the general—a very brave move in those days when government was a scientist's only possible employer. To his credit, the minister saw the injustice. A second telegram followed:

Reinstalar [reinstated].
Flores Muñoz.

Still and all, the situation remained worrisome. No one knew whom the excitable general would strike next. Or when. Or how. There was even a rumor that Norm himself was to be deported.

One Sunday afternoon in Sonora, Aureliano Campoy strolled over to the field at the old station. "How's everything going?" he asked.

"Jeez," Borlaug blurted, "the Minister of Agriculture wants to shut us down and I'm to be thrown out of the country!"

Those words sparked an explosion. Fire flashed from the old farmer's eyes and his arms pumped up and down. "To hell with that," he yelled. "My nephew [he was referring to a second nephew, Godofredo Chavez] is the head of the Ejidal Bank in Cajeme. He knows Flores Muñoz; he served on his staff once. I'll go see him."

Then he added a second thought: "You better go see Don Rodolfo."

By this time Rodolfo Calles was testing a field of Kentana and was developing a solid, if still suspicious, regard for the winsome wheat breeder who'd descended on his territory like a parachute. Borlaug caught him at home and spoke in emphatic terms: "If this problem isn't solved our work will be stopped. We'll get a telegram from Flores Muñoz and I'll be gone—for good."

Calles said he'd look into the matter, and next day telephoned back, confirming the worst. *All the Rockefeller personnel* were about to be deported. The order was even then sitting on the minister's desk. "We've got to stop this right away," he said. "I'm going to Mexico [City] tomorrow."

In the capital, the former governor arranged the meeting. He and Roberto Maurer and a representative of the government-supported poor

(Ejido) farmers flew to the capital, where they found General Flores to be cool, smooth, soft-spoken, even friendly. He admitted he was about to banish the Rockefeller Foundation. His decision was based on evidence his staff had submitted. If, however, there was contrary evidence he might be persuaded to change his mind.

Sending for three of his staff, the general demanded they publicly state their charges. The federal functionaries recited a list of corn, wheat, and beans varieties the OEE had claimed to be its own creations but that, so they said, had been bred by Mexicans on Mexican research stations. The list included several wheats.

Having been forewarned of this claim, Roberto Maurer passed the general a page detailing the pedigrees of these particular wheats, all of which were true-blue Borlaug creations. Both Maurer and Rodolfo Calles had signed the statement as witnesses to its accuracy.

The general scanned the plant genealogies, looked at the signatures, and handed the page to his underlings, conveying his question by raised eyebrows. The answer came in the form of embarrassed, even fearful, downcast gazes.

With an imperious wave of his hand, Flores Muñoz dismissed his aides. As he shook hands with the Sonora supplicants, he said: "They will be dealt with in a most proper fashion, señors. But you were lucky. You were just in time." He tapped the document on his desk. "Once I'd signed this, I'd have fought you to the end before changing my mind."

Thus it was that a voluntary intervention by Sonora farmers saved the future from duplicitous simpletons consumed by jealousy and the base motive of malice.

Knowing nothing of this intercession, Wellhausen and Stakman arranged their own meeting. The situation seemed so perilous for the Rockefeller Foundation's reputation that Stakman suggested the president attend. Dean Rusk, however, was otherwise engaged, so one of his vice presidents, Lindsley Kimball, and another senior officer, Kenneth Wernimont, flew down from New York to meet with the militant minister.

This meeting was rougher than its forerunner (about which, for some reason, they remained in ignorance). Flores Muñoz ranted over what he said was an effort to bind Mexico's agriculture to American interests and make it dependent on gringo goodwill. This was a reasonable concern but he next declared that the American scientists were claiming credit for Mexico's own agrarian successes.

In his rebuttal Stakman told Flores that he'd been fed untruths but then admitted: "No one is without fault. But we've given many years of work and effort and money for Mexico. We make no profit. We seek to help your people to get the very best life possible. However, there are many countries—some of them in South America—that are waiting impatiently for our science, our skills, and our help. If you don't want us to continue what we've done so far, then say it in a friendly way. We will shake hands and go."

Stakman's speech impressed General Flores, who confessed his country's food supply needed more help, not less. Acknowledging that he may have been misled, he treated them all to dinner.

Thus at the Mexican end all was happily resolved. Yet at the New York end the episode catalyzed endless unhappiness. Propelled by the charges from so high in the host government, frissons of alarm ran up and down the old Rockefeller building at 49 W. 49th Street.

In the end, the command decided to revamp its basic operating premise. Lying at the heart of the concern was Borlaug's bad behavior. The incorrigible employee had overstepped the boundary of science one time too many. From now on foundation programs would never proceed past the point of pure experimentation. Any steps to put research results into practice *must* be left to local authorities.

It was a policy that would in time become popular among scientific organizations trying to boost food production in developing countries. And it would do much to make them failures.

■ LESSON SIX: Circumvent Entrenched Interests

This whole incident produced his last basic principle for building an embracing and enduring food supply: *Recruit farmers and young scientists to the cause. Then leave it to them to battle apathy, anger and umbrage among their own officials. Aroused rural awareness is a force more powerful than foreign scientists or even local functionaries.*

When Norm returned to Sonora in January, he found that the seedlings from Vogel's seeds were certainly small compared to all the others in his vast panoply. However, they're still seedlings. Since December they've merely lounged around like lazy hockey jocks awaiting the advent of winter. Of course, by northern standards cold seldom calls in on the Yaqui Valley (which is at the same latitude as Central Florida). By the time the prissy plants had given up on climate change and begun exposing stems and flowers, the regular-sized wheats were long past flowering. Norm was stuck. He had no source of pollen. The newcomers couldn't be fertilized. He'd squandered Vogel's priceless gift.

Then by scouring his vast fields he discovered three late-blooming side-shoots (tillers) on a solitary plant whose biological clock had run amok. This calendar-challenged freak (Yaktana 54) had come from Joe Rupert, who was now at the new OEE operation in Colombia. Precious PhD in his pocket, Joe was introducing Borlaug wheats to South America, and repaid his friend by sending interesting local seeds back.

Joe's donation proved a godsend. Norm used the three freaky flowers to satisfy Vogel's dwarfs.

By this time, though, the effort seemed hardly worthwhile. Vogel's plants were certainly small but they were supremely susceptible to stem rust, leaf rust, and stripe rust. Indeed, most were pocked with so many red outbreaks they appeared to have contracted whole-body acne. Eventually, all succumbed without producing a single viable seed.

Wheat's last chance for heavy-lift capability was gone. There was nowhere to turn. Having reached the end of that string, he gave up hope of ever visiting the sunny uplands he knew lay just over the horizon. The quest for smallness was abandoned. The world's preeminent food crop would have to go on producing less than it told him it could.

That same year, Norm and Ed Wellhausen chatted several times about the difficulties of working at the decaying dump at El Yaqui. The wheat program could no longer operate way out in the wilderness, using borrowed land and neighbors' machinery. Wellhausen agreed. During a visit to New York, he approached George Harrar and asked that the foundation put up the money for a new experiment station in Sonora.

Harrar turned the request down with such asperity the researchers felt mortified for even raising such an outrageous possibility.

As the summer of 1954 advanced past its midpoint the messages dropping down from Canada and the upper Midwest turned evermore menacing. Up there, rust remained radioactive. That fall, for the second year running, Race 15B took out three-quarters of the pasta wheats and a third of the bread wheats. Canada and United States together ceded 200 million bushels to the gluttonous microbe that now possessed the master key to a continent-wide crop, and was intent on consuming the lot.

For the second time in American history there loomed the possibility

FIRST DWARF

The original plants from the cross between Japanese dwarfs and Yaktana. The former bird boy is holding the standard sized wheat to show the difference in size. This was a revolutionary change for a crop that had been that high throughout its 10,000 year history as a food plant. But these plants were riddled with rust and imperfections that made them worthless. This was a publicity shot of a historic achievement. Too bad these first ever spring wheat dwarfs were riddled with stem rust.

TECHNICAL PROGRESS, 1954

By the close of Round 19 in November '54, following ten seasons in Central Mexico and nine in Sonora, he's 4.5 years ahead of schedule.

On the upside 1954 has brought advances:

- Wheat production leaped like helium, rising another 100,000 tons to reach 600,000—a 50 percent increase over the level before his varieties gained traction.
- Farmers by the thousands are seeing results they'd never imagined possible. More and more are making the ultimate leap of fate and faith. Wheat acreage has thus begun increasing.
- American and Canadian wheat breeders have been to Sonora to harvest and assess their own plants—the first tentative step in international cooperation against stem-rust 15B.

On the downside this year:

- He's nearly been deported;
- The bosses in New York want him to do nothing more than experimental research; and
- The dwarf winter wheats have failed in Mexico. There's now absolutely no way to downsize spring wheats so they can carry the grain load their genes can deliver.

Borlaug's finds his sixth basic principle: *Forget functionaries, foster farmers.*

As 1954 comes to a close, he's glad to move on past the year when his career came close to destruction by misdirected friendly fire.

In the 10 years since his arrival, the number of mouths in Mexico has risen by 7.6 million, or 34.5 percent, to reach 29.6 million.

of government-mandated wheatless days. Indeed, there seemed no way to avoid it. Soon the silos and general stores would be running out of flour and everyone would have to forego bread, cookies, crackers, cakes, pastries, pancakes, doughnuts, breakfast cereals, rolls, bagels and maybe very much more. Just like in 1916.

In 1954 Little League was barely over a decade old. It was purely American; the very thought of introducing it elsewhere seemed downright unpatriotic. Nevertheless, the sport's headquarters jumped at the chance to go international. From Williamsport, Pennsylvania came not just the requisite authorization but also advice on establishing a league, arranging venues and maintaining a roster of matches.

That was all the incentive Norm and Niederhauser needed. By year's end they'd brought into being the enterprise they grandly dubbed Aztec Little League. It had all of four teams.

This venture was so miniscule that valiant organizational efforts were unneeded. Even finding players, umpires and volunteer helpers proved easy. Baseball being barely known to Mexican youth, most recruits came from American families. Games were played on the American School's well-worn diamond during a season stretching from March through June. Borlaug and Niederhauser each coached a team and got two friends to do likewise. Norm's squad was named the Aguilas (Eagles). Billy played catcher and pitcher.

Although both parents were happy with this sideline, they kept their involvement secret from their colleagues. For one thing, boys' baseball seemed unlikely to have any future in a land of such deprivation. For another, they feared the formidable George Harrar would conclude they were goofing off. Oh yes, there was a third reason: The standard of play was too embarrassing to reveal—the scores being astronomical, the fielding inept.

As a spectacle, therefore, the season ended somewhat less than stellar. It seemed clear that Little League had no future in a nation where local youths were too poor to indulge in idle play.

12

1955

Defying Doom

Although this year brings up Round 20 in the battle with Black Stem Rust, Borlaug is as anxious and as demonic as ever. The fields and plots at the old Yaqui Valley Experiment Station now constitute a continuum of plantings for multiplications, tests and trials, selections, segregations, cross-pollinations, and observations. In addition, he's laid out a new series of demonstration plots for the field day still five months away.

With all that going on you'd scarcely credit there was time left for externals. Yet he keeps his promise to help the northern growers whose fields are snowbound. Soon he and the work crews are preparing the plots and sowing the seeds mailed in from Canada and the U.S. Then they carefully label thousands of rows for colleagues thousands of miles distant who know nothing about him, his operation or his workplace, all of which are well off the wheat map.

This second round of the International Stem Rust Nursery continued a unique era of selfless cooperation between industry, universities and three countries. His contribution, done without charge or publicity, was a mere courtesy—a bagatelle that went unmentioned in his job description, resume, research papers, internal reports or palmistry plans submitted to the big brass in Gotham City.

During the Christmas break, Borlaug and John Niederhauser approached the local offices of four U.S. corporations, asking each to sponsor a separate Aztec Little League team. With so flawed a first season they faced a hard sell. But as pitchmen this pair was perfect. The big-hearted, affable, unhurried, ever-cheerful Niederhauser projected the friendly funnyman. Borlaug acted the straightman; solid,

CAREER SAVER #26 . . .

. . . FACES HIS DEMONS

Fate's 26th facilitator, Rodolfo Calles. Formerly Sonora's governor, he'd built the Yaqui Experiment station thirteen years before Borlaug arrived. The photo shows him on his first visit in over a decade. Before this he'd not been able to face the ruination of the research facility that had been his brainchild, which his successor in the state house had refused to fund on the basis that it could never lift the state's agriculture.

Rodolfo had declared these experimental fields and facilities would drive his state's prosperity up and out of dust and destitution. Until this day in April 1955 he doubted Borlaug's work and remained reserved. His stiffness, however, was merely skin deep. Behind that firm façade resided a warm heart, a dry humor and a romantic idea of a prosperous, plentiful and peaceful Sonora.

After this visit, he'll become Borlaug's biggest supporter in the Yaqui Valley. More than once he'll save Borlaug's bacon and keep the wheat program alive. In time, too, he'll help disseminate Borlaug seed to the world.

In his turn, Borlaug will prove Rodolfo Calles's early expectations correct. Research done on the old station *will* lift Sonora's prosperity to the sky.

Norm is of course on the right; the figure on the left remains unidentified.

stable, but fundamentally likeable behind his seriousness.

This one-two punch pushed aside reluctance—perhaps even reason. Generous support was offered notably by Sears Roebuck, Colgate-Palmolive and Proctor & Gamble. The funds would arrive before the playing season opened in the spring of '55.

Shortly after his return to Sonora came February's frenzied cross-pollination period. Then he remained in the north, shepherding the plantings through to their April conclusion.

In the fields this was a year of incremental improvements with no discernable biological breakthroughs. The year's breakthrough actually came from a different direction. And it came as if heaven sent.

In the middle of April Rodolfo Calles finally faced up to his fears and asked to visit the old station. Norm was of course delighted, and with the plants then nearing maturity he suggested an immediate visit. The scion of the ex-presidente therefore got a personal tour of the whole operation, including scenic stops at the rust-resistant types, the improved-bread types, the "new bulls" observation plots and the various demonstration plots.

All this mesmerized the former governor who'd poured his youthful dreams into establishing this weathered old research palace. His hijacked hopes returned like prodigal sons after 20 years in the wilderness. "Now I'm convinced that this is serious business," he said as they ended the tour on an almost transcendental high. "How can we rehabilitate this place? What can we do to make it better for you?"

TECHNICAL CHALLENGES, 1955

Rounds 20 & 21. His tenth season in Sonora and eleventh in Central Mexico. That March, he turns 41.

STEM-RUST RESISTANCE. 1955 will see the 20th and 21st rounds with stem rust. He'll have to twice undertake the normal collections for observation, cross-pollinations, segregations, selections to establish and carry out.

DEMONSTRATION DAY #8. These are getting so big that he runs separate groups of farmers through the fields, where they are met by students using amplifiers to reach the crowds.

BETTER BREAD, Rounds 5 & 6. His attempt to build better bread continues.

INTERNATIONAL STEM-RUST NURSERY. This will be the second.

The notion of revamping the derelict station took Norm aback. Unconcerned by personal needs, he had no ready answer. He did, however, later mention it to Wellhausen.

First thing next morning Ed telephoned Calles. "Don Rodolfo," he said, "there's not much point in rehabilitating the old station. Dr. Borlaug cannot work effectively out there. There's not enough land. Also it's hard to keep staff, seeing there's no clean water for drinking, no schools for children, no market for groceries, and the access road is terrible. Don Rodolfo, it would be better to move the whole operation to a more convenient location and start again."

"If Dr. Borlaug wants a new station," Calles replied, "just tell us how much land he needs and where he wants it."

Wellhausen explained that 100 hectares (about 250 acres) was required. It should be on a paved road, and close to town . . . hopefully, within ten kilometers.

"We'll get that for you," the ex-governor declared. "You'll have it in ten days!"

Rodolfo Calles began working the phone and quickly located a farm that met the needs and could be bought. Next he did the rounds of local farm-machinery dealers, grain merchants, bankers, farmer cooperatives and the rest. By almost depleting a lifetime accumulation of local goodwill, he cobbled together enough promises to not only purchase the place but to also provide a modern research facility. Then, going way beyond any call of duty, he obtained official recognition for the proposed new entity. The state legislature in Hermosillo even went so far as to pledge pesos from Sonora's notoriously tight coffers.

Thus it was that grateful constituents came together to provide the gringo the work site his bosses had so dismissively denied. Together, they bought 250 acres of flat, irrigated, fertile land on the east side of the main south road and made it available for wheat research. It was 10 kilometers (6 miles) from town. And the commitment was signed in 10 days.

Then, on Rodolfo Calles' urging, a farmer-support group, the *patronato*, was established to collect cash from crop sales and contribute it to the new center. Later the *patronato* also purchased the property beyond the back fence, adding 600 acres for future expansion.

Thus it happened that in one giant leap the program advanced beyond that of a one-man band making lonely music in a decrepit old facility lost in the wilderness.

That April, several American scientists as well as a few Canadians once more wended their way to the sands of Sonora. Their impressions of the old experiment station have gone unrecorded but surely weren't complimentary. Although now spruced up, the facilities still projected a depressing aura.

During a rugged week immured in the dun-colored void the locals called Valle del Yaqui each harvested his own breeding lines and saved the seeds from the best. Then all rushed for the airport to haul their precious progeny home in time for spring sowing in locales from Arizona to Arkansas to Alberta.

Some also carried home seed samples of Borlaug's leading lines, including Kentana. This is the first way in which Borlaug's gene gems entered the bread and wheaten products Americans eat to this day.

Beyond speeding the development of American and Canadian wheats to resist rust race 15B, this cooperation first exposed Borlaug's work to professional scrutiny. Before then, he'd been a recluse toiling in a foreign desert and unknown to his peers. Now, the shades had been parted and the visitors realized that this guy was someone to watch.

Norm explains:

> During the International Stem Rust Nursery, outsiders got to see our wheats and our shuttle breeding. It was pretty much the first time we were taken seriously.

No wonder. The Mexican plants and the shuttle breeding procedure may have been suspect, not to say seditious, yet here in Sonora they certainly seemed to be flourishing.

This was when the professionals first began questioning the textbooks' claims and wheat-breeding's basic beliefs. And in time, all would learn that Borlaug had been right all along. The smart set had blinded itself by building bricklike arguments upon the sand of falsehood. As scientists they should have known better. After all, the British polymath Bertrand Russell years ago cautioned: " . . . it's a healthy idea, now and then, to hang a question mark on the things you have long taken for granted."

May 1955 sees the start of Year 11; behind him now are 20 seasons of nonstop research. In each he's tried to block stem rust; in a few he's also tried to oust bad bread-making genes. This summer brought progress in Central Mexico too. One unexpected surprise resulted from an investigation of the Toluca dealer who'd sold Spurlock's neighbors fertilizer. The government ran a chemical analysis, and found that the man had taken a little shortcut. Locating some red volcanic cinder in the mountains, he'd crushed it and peddled off the powder as high-priced fertilizer. The stuff looked like the real thing. But as plant food it was no better than sand. Small wonder Toluca's wheats had been starving. They'd been on a sand diet!

The outcome gives Norm no pleasure; he still feels responsible:

> Dozens of Toluca farmers followed my advice and bought fertilizer. Some put themselves deep in debt. A few came close to ruin. And I hadn't been vigilant.

That Summer stem rust launched a new and unique fungal phantom. It was a stealth assault. Among the wheats then ripening across northern Mexico the fungus silently detonated its second dirty bomb. Thankfully, it made the strategic mistake of bombing Borlaug's place of work.

He was of course focusing everything on the fight against 15B when the horrifying truth hit: The diseased stems brought in from a farm in Toluca had been caused by some strain no wheat developer had ever faced. Those stems, it would turn out, carried Rust Race 139.

Known for 20 years in United States and northern Mexico, this rare strain—the 139th to uniquely disfigure the standard-wheat blocks in Stakman's greenhouses—had never been of concern. Its occurrences were small, sporadic, strictly localized. Besides, it lacked the power to penetrate Yaqui, so out of all the 300 different rust forms it was among the blessed few Norm need not care about.

However, on that particular farm in 1955 Norm, with sinking heart, noticed that the red dabs were disfiguring Kentana. That put a very different face on things: Obviously, Race 139 could unlock the Kenya-type resistance. And, given Kentana's soaring popularity, there was nothing to stop the fungus going forth to multiply across Mexico's burgeoning million-acre wheatlands.

This realization raised an excruciating personal issue: He'd gotten Mexico's wheat growers to abandon their traditional types and switch to his Foundation Foursome [Frontera, Supremo, and the Kenyas]. Then he'd gotten them to switch to his Follow-Up Foursome [Kentana, Yaqui, Nazas, Chapingo]. Finally he'd gotten them abandon the last three and switch solely to Kentana. And now Kentana was toast.

The thought was terrible: He'd led thousands of farmers down a daisy chain to disaster. He'd exposed the country's wheat industry to ultimate ruin. He'd not been vigilant. And Mexico's food supply was stuck in a microbial pincer.

Beyond contrition, this presented a quandary: What the hell to do?

Indeed, could anything be done? The brightest flowers in his garden had proved so inadequate that Mexico's future course could parallel that of Europe in the 1840s when another fungus knocked out every potato type, producing a famine that took two million lives in Ireland, not to mention millions more in continental countries all the way to Russia. Indeed, on their single-acre beside Sogne Fiord, Ole Borlaug and his young wife Solveig had lived on potatoes. After the blight struck, they'd migrated to America to escape starvation.

Now, a century onward, Ole and Solveig's great-grandson could see in awful detail a latter-day reprise materializing before his professional gaze. And, in a sense, it was his personal doing. Vulnerabilities deep within his own varieties had created this catastrophe. By attacking the flank from separate directions, stem rust could now wipe out this hungry land's whole wheat crop.

At that point he faced the following perplexity:

- Kentana's Kenya-type defense resists Race 15B but remains susceptible to Race 139;
- Yaqui's combination of Hope- and Newthatch defenses resists Race 139 but remains susceptible to Race 15B.

This is where the manic effort six years earlier paid off. During those trying months during the winter of 1948/49—the months when he and Enciso had worked alone as if the weight of the world was upon their backs—a few days had been devoted to crossing Yaqui with Kentana. For good measure, they'd crossed several hundred specimens both ways, with half the plants of each variety acting as the female and the other half as the male. Even though not proposed in the research plan submitted to his superiors, it had at the time seemed prudent to build in redundancy.

Though representing merely a contingency against the unthinkable that line of plants had been cycled forward season after season. Now, eleven seasons onward, the progeny had passed through segregation and had settled into stable lines combining Hope-, Newthatch- *and* Kenya-type rust resistances. Put another way, they combined the contributions of Edgar McFadden in South Dakota in the 1920s, Stakman and Hayes in Minnesota in the 1930s and Burton in Kenya in the 1940s.

Now in 1955 his prescience proves out when he released the five best to farmers in the areas infected by both Race 139 and 15B. That this Fabulous Five (Chapingo 52, Mexe 52, Chapingo 53, Bajío 53 and Bonza 55) could repel two fungal foes never known in Mexico at the time of their conception seemed almost miraculous.

Yet they were real: five new wheats stood strong and healthy beneath the deadly bipolar spore showers.

W e've already said that several years pass before a new fungal foreign body feels out its future and adopts the career of a crop killer. That delay is a blessing in disguise since plant pathologists can use the interim to find an antidote and get it into farmers' hands. In this case, the "phony war" following Race 139's debut also saw Kentana move out into the mainstream and begin making its mark on Mexican commerce and consumers. No farmer, let alone any national leader, was aware that this stellar variety drawing rave reviews was in fact headed for failure. They still thought it fabulous.

Actually, most Mexicans now considered wheat fabulous. When the data was compiled it was seen that 1954 had been a banner year: National production had risen for the third straight year, to approach 700,000 tons. The average yield had reached 1050lb per acre. And the planted acreage now surpassed the 1944 figure by 20 percent—a clear sign that the new wheat had more than nudged farmers' minds . . . it had nourished their ambitions.

Profit was the fizz fueling this excitement. Mexican farmers saw that the new high-yield seed could lift their families out of poverty. The sight was heady. As in Iowa a generation earlier, it allowed millions to pursue their self-interest and properly profit from their own labors. Once more, the sky seemed bluer and higher. Even in the backward Bajío, farmers lurched from fear of change to fear of no change.

Perhaps there's no surprise in all that; money, after all, matters most to the poor. On the shoulders of Kentana, rural Mexico—or at least the vast wheat-growing sections—promised to become prosperous.

Still and all, there was a catch: Though it was the pivot around which the wheat supply swung upwards, Kentana was predestined to perish.

Only Norm knew that.

He'd reached another make-or-break point.

Later that same year the Mexico City polytechnic awarded a BS in Biochemistry to the penniless girl from the barrio. While earning her degree Eva Villegas had of course kept on working, and within the group she was blossoming both as a personality and a professional. Having spent almost six years part time, she now moved up to fulltime. Her assignment: analyze Norm's breeding lines and determine how good each one was for making bread.

Sadly, plants cannot articulate that particular trait. Typically a pound or two of grain must be milled into flour and baked into a loaf—not for eating but for entering its height, color, texture and taste into screw-bound notebooks. To do this on thousands of lines a year was a huge task. But Borlaug insisted it be done to ensure his efforts would never fail at the last hurdle: the quirky concerns of consumers and commerce.

Beyond that Eva still oversaw the education fund. Thanks to her natural ardor, almost every bird chaser had already graduated high school. A surprising number had gone on to higher levels of learning. Several were agronomos (agricultural engineers) and a few had earned a Masters degree.

The sole exception was the first and foremost bird boy. Reyes Vega had earned a high school diploma but not even the group's conscience could coax him to go further. "We never could get him into college," Eva explains. "He had too many brothers and sisters, and needed to work fulltime to support the family."

Nonetheless, Reyes Vega mastered wheat breeding. He became, in fact, one of its great exponents. During fifteen or so years, each with two planting seasons, he turned out more crosses than maybe any individual in history—a triumph far greater than some scholarly calling-card fashioned for framing and nailing on a wall.

And transforming the process of wheat breeding was not the end of the former bird chaser's contributions. It was in 1955 that Borlaug made him the team's logistics specialist.

By this time administering the enterprise had become as important as the research itself. Among solitary scientific endeavors pedigree breeding is one of the most operationally complex, and in that era before computers, barcodes and digitized data it was a logistical nightmare. Tens of thousands of plant lines needed to be inspected, assessed, recorded, and harvested. The winners' grain samples had to be separated and thrashed, sorted, protected, stored, and prepared for replanting. Then everything had to be packed up and trucked to the next stop.

At each step the paperwork had to be complete and faultless. Keeping track of tickets, tags, labels, bags, plots, experimental reports, notebooks and pedigree records required vigilance, not to mention intelligence.

Reyes Vega accepted the challenge without hesitation. Together with the scientists, he now commuted to Toluca during the summer season and each winter he migrated to Sonora and back with intermediate stops in both directions. Acting as the organizing genius behind the scenes he kept everything in proper motion at stop after stop. And he did it well. Norm never had to worry about all the complex dovetailing of details, even though his logistics' manager had little book learning.

Cash for the boys' baseball league arrived just in time for the season's March opening. And it was very welcome because interest was soaring and Little League was verging on becoming a social phenomenon. Saturday mornings, whole clans showed up to cheer and sing and dance with delight following passages of good play. To those whom life was to be endured, not enjoyed, it gave a special lift.

Eventually, thousands would profit from the ingenuity of the two scientists who'd only wanted to straighten out their sons. As a wise person has said, "Some of the best lessons of life are learned on the baseball field: teamwork, communication, competition, respect, being responsible for yourself, and character."

Both Bill Borlaug and the Niederhauser boys benefited, though for them this was not sport as savior, as it had been for their fathers during the Great Depression. Still, they hold golden memories.

Little League of course occurred in the big city and during the early weeks of the season this fact raised an exquisite scheduling difficulty. Although the season began with March practices, Norm didn't reach the capital until late April. His last stop before home was La Piedad and, despite a round trip of almost 500 miles, he fulfilled his duties as coach. Dashing south after dark on Friday nights over bad roads and then back again on Sunday evening.

When Norm arrived in March 1955 he found professional progress in the Bajío too. In the spring of '55 the younger of the Massey Harris tractor dealers decided to grow wheat on his family's farm near Irapuato the coming summer. Pepe Huerta planned to sow 250 acres of three of Borlaug's triple-protected Fabulous Five [Chapingo 52, Chapingo 53 and Bajío 53]. His goal was to distribute the harvest and help insure his customers against the double-fungal disaster bearing down on his franchise region.

Unfortunately, though, this machinery salesman knew little about farming. The elder Huerta was downright worried. "Dr. Borlaug," he said in exasperation, "Why didn't you help young José? He needs you."

Eager to gain more real-world experience, Norm agreed: "Okay," he said, "I'll do it, gladly."

In truth, what he learned had more to do with people than plants: When the planting season arrived in May the foreman, a Japanese-Mexican, took exception to letting a stranger meddle in the Huerta farm's management, which was his personal responsibility. Whenever Borlaug requested irrigation water and tractors, it turned out the strawberry crop required them. Mr Tanaka was polite but persistent. Neither water nor tractors ever showed up.

Faced with 250 dry-as-dust acres, Norm couldn't even get the grain into the ground. Having wasted three weekends during April driving from Mexico City to Irapuato he turned desperate; May was nigh and soon there'd be too few warm days for the plants to mature before winter. He laid the situation on the line to José Jr.: "I can't help you, Pepe," he said: "Without water and equipment we'd better forget this."

"But I gave orders."

"That makes no difference; you've got to tell Mr Tanaka to his face, and in my presence."

So Pepe called in the foreman and the three spent some minutes in close counsel. In the upshot, Norm sowed his seeds just in time. During the next five months he devoted several weekends, supervising weed control, applying fertilizer, and overseeing supplemental irrigation. Typically, he spent Saturday night behind tractor headlights as he'd done the year before on Spurlock's rented land, which happened to be nearby.

Most of this frenetic activity was of course off the books, and ethicists today might censure a scientist who allows a business to benefit from his professional insights. Norm, however, was unpaid and was merely acting as an extension agent for the betterment of Mexico's food supply.

In the outcome his contribution proved pivotal because at season's end

TECHNICAL PROGRESS, 1955

By the close of Round 21 in November '55, following eleven seasons in Central Mexico and ten in Sonora, he's 5 years ahead of schedule. Without his doubled-up dedication he'd not have reach this level of advance until 1960.

All in all, 1955 has been the year of defying doom:

- Wheat production has risen yet again, to approach 700,000 tons.
- Average yield has reached 1050lb per acre.
- The planted acreage now surpasses the 1944 figure by 20 percent.
- He's produced tons of seed of the new, triply protected varieties that can withstand both the mass-killing 15B and 139 rust races.
- The tractor salesman, Pepe Huerta, has delivered the seed to customers throughout the Bajío—the region Henry Wallace despaired of back in 1940.
- After 6 rounds in the fight for better bread he's beginning to isolate stable plant lines from the segregates—the first to combine three of the Borlaug "Pillars of Strength: Speedy maturity, stem-rust resistance, and adaptability to different latitudes.

On the downside:

- Based on performance to date, the short-stem genes from Japan had no prospects in Mexico. Beyond succumbing to three major fungal diseases, they flower out of season.

As the Sonora season came to an end he was gratified although still not satisfied because of all the remaining things wheat had told him were possible.

the robustness of the plants and the hugeness of the harvest galvanized young Huerta into furious action. Loading his truck with the bags of freshly harvested Chapingo 52, Chapingo 53 and Bajío 53, he visited his customers, handing out excitement along with the seeds that could thwart Mother Nature's incoming multi-warheaded microbial missiles.

Thus it was that a scientist working off the station and a salesman who barely knew a stigma from a steering wheel freed Mexico's breadbasket from the onrushing duo of Rust Races 15B and 139.

We must mention here that another soul-restoring lift occurred around this time. Almost two years had passed since Norm abandoned hope of finding dwarf wheats. Still nothing useful had showed up. But in the summer of 1955 he had a sudden flashback, and recalled Vogel's envelope, which had languished untouched on a shelf at Chapingo. On an impulse, he checked again and found eight seeds he'd left behind in 1954 as a possible reserve. Rather nonchalantly, he added the tattered envelope to the pile to be hauled north in the fall.

It seemed like nothing at all.

13

1956
Rust on the Run

During that previous year, the research program departed the Yaqui Valley Experiment Station. The seeds, equipment and hundreds of screw-bound notebooks were trucked to the brand new operation the grateful locals had built for Borlaug.

Constructing the complex enterprise had taken a year. There'd been permits to get, legal titles to transfer, fields to lay out, and offices, warehouses, storage facilities, cold stores and lecture rooms to design and construct. But Rodolfo Calles and the farmers' organization, the *patronato*, had overcome all bureaucratic barriers and bumbling.

When Norm arrived that November it was to find a magnificent facility. Known as Centro de Investigaciones Agrícolas del Noroeste, it would become internationally famous by its acronym: CIANO [see-AH-no].

Wheat researchers now had the perfect place for progress. The same could be said for the wheat farmers, who demonstrated their approval by opening their pocketbooks. For every ton of grain sold, their *patronato* donated CIANO a dollar.

That was the best indicator that those who grew food had learned not to scoff at science, let alone its harbinger Norman Borlaug.

He'd won their confidence.

Certain others in the society, however, didn't see things that way. Federal functionaries, for instance, felt no sympathy for the Sonora self-starters who blithely bypassed bureaucrats to build their own research palace. Indeed, the agriculture ministry retreated into high dudgeon over this socialist indecency. For several years it refused to countenance, let alone contribute to, CIANO. The ministry's research

TECHNICAL CHALLENGES, 1956

Rounds 22 (Sonora) & 23 (Toluca). His eleventh year in Sonora and twelfth in Central Mexico. That March, he turns 42.

This is the first year in which stem is not his primary concern. He nonetheless continues back-crossing his most promising lines, building up a cohort of possible understudies:

MULTILINE BREEDING. He also begins a new approach that aims to produce plants that are identical in performance but that have different lines of disease immunity coded into their genes.

THE FIGHT FOR BETTER BREAD. During this year he'll make myriad crosses in Rounds 11 and 12.

INTERNATIONAL STEM RUST NURSERY, Round 2. He'll oversee hundreds of plots for the colleagues above the border.

DEMONSTRATION DAY #9. Of course he'll also plant the pairs of plots that at season's end will be the main attraction for hundreds of farmer visitors.

THE FIGHT TO DOWNSIZE WHEAT. He'd of course previously scoured the USDA's World Wheat Collection for short wheats and had squandered most of Vogel's seed back in 1954 but it was here in 1956 that the campaign for dwarf plants really begins. In Sonora this winter he'll grow the eight special plants and cross-pollinate them with his own creations in the world's first attempt to create dwarf spring-wheat.

arm thus boycotted the most up-to-date agricultural facility in the land. Or any land. For a still hungry nation how silly was that?

Norm, however, took full advantage, and CIANO's initial operations included nurturing the eight tiny, wrinkled seeds of the Norin-based dwarfs forgotten these two years and more in an old torn envelope.

Thus began Round 2 of his endeavor to downsize the wheat plant. As before, it was a crapshoot. This time, however, he did things differently.

First, he followed Burt Bayles' advice, moistening the grains on a bed of cotton and consigning them to six weeks confinement in the cooler.

Then he took those refrigerated seeds, planted each in separate pots, which were placed in a corner deep inside the building designed as a plant-protection laboratory. There, surrounded by walls, ceiling and concrete floor, the seedlings would be beyond the long reach of the rust that had killed their predecessors.

Although they were quite safe deep in that dungeon, he dressed them in muslin shrouds to intercept any sneaky rust spore that might perchance float down the corridor looking for opportunity's door knocker.

As expected, the well-winterized seeds now sprout properly and proceed to surge past the seedling stage. With the coming of December he admires the eight seedlings sitting in pots under grow-lamps deep inside the building. They're maturing in synchrony with their Mexican counterparts outside the building. And they remain exceedingly small.

While Norm relaxed at home during the Christmas break the attempted total-body overhaul of the ten-thousand-year-old crop continued apace a thousand miles to the north. During his absence two colleagues—John Gibler, a visiting scientist, and Alfredo Campos, the one-time weekend warrior—watered and watched the plants in the eight pots covered in muslin and energized by beams of artificial sunlight deep within the bowels of CIANO's plant protection laboratory. They similarly scrutinized an equal number of Mexican plants that Norm had chosen for the female partners. Those were clustered together in a tiny plot right behind the same building.

Although this work seemed merely a minuscule sideline to the chores involving acres of wheat plants, it could prove pivotal. Everything rested on just how these eight specimens reacted.

Most likely they would react badly. Not only was the dwarfing character limited to just eight plants but all were the kind of wheat that couldn't succeed in Mexico. Moreover, those miniatures were so receptive to rust they had to be housed far behind concrete and plaster and grown under cloth and colored light.

Still and all, he's far from disheartened; whatever the odds, pessimism must not be entertained.

Upon arriving back in Sonora late in January he's delighted to find the plants progressing. To a casual observer, size was the only difference: the eight bathed by grow lamps inside the building were half the height of those bathed by the sun outside.

When February rolled around, the plants inside and their counterparts outside set flowers concurrently. This time, however, Norm reversed the direction of pollination, using the eight special dwarfs as the males. He was hoping that reversing the gene flow might help the Mexican "mothers" exert more rust resistance in their offspring. Strictly speaking, that was more akin to faith than fact. In this final roll of the genetic dice for dwarfness he reverted to instinct.

When the flowers were about three days from maturity the cross-pollination procedure was begun. For starters Norm, John Gibler and Alfredo Campos prepared the putative brides growing outside the building. For the honor of receiving the priceless pollen, he'd selected

THE GIFT FROM . . .

CIANO, 1956. Farmers paid for and built this facility after Borlaug's bosses rejected a request for a better place of work. It was yet another manifestation of grateful users shouldering responsibility for the research that made life better. From this point onwards the work in Sonora was performed here.

...GRATEFUL FARMERS

This place was unique in its funding, its responsiveness, its relevance, and eventually its results. Among the first research carried out here was the cross-pollination that produced the first dwarf wheats, which were made in the foremost building. Visible all round are all the blocks and plots and fields of Borlaug's many plantings.

specimens of eight of Mexico's finest—including Kentana, Yaqui, Lerma Rojo, and Chapingo 52 and 53. The first task was to excise all trace of their own male organs, and after every pollen sac had been removed, the feminized heads were quickly enclosed within paper tubes, the tops sealed with paperclips.

Three days later the nuptial moment arrived: the three scientists entered the inner sanctum, removed the muslin shroud, snipped the head off one pygmy plant and carried it gently outside. Following the Reyes Vega innovation they cut off the glumes, propped the precious flower stalk in the soil for five minutes of sunning. Then, removing the paperclip on the tube of its chosen mate, they showered the newly emerged pollen over the unrequited stigmas. Then they repeated the process for the remaining seven brother wheats and their seven brides.

Next came days of waiting, filled this time with nothing more certain or satisfying than forlorn hope. Would these Borlaug-brokered marriages end up star-crossed? Or spectacular? Was this productive genetics or a practical joke; reality or unreality; farce or finesse?

The answer would remain in hiding for many years to come.

By this time hundreds of Yaqui Valley farmers had lifted their eyes to the skies and were seizing control of their own destinies. For one thing, Rodolfo Calles, Jorge Parada, Roberto Maurer, Rafael Fierros and others had established a cooperative to purchase fertilizer and other farm inputs in bulk. Its modest building housed not only warehouse space but also offices and a meeting room wherein members could thrash out technical, financial and operational problems.

Just one among several cooperatives getting underway, it included a credit union to help smooth out rocky patches in the members' finances.

The Cajeme Farmer Cooperative quickly took up the process of multiplying Borlaug's seed. It thereby replaced the amateurs Dick Spurlock and Pepe Huerta. It did it on a grander scale. It supplied its members certified Borlaug seed in good time for the planting season. And eventually, it would supply them to the world.

As the season advanced the eight plants enjoying the Sonora sunshine provided the researchers a daily delight. In March the fertilized flowers began swelling with seeds. All seemed normal, and that April the plants yielded about 1500 seeds. Though getting just one seed would have signified progress, these were merely F1s. Whether any of the 1500 would express the elusive smallness gene *as well as* rust

CAREER SAVERS #27

Fate's 27th facilitators, The Bird Boys. Without them, the world would be a different place. They allowed Borlaug to make thousands of cross-pollinations twice a year. He and they were associates rather than apprentices. He worked alongside as together they advanced the wheat plant.

resistance *and* the ability to grow without first being chilled cannot be known. They'll have to go through many generations before their qualities will shine through and he'll learn if he's got dross or diamonds.

Ever the enthusiastic coach, Norm spent happy hours with these young players. Back row: Borlaug and Niederhauser. Second row David Grossbeck, Alan Spielberger, Bill Borlaug, Jimmy Lorreta, Luis Nino, Tommy Chavez. Third row Jimmy Schneider, bat boys Steve Niederhauser, Rick Spielberger. Front row Dick Sneider, Mike Glawe, Bob Gerdes, Jimmy Niederhauser, Greg Stringer, Raul Castro.

That April Borlaug's work attracted its first international recognition when the Second American Stem Rust Conference was moved to Sonora, over a thousand miles from Minnesota, Manitoba and the other areas 15B was mauling.

Nothing about this change of venue seemed to make sense. The participants surely resented traveling to so remote and so irrelevant a location to discuss a local issue. But the place they found in the middle of the Mexican wilderness proved so surprising they could barely believe their eyes. In this ultra-modern facility with the alien name none had ever heard of wheat research and farm practice operated on a continuum, with results moving outward to farmers and practical needs feeding seamlessly back to researchers. At CIANO trust was the operating ethos. This was no science center . . . it was a service center. And its directors were the district's dirt farmers.

Late that April Norm moved south for the summertime plantings in Toluca. On the southward journey he spent two weeks at La Piedad harvesting the experiments sown when he'd been going north five months earlier.

During several weeks this insanely hard worker drove home on Friday nights—not to sneak in a restful weekend but to coach his baseball team. In this, the start of his third Little League season, he'd toil in the fields until dark, then hazard the 250 miles of dim and dangerous roads, arriving at the apartment at two in the morning, snatching a wink, and getting himself to the ballpark at nine in time for the game.

To him, it was well worthwhile. In just its third year, the Aztec League had increased to 14 teams. Over half the players were Mexican. And, not coincidentally, the quality of play was soaring. Indeed, it was reaching a point where observers wondered if it might not be international class.

Most of the Aguilas now came from a spirit-crushing slum near the American School. For that he made no allowances, treating each as if he were a born champion. "There's no damn messing around here," he yelled in Spanish. "Give the best God gave you, or don't bother competing!"

Even these days he sometimes wonders whether it was wrong to subject unlettered young destitutes to the same physical and psychological treatment Bartelma employed. But the disadvantaged boys responded. A surprising number developed into fine athletes. On the baseball diamond they'd gotten their first taste of talent, and it was terrific. That season, the Aguilas went *18 games without lo*ss.

May 1956 sees the start of Year 12; Norm's now put in 22 seasons of research without rest. During this summer, however, a new kind of ruckus arose. His plants are toppling like tired drunks. Lodging is becoming a national disgrace. His varieties' weak stems were killing production and profits. Actually, the plant's failings were only partly to blame; excessive fertilization was equally at fault. Farmers had fallen for the common fantasy that if a little is good, a lot must be better.

He issued instructions to *NEVER* apply more than 80 pounds of nitrogen an acre. That amount stopped the crop from crumpling but kept it from attaining its true potential. Although a grain yield of 3500lbs an acre was over four times the previous national average, he found it immensely galling to cap a hungry country's food production.

The real answer lay in strengthening the stems, and this summer his mind became transfixed by the plants arising from the special seeds whose parents hailed from separate Pacific shores.

This is why he exhibited an unusual tension as the seedlings of the F2 generation emerged from the warm soil of Toluca in the spring of '56. This was when a dwarfing gene might make its first appearance. As the season progressed, he scanned the fields like one obsessed.

At first, nothing strange could be seen. But as the days passed some of the plants looked distinctly odd. Those in the surrounding fields were surging toward the sky. These few among his special brood materialized much more slowly. They were roughly half height.

As the summer progressed most of the 1500 plants peopling that cherished plot got hit by rust. Those were ruthlessly ripped out, as were every taller specimen as well as every poorly performing petite.

That left about 50 true *half-pints*, which in July he cross-pollinated among themselves, sharing the pollen so as to lay down a broad base of low-rise genetic diversity.

That was the first step down a road leading, or so he hoped, to revolutionary spring wheats that would rise no higher than his waist. How far the journey would take him he didn't know—most likely this road would lead nowhere. They were riddled with defects.

Despite the depressing sight of these few sorry survivors, he decided to bet his career they'd carrying wheat to the next horizon.

TECHNICAL PROGRESS, 1956

By the close of Round 23 in November '56, following twelve seasons in Central Mexico and eleven in Sonora, he's 5.5 years ahead of schedule.

On the upside 1953 has brought advances:

- The battle between Borlaug and black stem rust is finally over. Borlaug-built plants have the exquisitely rare, mysterious, almost mystical, ability to deny *every spore* access to its innermost tissues.
- His fast maturing, rust resisting, standard-sized plants—primarily Kentana and Yaqui—have increased Mexico's national average wheat yield to 1370lb per acre, an 83 percent jump.
- His own fields produce up to 3500lb per acre.
- Overall wheat production has doubled. For the first time, Mexico produces all it needs. Also for the first time, it's begun handling grain in bulk.

On the downside this year:

- He knows that the real revolution is still ahead. Pint-sized versions can lift the yield several fold. Unfortunately, his are riddled with rust.

This success rode in on the backs of his second-generation varieties.

The Cornucopia Combo now has four legs. His plants mature fast, grow in any wheatland, resist fungal disease, and yield exceptional amounts of food.

In the 12 years since his arrival, the number of mouths in Mexico has risen by 8.5 million, or 38.6 percent, to reach 31.5 million.

By year's end the battle between Borlaug and black stem rust was finally over. Combining Hope- and Kenya resistances has got rust on the run. From October 1956 onward he works on rust resistance only for insurance, not for necessity.

From here on, healthiness becomes the third pillar of power behind Borlaug wheats. The Cornucopia Combo previously included fast maturity, which had virtually fallen into his lap when he picked up a Marroqui seedhead during the maverick trip to Sonora, and the adaptability generated as a byproduct of his shuttle breeding between Sonora and Toluca. The third pillar of power has taken 11 long and action-packed years, totaling 22 seasons of nonstop toil. But from 1956 onwards stem-rust resistance is a basic support behind every seed he supplies. All Borlaug varieties now grow fast, grow well across the world's various wheatlands, and resist the crop's vilest enemy.

The 1956 national harvest proved sufficient to provide all the flour Mexico needed to fulfill its burgeoning hunger for bread, flour tortillas, bolillos, cookies or crackers. Grain merchants now troop to places like Torreón and Toluca rather than to Texas. And farmers are paid promptly, properly and respectfully.

This success rode in on the backs of the Fabulous Five (Chapingo 52, Mexe 52, Chapingo 53, Bajío 53 and Bonza 55). These fast maturing, disease resistant, standard-sized plants lifted Mexico's wheat yields 83 percent to an average of 1370lbs an acre.

High yield becomes the fourth pillar of power behind Borlaug wheats. The Cornucopia Combo now has four legs: fast maturity, extreme tolerance of climate and conditions, disease resistance, and high yield.

Until 1956 all of Mexico's wheat had been handled in sacks—by hand. This year brings a historic change: the construction of modern elevators and the use of loose grain. Large combine harvesters are appearing. Trucks piled high with grain are seen commonly on the highways. And the railroads provide freight cars designed for handling grain in bulk. A massive new industry is underway.

Success nonetheless caught Borlaug in yet another surrealistic situation. Despite the general exhilaration and ever-rising confidence, he knew the plants were too tall. They fall down when fertilized. Farmers must restrict the plant's diet for it to stay straight. If he could just shrink the plant it would so much better.

Eva had become the rock behind the advances in bread-making qualities. However, genetically combining the best bread-making plants with the best rust-resisting types was a huge challenge. Borlaug has so many lines of ongoing research and he wants them all tested so he doesn't waste time producing grains no one wants. Clearly, she needed better facilities.

Ed Wellhausen approached George Harrar with a request that the Rockefeller Foundation provide special funds for a laboratory to evaluate bread quality. Now that Mexican bakers were using flour from locally grown wheat, Ed explained, OEE needed a laboratory to find the right strains to carry forward from the myriad lines Borlaug was trying to perfect. The savings in time and money would be immense. And they'd avoid any possibility of consumers rejecting the result of years of effort.

This request was approved, though not the part for an actual laboratory. The noncoms occupying ornate thrones in the ice palace were willing to support three salaries and the purchase of small mixers and baking ovens. For the hunger fighters in the frontlines there'd be no dedicated laboratory to determine protein levels, protein types and bread quality. They'd just have to make do.

14

1957

Bread & Circuses

A s the new year of 1957 got underway, Mexico's wheat farmers went wild for fertilizer. Soon thousands of acres of Borlaug-creations were groaning under more grain than their slender stems could bear. Whenever the late-season breezes blew their best, which they aspired to do most afternoons, whole fields bent over and gracefully bowed to the ground.

No matter what means of persuasion Borlaug tried, farmers in ever-increasing numbers willfully and wantonly broadcast more than 80 pounds of fertilizer. Thus, although their acreage started out a delight for the soul, it ended up doing nothing for the stomach.

Given that these human propensities were unstoppable, he faced even greater pressures as he launched the third round of his contest with the genes that could contribute heavy-lift capability.

Those cranky DNA segments were proving wily adversaries. Although he's got them corralled, and their short, stout stalks hold up heavy heads, none can feed the masses because:

- The male flowers are mostly sterile;
- The leaves and stems are susceptible to several rust diseases;
- The seedheads refuse to hold the grain—a trait, called "seed shattering" that sees the harvest scattered over the ground; and
- The grain has a soft texture and weak gluten, and makes bad bread.

That winter he tackled the first stage in the colossal effort that will absorb most of the next decade: piling together genes for short plants and for tall bread while still retaining all the powers for fast maturity, climatic adaptability and immunity to the prevalent races of stem rust and leaf rust.

237

TECHNICAL CHALLENGES, 1957

Rounds 24 & 25 (Toluca). His twelfth season in Sonora and thirteenth in Central Mexico. That March, he turns 43.

This year he'll undertake:

THE FIGHT FOR BETTER BREAD, Rounds 9 & 10.

THE FIGHT TO DOWNSIZE WHEAT, Rounds 3 & 4. He needs to outflank the flaws that still control the dwarf's chromosomes.

THE INTERNATIONAL STEM RUST NURSERY #4.

DEMONSTRATION DAY #10 the demonstration-day plots,

You might call his efforts "affirmative action" for disadvantaged wheat genes. But most of all he's hoping some will show their gratitude by turning into cereal stars.

In a career defined by the conquest of challenge, this was the ultimate proving ground. His target: a plant in which *all* of the rare and deeply recessive traits (for speedy maturity, adaptability, healthiness, high yield, smallness, and more) are prominent, dominant and functioning fully. This grand "meta-mission" would ennoble an array of shy genes that— even in the classless world of wheat—had never had a chance to shine individually, let alone collectively.

For getting multiple layers of recessive genes to settle simultaneously into the upper cellular sanctum his only tool was the flower's male element. By launching pollen grains like genetic grenades he could, in principle, jolt good genes into prominence. However, pollen (like most males) also carries a few bad genes. Purging this bad seed from his crossbred beauties would occupy most of his time from here on.

Compounding his burden was the fact that the desirable genes were reluctant to reveal themselves. Whenever they met their counterparts in the push-me-pull-you power plays along the chromosome they hastily withdrew into the dark shadows of the gene underworld. Getting a whole array of these ever-so-timid DNA segments to accept celebrity in the face of heredital harassment seemed impossible.

For the huge and risky effort to compel bold "bad" genes to submit to their bashful brethren a new ground force was recruited. Youthful as ever, its oldest members were in their mid-twenties.

One was Ignacio Narvaez, who's become Norm's chief assistant. He's recently returned from Purdue University in Indiana, bearing in his suitcase that most sacred of modern good-luck charms, a PhD.

Two more were Teodoro Enciso and Alfredo Campos, the former

weekend-warriors who've now toiled by Norm's side amidst heat and flies and dirt and diseased plants *for a full decade.*

Contributing further heft was a new platoon of young plant pathologists, including Gregorio Vasquez, Alfredo García, Jacobo Ortega and Aristo Acosta, all of whom came from George Harrar's commitment to "train Mexican students on the agricultural sciences." Each had weathered a withering apprenticeship in Borlaug's fields. They knew their stuff, knew what they were in for, and welcomed it.

Supporting these toilers of the sea of genes were "enlisteds" who accompanied the research squadron on its endlessly repeated annual expeditions up and down the country. This support staff was now led by Reyes Vega, who at the ripe old age of 20 still indulged in wheat breeding but now acted mainly as "Master Technician." The title was made up but went down well because good management was as vital as good science, and he had proved the best manager. Norm explains:

> Reyes Vega deserved the honor. We turned the logistical support over to him. He organized all the field operations and kept track of the details. Along with several other field boys who later also became Master Technicians, he played a helluva role. They relieved us of mountains of work. And they did it better than we ever could. Without them, we scientists wouldn't have gotten very far.

Mexican Civil Service paychecks were predicated on the laurels of academe, rather than anything so lowbrow as competence. So, exerting his maverick streak, Borlaug elevated the technicians to pay levels comparable to an Ingeniero Agronomo (agricultural engineer). He treated bird-chaser graduates, in other words, like college graduates.

By this time, the little gadflies, once cocooned in lowly lives, had coalesced into the world's most accomplished wheat-breeding assemblage. Their liquid-motion fingers now manipulate pollen, plants and people on a grand scale.

The boys' metamorphosis touched him deeply:

> Those guys were truly impressive. I'd always been an advocate of youth. "Give the young fellows a chance" was a comment I repeated to colleagues and counterparts. But in this case words were not up to the task. In their own research all the professionals I knew refused to elevate rank amateurs to positions that traditionally demanded degrees of higher learning.

His bond with the bird boys thus remained unique. All members of this ragtag research team were friends, and that togetherness transcended

THE BOY . . .

The boys, most of whom came from impoverished backgrounds, rose to become t
best group of wheat-breeding technicians perhaps ever known. Borlaug opened t
chance to challenge themselves at a technical pursuit, and they seized it.

. . . WHEAT BREEDERS

Borlaug never lost the ability to move young minds. Indeed, molding groups of youngsters into formidable professional teams lay at the heart of his efforts. He imbued youngsters with a sense of purpose and got them producing a product not a paper.

the group "worked as only zealots can work," which was true enough but this campaign to give wheat's double helix an extra twist was complex almost beyond belief. Every talent was called up for duty in this career gamble that he could rearrange the genetic instructions for assembling and running the greatest crop on earth.

Mankind's existence is contingent on the consent of plant genes, and although such consent is never given easily, in this case it was withheld with the tenacity of desperation. The progeny of the tall Mexican spring wheats and small Japanese winter wheats popped up such a profusion of grouchy genes there seemed no possibility of ever furnishing food this way. His sole option was to submit to the entropy of heredity and trust that in time something worthwhile would emerge from the eternal disorder.

Despite the wall-to-wall DNA defiance, he remained committed to cutting the crop down to size. There was nothing else on his agenda these days . . . not even progress:

> We always seemed to face barriers beyond barriers. To get where we needed to go there were no guideposts. It was way off the known map. Somehow we had to find the passes and passages through the obstacles. And it seemed there were none.

That winter of 1956/57 he surveyed the thousands of diminutive plants, selected the gems, and crossed them among themselves in combinations by the hundreds. Then, with that season's program completed without practical result, the group gathered up the seed from their most promising candidates and, like transient stagehands, moved on for a repeat performance in another season, another show.

Throughout all these endeavors Norm was peering into the genomic depths hoping to glimpse a faint gleam. Where others saw a sea of green promise, he saw a sea of insignificance concealing an odd sparkle that just might reflect a pearl worth polishing.

Lacking computers, he navigated these murky seas with only eyes, memory and screw-bound notebooks. And the pursuit remained so ephemeral that things could careen off track in almost infinite ways. Maintaining focus was vital. Norm recalls his words to his young colleagues:

> There are millions of wheat plants here. Each head will produce a couple of dozen grains—and not one in half a million will be suitable for what we need. Even it will not be perfect but that shouldn't

bother us. Perfection is a butterfly academics chase and never catch. If we go on looking for the ideal, Mexico will go on being hungry. We must find the best we can, and make the most of it.

Although the youths imbibed such maxims along with his methods, and although they performed like seasoned veterans, progress still proved elusive. The bad genes that needed exorcizing didn't want for inventiveness, and of these antagonists the wiliest were those rendering the pollen sterile.

Wheat, as we've seen, is incestuous—its bisexual flowers go so far as to pollinate themselves before letting any other pollen have a chance. Males in many of Borlaug's dwarf crosses, however, were incapable of satisfying all the females within their amorous embrace. When, in the natural course of events the flowers opened, the unrequited stigmas accepted whatever pollen the breeze happened to blow in.

This so-called "promiscuous outcrossing" is the wheat-breeder's curse. And no wonder: After directing the pollination between select parents the breeder relies on boring old-fashioned monogamy to keep the desired genes stable throughout all the years of subsequent crossing and backcrossing.

Since the underperforming male parts could send Borlaug's dwarf lines veering in dozens of diverse misdirections the systematic development of practical varieties seemed improbable, perhaps impossible. With pollen floating in from every neighborhood Tom, Dick and Harry these plants could never support a steady forward advance.

That genetic instability was now the primary obstacle, and he began desperately searching among them for fully fertile male parts.

Other hurdles he was at the same time facing included:

Seed shattering. With Sonora farmers now moving to mechanical harvesters, new varieties had to hold their seed during rough handling. His dwarfs, by contrast, held theirs so loosely the slightest shake sent it flying. They needed genes that specialized in gripping grain.

Susceptibility to disease. His putative dwarfs were a sickly lot. The end-of-season scenes brought back painful memories. These graceless grains seemed bent on breaking his spirit by reintroducing him to the sour-smelling ugly brown decrepitude not seen in his fields in a decade.

Genes for bad grain. The soft centers in the dwarf-line seeds meant that on drying they shriveled like peas—a mortal condition because millers can stand the sight of wrinkles no more than a socialite. Worse, in gluten strength the flour was so feeble the bread fell short of the altitude

Navajoa, Sonora, April, 1957. The Yaqui Valley now produces so much grain that for the first time in Mexican history there's a big change in scale and perspective in handling grain in bulk rather than in sacks loaded by hand.

demanded by bakers and their customers.

It was all very dispiriting. The assemblage of impediments appeared overwhelming.

May 1957 sees the start of Year 13; Norm's now put in 24 seasons of nonstop research. This time the team plants the winning F3 selections of the dwarf plants at Toluca. The results were no more uplifting than before. That fall, the panorama painted by the F4 fields appeared as abstract as ever, evidencing the sobering fact that, despite two years of unremitting toil, no advance had been achieved on the dwarf-wheat battlefield.

The momentum in Mexican wheat development had died. The dwarfs were a disaster. There was no way to navigate around the labyrinthine barriers heredity had erected against anyone shrinking spring wheat several sizes.

Also in 1957, thimbles containing U.S. and Canadian wheat seeds were migrating up and down the continent searching for the cure. Following the fall harvest, wheat breeders in Alberta, Saskatchewan, Manitoba, Minnesota, Wisconsin, North and South Dakota and Montana dispatched seed samples from their best 15B-resistant lines all the way to that distant place of mystery, Sonora. Then in November Norm and his young staff sowed the lot.

Though that may seem inconsequential, the International Stem Rust Nursery was no longer a mere sidelight. With the mail delivering as many as 10,000 thimbles, the group had to manage 10,000 rows, each separately sown and labeled as well as cared for during five long months. And on top of that, Norm's group had to multiply certain advanced lines—helping their northern colleagues, who by then couldn't see soil for snow.

Thus, even from the heart of Mexico Borlaug was contributing to the wellbeing of his own countrymen. As the time of harvest approached in April, the airport bustled with a gaggle of suits, each needing a ride to town, not to mention accommodations, transportation, supplies, fellowship, and beer. In CIANO's fields the newcomers addressed the plots containing their own seed, identified rust-resistant specimens and gathered and threshed their grain. They also harvested their own multiplication plots. Then the Rust Prevention Association trucked the botanical booty back north 2000 miles in time for planting in the northern states and Prairie Provinces.

All this exemplified international cooperation at its finest. It was based on that quintessential American phenomenon, a volunteer association of professionals conferring not for cash but for the common good. Norm contributed his time without charge or complaint.

Then, the whole uplifting undertaking became threatened by a particularly parochial issue: proprietorship.

Most plant-breeders regard their lines like a mother hen regards her chicks. Many now refused to contribute their best to the rust nurseries in Sonora. Only after each gene gem had been perfected, named and officially recorded would they expose it to possible appropriation.

Borlaug couldn't accept that attitude. Given the looming threat of crop collapse, what did it matter if progress was shared? Saving wheat was in *everyone's* interest. But his was a minority view, possessiveness being a force that emanates from deep within the primitive part of the brain that regulates emotions. The amygdala is a sucker for fear and fantasies, not facts.

Among the most overprotective were professors. Before this time, publicly supported crop breeders—Vogel, Stakman, McFadden, and the Saunders brothers, for example—saw themselves as service providers to society. Members of the new generation, though, saw themselves as representing the financial interests of their institutions, if not of themselves. It was another momentous turning point in the relations between scientists and the society supporting them.

Having suffered through agonizing hours of wrangling at a Rust Prevention Association meeting, Norm suddenly leapt to his feet and loosed a new announcement that shook the cereal-science world:

> Look, whatever everyone else decides, we in Mexico are *not* going to wait until our varieties are properly registered. We'll contribute seed of *everything* we've got that looks promising. If someone wants to use our lines in their own breeding programs or in commercial production, God bless 'em. We ask only that our program be credited with providing the seed.

That sweeping gesture with its spirit of cooperation for the greater good melted the mental deadbolts. At bottom most knew that allowing a staple food to fail for personal pique would be judged a capital offense in the court of civilization.

During that same year the Wheat Quality Laboratory was established to test the bread-making ability of Borlaug's many candidates. Seeing that he toyed with thousands of lines a season, the staff couldn't be called exorbitant.

Eva Villegas was in charge. Her assistant was Federico Chacon, an agricultural engineer who'd converted himself into a skilled miller and baker. Support personnel were Arnoldo Amaya, a young agronomo, and Antonio Rodríguez, a one time bird boy. This last, a grade-school dropout had blossomed into a brilliant electrician and mechanic who wired up the equipment and kept it running.

Keeping everything running was hard. As funds for a proper facility had been disallowed, the operations had to be shoehorned into the already tight quarters at Sonora and Chapingo. In the latter location it was compressed into a crude wooden hut hardly bigger than a garden shed on the ag school campus. The place lacked a foundation, and its cracked floorboards admitted competitors. The staff was forever stepping over mice.

In 1957, to the surprise of all, Little League soared so fast its originators couldn't keep up. Seemingly, all Mexicans embraced youth baseball in a rush. To handle the press of boys wanting to pitch or bat or catch fly balls on a Saturday morning John Niederhauser helped set up three more Mexico City leagues—Maya, Toltec and Metropolitan. Then that OEE potato expert helped arrange a citywide championship. Other cities were already establishing their own. Even a national championship was underway.

The two plant pathologists had tapped into a deeply hidden human need—the need for athletic amusements in luckless lands where children are required to work rather than write and read and reason.

Amazingly, they'd also tapped into a talent pool. Borlaug's team topped the Aztec League, with each player lifting his game high enough to brush the stars. In 1957 the Aguilas won 10 more contests without loss. They'd coalesced into a committed, almost instinctive, group. He recalls them with an admiring chuckle:

Those little guys were mean . . . I tell you, they were tough!

In fact the whole country's pre-teen talent was getting terrific. That same year the team from the industrial city of Monterrey in northern Mexico won state, regional and national championships, and then took

TECHNICAL PROGRESS, 1957

By the close of Round 25 in November '57, following thirteen seasons in Central Mexico and twelve in Sonora, he's 6 years ahead of schedule. Without his doubled-up dedication he'd not have reach this level of advance until 1963.

As 1957 comes to a close he's focused on bread but the months have seemed more like circuses:

- In Mexico he's no longer a no-name.
- His seeds are being spread throughout the Americas.
- Wheat production has made a fantastic comeback in the Bajio region, where in just the last six years yields have doubled and tripled.

On the downside this year:

- The dwarf plants remain fractious. He's caged the chromosomal blends from dissimilar parents from dissimilar shores of the wide Pacific, but they remain undisciplined, not to say insolent. This tug-o-war between campaigner and chromosomes is one he seems to be losing.

off for Williamsport to test themselves against the best of the rest.

Norm couldn't leave his wheat fields to watch the first non-U.S. team compete in the Little League World Series. Niederhauser, however, got himself to central Pennsylvania and was on hand to witness the triumph that upended the known universe. The score in the final was Monterrey, Mexico 4; La Mesa, California 0.

Just four years after the Aztec League's founding, Mexican boys were World Champs. President Eisenhower invited them to the White House to receive his personal congratulations.

15

1958

Musical Chairs

Through the spring of 1958 the F5 generation of dwarfs emerged in Sonora's irrigated fields. Segregation was by now rampant, and the wheat team confronted an awesome mindscape of genes, chromosomes, rust pustules, stem-strength, stem height, seed shattering, pollen sterility, multiple stalks, bread quality and more.

The basic problem was that every step threw up false positives and false negatives, and there was no way to confirm a gene's presence or absence. He couldn't even create a data base to track the intricate efflorescence of diversity. Personal computers were still several decades in the future.

Amid the ever-changing outcomes in these gene swapmeets every result required keen observation, massive memory, exceptional brain processing power and not a little faith. He literally felt his way forward like a blind beggar, groping for the genome's outer extremities. For this unprecedented chromosomal renovation his only tool was pollen, and his only available strategies were backcrossing and double-crossing in hopes of piling in enough of the Mexican parents' genes to trump the problem genes from abroad.

He was also under the clock. "For him," wrote the astute observer Donald Paarlberg, "breeding better wheats was not just a matter of genes but also of time. True, he seemed cut out for work, which he apparently treated as synonymous with life. But there was something else to spur and inspire him, and, by example, others. Few people could read the temper of the times with such uncanny foresight as Borlaug did, and few could detect so unerringly the early symptoms of an emerging food-population crisis. No wonder that he should have developed what his colleagues called the 'wheat fever,' which he successfully transmitted to his Mexican associates."

That was true for the inner circle, but by and large "wheat fever" remained contained: few others realized the fundamental significance of this maniacal enterprise.

Even the world's wheat breeders were hostile. The conception of dwarfing the 10,000 year old crop was so radical it presented a professional threat. If he was right, everyone else was wrong. Not unexpectedly, they tut-tutted themselves into a twitter. "Sure," they said, "short wheats might work under irrigation in Mexico but *never* under rainfed conditions in the U.S. Why, those shrunken misfits would be so low the reel on a combine-harvester could never reach them. American farmers could not gather their grain. Yes, no doubt about it . . . this was folly. Borlaug's folly!"

In his parallel efforts for winter wheats in the Pacific Northwest, Vogel was suffering a similar estrangement. Indeed, both Borlaug and Vogel were considered heretics, and both were relegated to the very dank dungeon reserved for professional outcasts. Whenever they spoke at cereal science meetings hostility hung in the auditorium. And during question time the listeners, almost in a body, challenged the notion of tampering with the size of a plant that had been shoulder high since the dawning of domestication.

The fervor of the opposition served to bring the pariah pair together. Both Vogel and Borlaug had ventured into a wheat warp before everyone else. It was lonely out there, so it was good they had each other. It was also good that each knew what he was doing.

May 1958 sees the start of Year 14; Norm's now completed 26 seasons of nonstop research. This time he found it infinitely refreshing to return for the summer and a few months working out of home. The family had learned about the changes occurring in Mexico's wheat fields, though not from him. He didn't mention accomplishments . . . never thought much about them. With so much still awaiting attention his mind remained rooted in the future. Past and present were merely forgettable way stations.

Outside observers believed that his dedication, which appeared to border on the fanatical, had to be drifting the family apart. Luckily, though, Margaret remained infinitely forbearing of her unfair life. In two decades of half-yearly estrangements she'd learned to cope. "He's just the man who shows up here from time to time," she said. And she said it with an honest chuckle.

Margaret's tolerance rubbed off on the children, who were so inured they took their father's absence as just part of the human condition. Nonetheless, Norm did his best to bridge the generational gap. In November 1957, for example, he hauled Billy north to share the coming campaign.

Air connections to Sonora were getting almost modern, and for a ten-year-old this was a high adventure. Father and son spent several days in the fields but failed to achieve the sort of bonding found most frequently in a movie's final scene. Somewhat to the father's chagrin, the son trotted off to stay with the Maurers and play with the twins, thereby escaping the hot, sweaty fields seemingly stuffed full of millions of plants all identical.

Next Stakman arrived, and for the first time the old mentor seemed troubled. Long retired from active research, he'd shucked all trace of the hard carapace and replaced it with an almost paternal softness. His mission this time was to stop Norm from further harming his loved ones. During a walk through the fields behind CIANO he offered his considered advice: leave the Sonora part of the project or, at the very least, take a long break and go home to his wife.

But to Norm delay was unthinkable. Hunger would soon be taking a fresh peek over Mexico's shoulder. If he could just smoke the evil genies out of these chromosomes that vicious voyeur might go searching for pleasure somewhere else.

He pointed out the plots to Stakman. The wheats were certainly tiny but otherwise lacked any notable quality. Stakman looked and was skeptical. Nonetheless, Norm talked up the diminutive specimens. They'd come out all right, he declared.

Sometimes even a scientist of Olympian confidence must entertain some faith in miracles.

By now the new squad had forged a bond akin to that of troops sharing a life-or-death struggle demanding every member contribute feats of skill and endurance. Given the obstinate chromosomes' hectic resistance to genetic reorganization, the key to progress was the mystical union between scientist and staff. With their work teetering on the brink of defeat, it was a time for the ultimate effort.

Australian biographer Leonard Bickel, writing shortly after these events, summed up Ignacio Narvaez's recollection of Norm at that time: "[I]n all his years with Borlaug he'd never seen his teacher concentrate with such intensity on a single variety. He watched Borlaug's mood change as he studied the dwarfs—now angry, now delighted, now frustrated but always, always patient. Month after month Narvaez saw Borlaug shaking a problem to pieces like a terrier with a knotted rag, worrying and tossing it back and forth, never letting it go."

Most galling of all was the fact that despite all the devotion no practical variety was even on the horizon. Most observers were sure he'd lost his way. This gene pool was just a cesspool.

Despite the obvious fact that the genes had him outclassed, he never doubted eventual victory. And it would be a victory not just in shrinking the plant. The historic fusion of tall and short trans-Pacific wheats had already exposed several astonishing and unique features:

For one thing, he'd located a few plants whose spikelets carried six grains—three times the normal number and twice as many as even Yaqui. An acre of those would produce *three times as much* as anyone had ever seen.

For another, he'd reeled in some plants that sprouted six or more stalks instead of the usual one or two. Moreover, each stalk produced tightly packed clusters of seedheads.

And beyond all that he'd spotted the odd specimen that resisted the prevalent races of leaf rust.

Although these were heartening developments, they were incidental to the main thrust, which was to get a usable shrunken-stemmed plant. Nonetheless, how could he ignore the extra contributions? It was unthinkable not to incorporate those amazing yield-multipliers of production into the world's main food crop.

Thus from here on, he knew he had to do more than complete the chromosomal house-cleaning, he had to also fuse in five new qualities that had never been part the wheat's genetic spine. His horizon lifts to the stratosphere. The goal now is to build super wheats with:

- Short, stiff stalks;
- Six seeds per spikelet;
- Six stems per plant;
- Leaf rust resistance;
- Great bread quality;
- 15B- and 139 stem rust resistance;
- High yield;
- Adaptability; and
- Speedy maturity.

While raising the sights to the stars, this lowered the chance of success to the depths of despair. He hadn't even accomplished the first trait and now will attempt a complete reworking of a crop plant with *nine* qualities it has never before possessed.

It should be understood, too, that the struggle was not solely plant genetics. Field management was equally important. He quickly found that the half-height version refused to follow normal wheat-growing dictums. Thus even while he was rebuilding the species he was also striving to work out how best to handle plants that differed so greatly from any before.

It was this summer in Central Mexico that he learned the seed needed to be sown at a depth of 2 inches rather than 6 inches. Moreover, weeds had to be carefully controlled to keep them from overwhelming so small a seedling.

In addition, the seed had to be sown at the right time. And the seedlings watered just so, because the roots were short and so near the surface they were prone to desiccation.

Finally, to extract the ultimate performance fertilizer had to be supplied at exact points along the growth cycle and in amounts generous enough to power the plants all the way to their uttermost potential.

That year 1958 also brought five items that were, or at least seemed to be, ancillary to the attempt to roust the bad actors from the quirky chromosome cast:

One. In April when Don Fletcher—the Rust Prevention Association leader—arrived in Sonora to harvest his members' seeds, Norm went out of his way to accommodate this former Stakman student. One morning they were checking over the best of the small plants, which were still looking pretty sorry. Fletcher, however, expressed keen interest. "Do you mind," he asked, "if I take a head or two?"

"No problem," Borlaug replied, "you're welcome."

For North America, those 200 or so seeds—the first spring wheats expressing the dwarfing trait—were actually treasures beyond measure. On his return home, Fletcher distributed them among the various U.S. companies that bred wheat. This is another way in which Borlaug's gene gems got into the bread and wheaten products Americans eat to this day.

Though Norm seemed to have given away the store, he thought nothing of it. It was another indication that he wanted *everyone* to prosper and eat well. This time we were included.

Two. More countries were these days clamoring to participate in the International Stem Rust Nursery. For several years he'd shared seeds and discoveries with Latin American wheat breeders, and now he helped them join this continental crop-care initiative.

Thus, in 1958 the International Stem Rust Nursery expanded southwards. Eventually, the thousands of thimbles of wheat seed would be dispersed annually to each of 14 locations scattered between Canada and Argentina. It was not unlike a coordinated campaign for hemispheric health but it was a voluntary effort, operating not just without money but without publicity, not even a mention in the scientific literature.

Incidentally, the plantings showed that Mexican wheats performed up to snuff throughout Latin America's many and varied wheat-growing regions. Now even dogmatists could see that these varieties performed well across two continents without needing acculturation. It was enough to break the mental mold; from here on, the belief that wheat be bred for individual conditions was quietly shelved. It was an embarrassment.

That of course arose from Borlaug's shuttle breeding. Had he listened to his bosses and stuck with professional precedent his plants would have performed properly only in Mexico. By developing them successively in different season, altitudes, latitudes, soils and moisture conditions he'd made them capable of performing throughout the Americas, from near the Arctic Circle all the way to Argentina.

Three. That spring, boy's baseball lit up every corner of the land. The youthful energy—not to mention the skill and joy—now brightening Saturday mornings became a phenomenon. In 1958 the Monterrey Little League team returned to Williamsport, PA. This time, the World Series final ended up Monterrey, Mexico 10; Kankakee, Illinois, 1.

Norm of course had no direct connection with this team from northern Mexico but his Little League participation would extend well into the 1960s. No longer was he an organizer; just a coach. For the Aguilas he typically engaged spirited kids from the barrios, who seemed to extract a special essence out of *beisbol.* Quite a few Aguilas went on to achieve success in life. Pitcher Alan Spielberger moved to California and played in the Pony League World Series for Santa Clara. First baseman Luis Nino de Rivera attended Indiana University and in time won the national NCAA high-board diving championship and twice represented Mexico in the Olympic Games. Shortstop Raúl Castro made such an impression he became an honorary Borlaug:

> We got Raúl excited about learning English and sent him to Cresco for the summer. He stayed with my sister Charlotte, and fitted in so well at the high school and picked up English so quickly that one of the locals said: "He's the best damn ambassador Mexico ever produced!"
> Later Raúl entered college and ended up a chemical engineer with the DuPont Company in Mexico City.

Through his experiences with baseball and bird boys, Norm knew that Mexican youngsters were no different from their counterparts in Iowa. Most rose to meet the pinprick of opportunity he provided, and then moved on to do themselves proud. He's still impressed with the way their skill and confidence grew:

> It was amazing how those young guys changed their lives around. It was really refreshing. That's one of the best things I was ever involved in. The boys were among our greatest successes. They came from really poor families but they had the makings of champions. They'd just never had a chance.

Four. Finally among the extraneous activities diverting him from the tussle with dwarf genes should be mentioned the scientific powwow in Winnipeg. The success of the earlier one had sparked a series of follow ups. In August 1958, the University of Manitoba hosted what was called the First International Wheat Genetics Symposium. Norm attended rather reluctantly but while there ran into a friendly Canadian who happened to be working on the genetics of rust resistance in bread wheat.

The two hit it off. The man's knowledge along with with his warm personality made a lasting impression. At that time, Norm thought nothing more of it than that. After all, Glenn Anderson had a solid career and responsibilities in Ottawa. He was a Senior Research Officer at the Canada Department of Agriculture. However, in the next volume in our series he'll do very much more.

Five. It was in 1958 that the Rockefeller Foundation moved into swank new quarters in the just-completed Time-Life Building at 1271 Avenue of the Americas. The first building in the expansion of Rockefeller Center to the west of the Avenue of the Americas, the 48-story skyscraper had an exterior of green glass with widely spaced, tapered, vertical limestone piers. The building was connected to a vast underground concourse, and its top floor was devoted to a private dining facility known as the Hemisphere Club.

It was from here that the leaders of the world's richest philanthropic organization presided over hundreds of programs dedicated to the improvement of the human condition. From that perch near outer space they peered down on the scientist struggling in the soil of far-away Mexico, and their gaze was not kind.

T hroughout his now three-year hunt for shorter, stouter stalks his old full-size plants continued their dominance across Mexico. The Fabulous Five continued performing prodigies for growers, not to mention consumers. Despite their susceptibility to wind blasts, Mexico continued producing all it could eat, and the growers did well. By the fall of '58 the Cajeme Farmer Cooperative was selling Borlaug seed throughout the state of Sonora as well as half a dozen other states.

Though seemingly innocent enough, those sales sparked a weird brand of petty tyranny. The concern this time arose from the fact that the government had its own seed organization, within whose soul resided a serious streak of spite.

Previously, PRONASE [pro-NAH-see] had renounced wheat and refused to produce seed for farmers. Now, though, it concluded that producing wheat seed was its own prerogative. Its leadership thereby issued an order blocking the Sonora farmers from multiplying and selling Borlaug varieties. This cease-and-desist decree declared the maintenance of seed stocks a government responsibility. Clearly, the processes were so exalted as to be done only by bureaucrats.

No such power grab had been authorized, and even in this socialist society it made no sense. Eager to exhaust his political capital, Rodolfo Calles marched on the City of Mexico and buttonholed certain biddable sausages occupying high positions in the PRI, the political party that had run the country since his father founded it in 1929. Only by that means was bureaucracy's attempt to hijack Borlaug's seed snuffed out.

Not even the former-presidente's son could, however, stop PRONASE seizing the seed wheat destined for the very poor farmers who were under governmental patrimony.

Thus from then on Norm divided his basic breeder seed into two portions. One went to the farmers' coops, which multiplied it for commercial growers. And the other went to PRONASE, which multiplied it for subsistence farmers struggling against starvation on tiny gifts of government land.

TECHNICAL PROGRESS, 1958

By the close of Round 27 in November '58, following fourteen seasons in Central Mexico and thirteen in Sonora, he's 6.5 years ahead of schedule.

On the upside 1958 has brought advances:

- The crop is now being grown on a large scale in summer as well as winter. That alone doubled the output of plants that had already doubled the output. Mexican farmers could quadruple their production and income.
- Borlaug seed is selling throughout Sonora and half a dozen other states.
- His plants are proving out throughout the Americas.
- He finds new prospects for great surges in yield, including clusters of six seeds (where the normal number is two) and clusters of six stems (where the normal number is one).
- He's working on field management and learning how to handle the dwarfs.

On the downside this year:

- Two of the staff drown while trying to save the seed during a flood.
- Like skittish colts, the dwarf genes are balking at being put into the traces. Nothing is going right, and Borlaug's friends are trying to get him to quit.

For all the deadly outcomes, 1958 reminds one of the child's game of musical chairs. The stakes are getting higher and the music threatens to stop.

In the 14 years since his arrival, the number of mouths in Mexico has risen by 11.7 million. or 53.2 percent. to reach 33.7 million.

Having even a partial monopoly clamped on his creations made him unhappy but as a foreigner what could he do?

Eventually, though, these schizoid seed sales would spawn problems, and not just for Mexico.

In September 1958 Mother Nature hurled her hardest blow at the upstarts trying to thwart her by cutting her design down to a different size. Right after the research plots had been harvested at La Piedad a hurricane swept in from the Pacific Ocean submerging western Mexico under a relentless combination of swirling winds and falling sky. Among other things, rainwater tumbled from the Sierra Madre in cataracts far surpassing what the rivers could dispose of.

Water piled up and piled up until at last the plains resembled an aquarium. The Lerma—Mexico's longest river, which normally ambled quietly past the experiment station—spread sideways to form a huge lake that invaded the research facilities, drowning fields and flowing toward what seemed like the ends of the earth. At first, things only looked bad. Then the swollen surge washed around the storehouse containing the seed just acquired from the hundreds of experimental lines of dwarf wheats.

Perhaps it is well that Norm was not present; there's no telling what risks he'd have run to save those seeds. As it was, the station's head mechanic (José Flores) a soldier (José García), an agriculturist (Abel Arredondo) and his field assistant (Abel Melgosa) improvised a raft out of empty oil drums and old wooden planks. The four scrambled aboard to cross the racing wind-whipped tide.

That afternoon, the gale and the gushing current happened to be working in violent opposition; pummeling the torrent into an ugly chop. The raft proved too unwieldy and too unstable.

In the middle of the flow it capsized.

Abel Arredondo and his colleague Abel Melgosa drowned.

And the precious seeds disappeared beneath the raging whitewater to drown as well.

16
1959
The Music Stops

Though the program is set back, duplicates of the seeds had been planted at the other facilities. Also, the loss was mitigated by the sad fact that nothing Norm's doing seems to be going anywhere. The breeding plots of this, the decade's final year, will produce the dwarf wheats' F7 and F8 generations in Sonora and Toluca, respectively. But not even eight investment cycles will yield a dividend. The genes still emerge in ragged confusion, and the petit plants again prove unusable.

People today generally regard Borlaug as a crusader, and they're right. In reality, though, he was more of a craftsman. He ground out thousands of crosses a season. And never was his craftsmanship more vital than in 1959.

Despite fourteen years of doubled-up duty, Norm remains as active and energetic as the youths around him, few of whom have reached half his age. He never acts, sounds, or looks persuasive. There is in fact no sense of the scientist or even of the intellectual about him. Day after tedious day he struggles alongside the field-hands, doing the same tedious tasks, sporting the same dusty khakis, cursing the same malevolent mosquitoes, and tugging at the same kind of sweat-stained baseball cap to thwart the angry sun.

To outside observers it looked like an endgame; most assumed he was utterly beaten and merely playing for pride. They decided he was constitutionally unable to face reality.

Actually, though, he remains convinced of victory. For such trying times, he possesses the right mix of temper and patience, and the group goes on functioning like a well-drilled squad of Marines hitting beach after beach with the same maniacal verve and devotion.

By the fall of 1959 he'd put the dwarfs through nine cycles of

TECHNICAL CHALLENGES, 1959

Rounds 28 & 29. His fourteenth season in Sonora and fifteenth in Central Mexico. That March, he turns 45.

This year he'll shoulder merely four major concurrent research endeavors:

BETTER BREAD, Rounds 13 & 14.

DOWNSIZING WHEAT, Rounds 7 & 8.

INTERNATIONAL STEM RUST NURSERY #6.

DEMONSTRATION DAY #12 in the series in Sonora.

development. During each round he'd introduced different genes on a scale never seen before. Yet nothing has turned out right. Not a single line is even close to farmer-ready. Indeed, progress is proving so glacial it could well be illusory.

About this time one of Europe's prominent wheat breeders dropped by. On seeing all that was being attempted and how little was being accomplished James MacKey was appalled. Taking Norm aside, he grabbed him by the arm and spoke with great earnestness directly into his face. "Stop wasting your career," he pleaded, "on such a hopeless mission!"

In that same year of 1959 the Rockefeller Foundation sent Borlaug on a survey mission to South America, instructing him to search out locations where the Mexican work with wheat and corn and beans and potatoes might be extended. It was a tiring trip that took him through Brazil, Argentina, Bolivia, Peru, Ecuador and Chile. It was also depressing because in every country he found that the agricultural scientists ignore farms and farmers. They stay within their own safe worlds, wearing lab coats or even business suits, never leaving the cool confines of the science building or experiment station. Typically the senior scientists sported prestigious degrees from great universities—mostly American and European—but pursued research endeavors based more on personal whim than people's wants. It was as if the all-pervasive realities of poverty, hunger and suffering didn't matter, or didn't exist. But it did exist and it basically stemmed from under-performing agriculture.

By contrast with South America's depressing scenes, the Sonora he came home to looked astounding. Across thousands of acres his tall wheats still prosper and rural resistance is dissipating like smoke as more and more farmers find that the path to personal wealth leads right through CIANO.

By 1959 the demonstration days had become something like fiestas. Farmers pour in not just from across the state but from across many states. Some come hundreds of miles by car, bus, truck, commercial airliner, even private plane. Many were there because the agricultural bank now demands its borrowers attend his demonstration day but most had come of their own volition. To a surprising extent it was due to the transistor radio.

Radios had always been big, bulky, expensive and tied to a plug in the wall. But these small, cheap, portable sets were beginning to show up, and they had a special appeal to farmers. CIANO's weekly radio broadcast attracted loyal listeners on Mexico's wheat, corn, cotton and soybean farms. Many came to the demonstration day to see whether the reality in the dirt matched the rhetoric on the dial.

Also, the Yaqui Valley no longer looked the same. Rodolfo Calles has been proven right: Agriculture was indeed lifting his state up out of dust and destitution. More than half the national wheat production now came from here.

The somnolent burg that 14 years earlier had resembled a stage-set for a matinee movie was now a vibrant metropolis of 170,000. Along with the dust of the past, Cajeme had shaken off its name. It was now called "Ciudad Obregón" after Álvaro Obregón, the local garbanzo farmer who by force and fair judgment rose to be presidente in 1920 only to be assassinated for the good work he'd done in stabilizing his war-torn nation.

Once a backwater lacking even a graveled road, this so-called Obregón City now was grid-ironed with wide, paved, well-lit streets, including several central avenues. The dusty main drag had become a wide avenue (which in the years ahead will be renamed Calle Dr. Norman Borlaug).

In addition to streetlights, there were sidewalks and storm-water drains, not to mention parks, playgrounds and other public amenities. And just beyond the city limits, a few miles down the highway past CIANO, a big new airport capable of handling jets—the amazing new aircraft that somehow could fly without propellers—was being laid out.

Urban planning set this place apart. And behind that planning lay a commanding emotion: civic pride. This was a city of success, and the people were more than satisfied . . . they were pleased.

Moreover, the burgeoning wheat harvests had attracted considerable investments in food processing. The place that was once just raw now

NEW WHEAT . . .

The revolutionary knee-high wheat no longer falls over in the wind. However, after four years of effort it remains susceptible to disease and to dropping its seed on the ground. Most observers judge that Borlaug is wasting his time working on it.

. . . AND OLD

Meantime, his waist-high Lerma Rojo is working wonders across Mexico. However, farmers must keep it from producing to its potential because that much grain at the top that the winds of fall blow the plant over. The stems are too long for the load.

exuded raw power, though few recognized that it was the power of a seed. On the city outskirts clusters of grain elevators stabbed the sky. Near them were massive flourmills. A big new Bimbo Company factory was baking bread and cookies for much of Mexico. A huge brewery had appeared, making liquid gold Corona—much of it for thirsty Americans—out of the abundant grain to be had around these parts.

Prosperity and social progress could be seen the length and breadth of the Yaqui Valley. The irrigation department had by then provided water to almost all the districts, which were also fitted out with electricity, paved roads and banking services. All were growing Borlaug wheat.

And the benefits reached past the state line. In Sinaloa, Coahuilla, Michoacán, and a dozen more states attitudes toward wheat were reversing, and with more farmers growing more than ever the national production was soaring at a rate to soon top 5 million tons—*a 14-fold increase since his arrival.*

This heady leap rested not only on the seeds but also on their management. Farmers now applied fertilizer, weed control, and irrigation water at just the right times for robust growth. And the plants responded with production and profits that people thereabouts had never possessed.

The sight perhaps upset sentimentalists flying over on their way to find fun in the sun on Acapulco's beaches. The vast stretches of uniformity certainly seemed to have robbed the romance gringo touristas expected of rural Mexico. But for those on the ground the happiness that comes from bettering one's self and one's family counted most.

Already dubbed the Quiet Wheat Revolution, this social upheaval was touted as the best and only bloodless insurrection in Mexican history. Of special note was the fact that it arose out of the countryside, out of local initiative, and everyone benefited, poor and not-so-poor.

May 1959 sees the start of Year 15; Norm's now put in 28 seasons of nonstop effort. And that year Mexico's agricultural research came of age. The Rockefeller Foundation was then awarding the last of 250 agriculture fellowships—mostly for study in the United States, Canada and Europe. Nine out of every ten previous recipients had returned home with good academic records, and at least three ascended to positions of national influence. From formerly having a mere handful of agriculturists with a Masters and none with a PhD, Mexico now had around 100 MS graduates in the agricultural sciences and almost 30 more with a doctorate.

Thus, as the 1950s came to a close Mexico possessed the competence to meet its own agronomic needs. Thanks mainly to George Harrar's foresight and John D. Rockefeller's funds it could carry on crop development without outside help.

Or so it seemed.

In situations like this, success seldom survives for long. Someone invariably makes a stupid decision. And would you believe it, the managers in Manhattan now sought to abandon Borlaug's thorny little project that seemed to go on and on without end. In the eyes of the elect, the mission had been accomplished. Even George Harrar declared that the time to pull out had arrived.

Thus, for all the satisfaction regarding the accomplishments visible across the rural regions, 1959 was a bittersweet year for the hunger fighters in the frontline.

Still and all, the news that OEE was closing came as no surprise. The scientific responsibilities would be transferred to the National Institute for Agricultural Research (INIA), a Mexican counterpart constituted to carry the projects onward under government management.

Borlaug was given one month to step aside. Strangely, he didn't demur. In his code of conduct the person paying the salary was sacrosanct. Also, this instant rebuff reflected an undeniable honor. After all, he'd been hired to do a job, and he'd done it.

Nonetheless, he was far from happy. Could he in good conscience walk away from the vast research operation he'd nurtured so long? Was it right to abandon the ongoing experiments in the Yaqui? In Toluca? La Piedad? Torreón? Could he turn his back on all the youngsters who counted on him for labor and leadership, if not for life? Could they make themselves over again and find paychecks of another sort?

And what would happen to the thousands of partially perfected dwarf plant lines? It was wrenching to see the summer sun bathing their gilt heads and ponder the swans these ugly ducklings might yet morph into.

But now they were to be abandoned. He'd lifted the crop that supplies a third of the food on Planet Earth but he'd lifted it a single step, and he knew that many even more wondrous steps awaited.

Norm was now 45, and the trajectory of his life had zigged to yet another turning point. Regardless of his wants or the fact that his motor was running in top gear his contract was terminated. The glory days were gone. The sequence of incredible coincidences—a chain of circumstance

NEW LOOK . . .

Ciudad Obregon after Borlaug. In 1944 when Borlaug began developing wheat, this was a small forgettable outpost raw and far from civilization and without any claim to fame, By 1959 the desert backwater was no longer raw. It was no longer far from civilization. And it had a claim to fame. It was the center of a great agricultural enterprise based around wheats.

. . . NEW GLORY

Half of Mexico's 5 million tons of wheat now comes from the Yaqui Valley. The culture hereabouts has changed from demoralized to radiant. Grain silos stand on the city skyline. Ciudad Obregon is a gentrified spot with the facilities of a modern city. Borlaug wheat had made it possible.

TECHNICAL PROGRESS, 1959

By the close of Round 29 in November '59, following fifteen seasons in Central Mexico and fourteen in Sonora, he's 7 years ahead of schedule. Without his doubled-up dedication he'd not have reach this level of advance until 1966.

He's now spent a third of his life struggling to make Mexican wheat healthy, productive and great to eat. He's moved the country to higher ground; Mexico had become self-sufficient in wheat production. And he's standing proudly in his own shoes.

On the upside 1959 has been spectacular:
- The Yaqui Valley is now among the world's great wheat-producing areas
- It produces more than half Mexico's wheat.
- The national production is soaring toward 5 million tons—a 14-fold increase since his arrival.
- The dump of a town he'd found in 1944 is now Mexico's most modern city, known as Ciudad Obregón.
- Corporations have moved in to take advantage of the abundant grain to make products such as beer and baked goods. They've brought jobs and commerce.

On the downside this year:
- He's out of work.
- The chances of combining all the possibilities wheat has let him see are remote, even if he still had his job.
- Super wheats might well double all his current accomplishments, but there's no way he can produce them now.

In the 15 years since his arrival, the number of mouths in Mexico has risen by 12.8 million, or 58.2 percent, to 34.8 million.

that had transcended the laws of chance, one that could happen only in real life, being too unbelievable for novelists or movie moguls—that could have parted at a dozen points but had held as if clasped by some Hidden Hand—was hereby broken.

Should there be any future battles, they'd have to be in some different theater of conflict. But where? The chain of challenges had ended so abruptly he'd never thought of any line of work other than researching wheat in Mexico. The dwarfs' seductive possibilities for helping the hungry had drawn him in so deep he'd forgotten his own needs. Or his family's.

So, mixed with the many other worries was one that for any Great Depression survivor rang with a truly terrifying clamor: unemployment.

Yes he's been let go.

The taming of the dwarfing genes seems far off. Dwarf wheats with giant candlepower are now unreachable.

He's at the top of his game.

The century has just passed its midpoint, the world is steadily getting hungrier.

But the music has stopped.

And this time the Hidden Hand is finally outclassed!

Or so it seems.

AFTERWORD BY NORMAN BORLAUG

The previous chapters accurately reflect the hardscrabble existence and tough times experienced during my first fifteen years in Mexico—roughly between my 30th and 45th birthdays. This was my professional testing time and it was also the foundation of my career.

As in my earlier days I could not have accomplished so much without the support of others. Thus, I'm especially glad these pages honor those who helped turn Mexico's food production around.

Henry Wallace started everything off. Later I got to know him, and he often said, "What's an Iowa boy like you doing in Mexico developing wheat?" Without his intervention I doubt the Rockefeller Foundation would ever have taken up agriculture south of the border, let alone around the world, as it later did.

Edgar McFadden and E.C. Stakman donated the seeds that—following many twists and turns—provided the stem-rust resistance upon which all our varieties rested.

Mrs Jones, Joe Rupert and Aureliano Campoy got me through the very rocky early years, when I was basically learning about wheat and its capabilities.

Richard Spurlock and the Huertas—both father and son—made possible the outreach to the farming community across Central Mexico. That was something beyond my capacity, so those amateurs made possible the ultimate improvement to Mexico's food supply.

Margaret, Jeanie and Bill provided the rock of my own life by putting up with my annual absences. And Margaret made everything possible by taking responsibility for the family chores, such as picking up the monthly paychecks and paying the rent, the utilities and the other bills. That would have driven me nuts; compared to bills, wheat was a breeze to deal with.

Without Burt Bayles I probably wouldn't have heard about the

Japanese dwarf wheat that Gonjiro Inazuka had discovered, that Samuel Salmon had sent home to the U.S., and that Orville Vogel had developed. And without Orville's generosity in sending the envelope of seeds containing the dwarfing genes we would never have completed the ultimate task of raising wheat's productivity beyond even my imagining. Furthermore, Vogel's special thrashers and tiny combines made possible the numbers of experimental blocks and plots and plantings that in the end meant so much.

At first neither Ed Wellhausen nor George Harrar understood the merits of what I was attempting, but in the end both provided institutional support that several times kept the wheat program from collapse. Without their courage and conviction my efforts would have fizzled in the 1950s.

Rodolfo Calles was a man of strict reserve, but in time we developed a warm and trusting friendship. He made possible the fantastic new research facility, CIANO, and would later help send Mexican seed wheat around the world. I was devastated when he died in a Houston hospital following a heart attack. He too kept the program alive when we were about to be shut down and I was about to be deported.

Of course I'm also grateful to all the young Mexicans who contributed to our enterprise. They made it possible for me to explore so many avenues—most of which went nowhere, while a few opened possibilities no one else had seen. Not all those youngsters began as bird boys; many were students from the agriculture college at Chapingo or from other Latin American countries.

During the years covered in this book I learned that the most important ingredient in uplifting food supplies for a whole country is research. And our research was of the conventional, mundane, mainstream kind involving laborious cross-pollinations between thousands and thousands of plants.

The first key to our success was the healthy plants that withstood diseases without chemical or other treatments.

The second key was productivity per acre. Our plants were capable of producing several times more than had been possible before. That in turn showed that the soil in Mexico was too worn out to take advantage of the power of our plants. Fertilizer thus rose into relevance.

Though it was an expense, fertilizer paid for itself many times over, so it became the third key to getting the most from every acre.

Also fertilizer helped the farmers get the most income from their land.

Indeed, the fact that our wheats provided a path out of poverty meant the seeds sold themselves and spread far and fast. For decades afterward I'd be inspecting agriculture in some remote area of a foreign land only to run across my own plants or their descendants. How they got there I have no idea.

All that came about because we were completely open about sharing seeds and because the plants had built-in adaptability and could grow with little or no adaptation wherever they went in the world's wheatlands.

Beyond acknowledging the plants and people who made my long journey possible, the previous chapters highlight an important incident that is today little known: Mexico's Green Revolution. Although we worked mostly in Sonora and Toluca where the farming community was most receptive to better seeds and better farming, the Bajío, the most impoverished, complex and resistant rural area, benefited equally. Though physically unable to match the huge leaps in the irrigated areas of northern Mexico the Bajío's rise from poverty to prosperity was of immense social significance.

Perhaps the saddest lesson from all this is that even the greatest uplift in food production will have difficulty keeping up with the kind of population growth that has occurred since the days described in this book. When I arrived, Mexico had 22 million people; now it is approaching 110 million.

Having heard Stakman declare that "Rust is a shifty, changing, constantly evolving enemy," I thought the resistance we built into wheat in the 1950s might last a decade or so. That resistance—which came thanks to Stakman, McFadden and Burton—actually almost outlasted the 20th Century. But now stem rust has found a way around that triple combination. A new and virulent strain has broken out in East Africa and is now spreading into Asia. Combating that is perhaps the greatest current challenge for maintaining the global food supply. An international project has been launched.

It is interesting to think that a new generation now must relive some of my experiences, which Noel Vietmeyer has so ably presented here.

NORMAN E. BORLAUG
September, 2009

AFTERWORD BY

JEANIE BORLAUG LAUBE

My thoughts on Dad being gone three-quarters of the year are mixed. Bill and I were excited to see him when he lived at home but even then he would leave at 5am and return around 8pm, so we really did not have much time with him.

However, the time we did have was always quality time. He was genuinely interested in our activities and events. He started Little League for my brother. He helped with my Girl Scout troop—instructing all of us so we could get the "Conservation Badge."

Dad took off six weeks every second summer to tour the U.S. and visit family and friends. Those were great vacations, and we had wonderful times—going to many baseball games and eating at a lot of Dairy Queens (he loved their ice cream). It was great for the family.

He never missed a graduation from high school or college—whether it was for me, my brother, or our five children. He attended family weddings and has been very interested in the welfare of his five grandchildren and now his six great grandchildren.

He has been a great role model for me, and I'm committed to passing his lesson on. I run a Community Service Program for two private schools, each year taking more than 700 high school students out of their secure environment to help those who are less fortunate.

Mother held the family together. She took total responsibility for my brother and me. She was an educator, a strong person, and did the banking and other family chores so Dad could work without that worry.

My brother and I and all our kids and grandkids are blessed to have two such role models in our lives.

JEANIE BORLAUG LAUBE
Dallas, Texas

AUTHOR'S NOTE

In August 2009, with the printer's deadline looming just three weeks ahead and with a manuscript that seemed incomplete, I was seized by the notion of visiting the Rockefeller Archive Center in Sleepy Hollow, New York. My hope was to find an odd photo that might bring the words and the underlying message into a more perfect union.

What I didn't anticipate was the Archive Center's photographic treasure trove. Turns out, the OEE had employed a professional photographer in Mexico, and his stunning 8 by 10 glossy prints have been stored under archival conditions ever since.

A number of those have been incorporated into the preceding chapters, but rather than let the rest remain unseen I'm presenting here a further selection that seem especially relevant to Borlaug's travails in Mexico between 1944 and 1959. I hope they'll help readers relive incidents from the previous pages and see them in a fresh light.

The images that follow were made possible by Michele Hiltzik and Bethany Francis, who were my hosts at the Rockefeller Archive Center. Bethany went to extraordinary lengths to scan 50 prints I'd selected and to provide them within just days of my visit. Later she discovered some great photos lost and forgotten in unsorted collections. Those in Chapter 1 showing Norm (page 24) and George Harrar (page 26) are examples. They are published here for the first time.

The images that follow were also of course made possible by Neil Maclellan, the professional photographer on the OEE staff during the late 1940s as well as the 1950s.

San Jacinto, Mexico City. This is the rundown edifice that housed the OEE's headquarters—the one where Spanish was spoken (page 27). The three hot and dusty rooms were on the third floor of the right hand building. This was also the place that was later invaded by students demanding it be made into a dorm for them (page 191).

This scene reminded me of Vicente Guerrero and the daunting muddle of metallic body parts of the TD8 International tractor (page 28). It was taken a few years later and at the La Piedad facility, but this is undoubtedly the same crawler tractor Borlaug used to scrape scrub, level planting areas, smooth exposed earth and turn the tawny wilderness at Chapingo into the research facility that would change the world(page 32).

El Yaqui Experiment Station. This must be Aureliano Campoy's "little" combine, the one he often drove over for Borlaug's use (page 95, for example). The picture was taken in 1951, but clearly reflects the scene in the years from 1945 onward. I assume Norm is driving and you can imagine Joe Rupert or Enciso under the other hat.

From the start in 1945 Borlaug established nursery blocks in every season in Mexico's wheat-growing regions. This happens to be at Chapingo, probably in 1955. Note the clear air Mexico City had then. These nursery blocks were test beds for promising plants as well as places to evaluate hundreds of newcomers.

Yaqui Valley Experiment Station. This is Rodolfo Calles' brainchild—the research facility he thought would lift his backward desert state out of dust and destitution. This photo was taken at harvest time, April 8, 1951. By then, the place had been considerably cleaned up. It was no longer the derelict wreck that had been looted of anything valuable and left to the forces of decay and desolation by a government with no faith in the power of research.

The fields surrounding the station are those where Borlaug went looking for wheat in April 1945 (page 42). Here's where he set out through the shimmering surroundings and found Marroqui and Mentana, the wheats his predecessor had abandoned as losers. Although in this view the surroundings look lush, daytime temperatures in April average 105°F. This is the scenery that gave raised the possibility that he could give Mexico all the bread it could eat.

The plants are of course the book's real stars. This is a Frontera cross descended from McFadden's gift seed that contained genes from emmer, the wheat beloved of Jesus and Judas (see page 66).

These are descendants from Supremo (page 57). These too come from McFadden's gift and carry the same emmer-based stem-rust resistance McFadden into the he called Hope. The awns (long bristles) make it look particularly robust.

This is Kenya White, part of a matched pair, one having white-skinned seeds and the other red. Both these awnless varieties carry the stem-rust resistance bred in by Gerald Burton in Kenya. These together with Supremo and Frontera have provided the rock of rust resistance for the world's wheat crop for about half a century.

Although unsure, I like to think that this shows Enciso in the field of rusted traditional wheats—the one where Borlaug reluctantly gave the farmer seed that would resist this devastation, and the farmer kissed his hand in gratitude (page 131).

Third Demonstration Day at the Yaqui Valley Experiment Station, April 1950 (page 153). I like to think that this is Jorge Parada waylaying Borlaug to insist that fertilizer had had no effect in the trial on his property (page 154).

Whatever the incident, Borlaug doesn't seem happy with what he's hearing. I'm also reminded of the fact that Sonorans were a scrappy lot, shrinking neither from a stranger nor silly questions (page 43). Borlaug has just turned 36.

Beer and the barbecue at the fourth Demonstration Day, April 8, 1951. This is not the famous one (page 120), but the scene is probably similar. Borlaug has just turned 37.

Clearly, he's developing a rapport with the local farming leaders. They in turn are appreciative of the gringo who's changing the prospects for Yaqui Valley wheat.

This is probably one of the valley-wide fertilizer trials (page 151). Sights like this were behind Borlaug's recognition that Mexican soils were worn out. The plants all come from the same seed. The healthy ones on the left received nitrogenous fertilizer. The malnourished ones on the right received no nitrogen.

This looks like an old style wheat crop. Maybe it's a field of Barigon, the pre-Borlaug wheat that was good enough only for soda crackers (page 42). Maybe too the farmer is Roberto Maurer (page 122).

One of Borlaug's young Mexican colleagues removes the pollen sacs to turn the bisexual wheat flower into a pure female. The process was challenging but rewarding.

The feminized flower spike is being covered by a paper tube the boy had previously initialed to signify responsibility. I wonder if he 'd missed a pollen sac and ended up buying Coca-Colas for the other crew (page 157).

I believe this is a publicity shot staged to show the yield improvement from Borlaug's early wheats over the scrub wheats that dominated before he arrived. This is presumably the production from an equal area of land. The young man looks like Norm's first student José Guevara, the Coahuila farm youth whose research notes had been taken by a whirlwind (page 47).

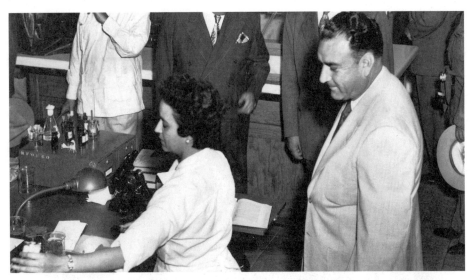

Marta Zenteno, one of Mexico's first two women agricultural researchers (page 54), and agriculture minister Gilberto Flores Muñoz.

Chapingo, August 2, 1954. Gilberto Flores Muñoz (white suit) hardly seems impressed by the discussion of OEE's wheat research. The agriculture minister was actually preparing to sign the paper to deport Borlaug and the Rockefeller Foundation (page 203). Harrar and Wellhausen are on the right.

President Eisenhower's agriculture secretary, Taft Benson, inspects Borlaug's first dwarf wheat. From left to right: John Gibler, Ed Wellhausen, Secretary Benson, agriculture minister Flores Muñoz, and Borlaug's first student José Guevara.

Dedication of CIANO (see page 225). Rodolfo Calles reads his speech to Mexican president Adolfo Lopez Mateos (left). On the right is Sr. Roldan, who will play an infamous role in Volume 3.

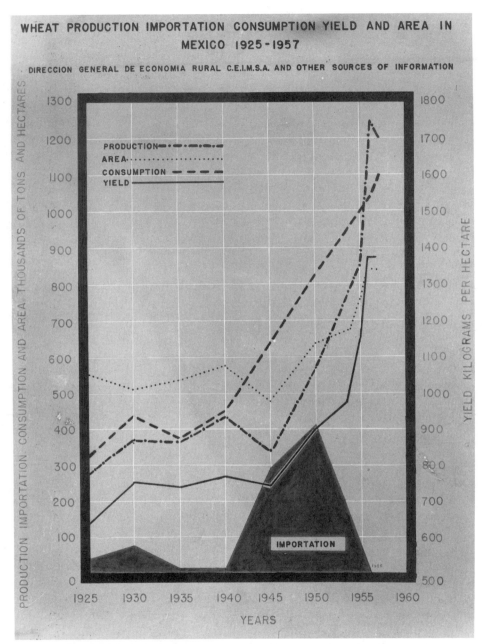

WHEAT PRODUCTION IMPORTATION CONSUMPTION YIELD AND AREA IN MEXICO 1925-1957

DIRECCION GENERAL DE ECONOMIA RURAL C.E.I.M.S.A. AND OTHER SOURCES OF INFORMATION

PRODUCTION
AREA
CONSUMPTION
YIELD

IMPORTATION

YEARS

The Quiet Wheat Revolution (page 264). A placard from 1957. Despite Mexico's soaring consumption of wheat, imports have plunged to nothing because local production has risen to meet the demand. Borlaug began work in 1945 (where the "I" in **IMPORTATION** appears). That's about where the production begins shooting upwards.

Sadly, by press time I hadn't found out who this is. I'm guessing Alfredo Campos or another of the many Mexican students who helped create the Quiet Wheat Revolution. Youths flocked to follow Borlaug as if he were the Pied Piper. His was not a formal operation with an organization chart—just a charismatic leader to whom young people were attracted and for whom they willingly worked their hearts out.

Stakman at Chapingo. The man who made Borlaug possible often came to visit the program in Mexico that was essentially his brainchild. I like to think that this was the visit when the formerly crusty professor pleaded that Norm slow down his research frenzy and devote time to his family (page 251). But maybe it was when his speech soothed General Flores who was about to deport Borlaug (page 207).

CAREER SAVERS

VOLUME 1

1 Sina Borlaug	1928	Got Borlaug to high school
2 David Bartelma	1930	Guided him toward success
3 George Champlin	1933	Got him to university
4 Frederick Hovde	1933	Allowed him to stay in school
5 Margaret Gibson	1933	Began a lifetime of giving him good advice
6 White Castle	1934	Kept him from starvation
7 Alpha Omicron Pi	1934	Fed him so he could stay in college
8 Eleanor Roosevelt	1935	Her NYA initiative provides his tuition
9 Edward Behre	1936	Provides a job so he can finish his BS degree
10 Hank Shank	1937	Reneges on an offer of a Junior Forester job
11 E.C. Stakman	1938	Offers tuition for a Masters in agriculture
12 George Harrar	1944	Induces him to go to Mexico

VOLUME 2

13 Henry Wallace	1940	Induces the food research program in Mexico
14 Edgar McFadden	1945	Provides seeds that initiate Borlaug's success
15 Mrs Jones	1945	Helps him survive in the Sonora wilderness
16 Joe Rupert	1946	Helps him overcome personal trauma
17 Aureliano Campoy	1946	Begins helping him succeed in Mexico
18 Richard Spurlock	1947	Begins providing his seed to Mexican farmers
19 The Family		Provide a lifetime of domestic support
20 The Huertas	1949	Father and son start donating his seed to farmers
21 Burton Bayles	1952	Informs him of the existence of dwarf wheat
22 Gonjiro Inazuka	1940s	Creates dwarf wheat in Japan
23 Samuel Salmon	1945	Sends Inazuka's seed to the U.S.
24 Ed Wellhausen	1952	Begins running interference to save Borlaug's job
25 Orville Vogel	1953	Sends him 80 dwarf wheat seeds
26 Rodolfo Calles	1954	Saves him from being deported from Mexico

ACKNOWLEDGEMENTS

The author gratefully acknowledges grants from:

- **The Rural Development Foundation**, Taipei, Taiwan, Republic of China; and
- **The Wallace Genetic Foundation**, Washington, D.C.

Both grants were administered by Professor **Edward Runge** (Department of Soil & Crop Sciences, Texas A&M University), whose efforts I also acknowledge with gratitude.

This biography is not the academic kind compiled from a collection of learned quotes and documents. At bottom, its content is entirely thanks to **Norman Borlaug**. These pages result from many discussions scattered over several decades. Most took place while we were on assignment for the National Academy of Sciences.

Borlaug family members also contributed. Norm's wife, the late **Margaret Borlaug**, twice provided hospitality when I visited College Station, Texas and we shared some good talks about old times. Norm's daughter, **Jeanie Laube**, provided recollections, photographs and relayed Norm's answers to my last-minute questions. Norm's son, **Bill Borlaug**, also helped by providing a photograph, answering questions, and reassuring me about an image in Volume 1.

Although the text reflects Norman Borlaug's own recollections, the overarching historical and philosophical comments and claims reflect my own reading of science and history. Most of Norm's claims (as well as mine) were double-checked via alternate means, including personal contacts, direct requests, library services and Internet sources. This meticulous checking proved once again the phenomenal quality of his memory.

Gathering the photographs was a separate saga. I'm especially grateful to all who went out of their way to help find the rare pictures enlivening these pages. I sought images that expand the reader's consciousness by enhancing the text as well as by being instructive and, above all, by being moving. In that regard **Bethany Francis** and **Michele Hiltzik** at the Rockefeller Archive Center were especially helpful. Without the images they provided the book would be just words. In addition, **Gay, Phil** and **Josh Courter** of Courter Films & Associates generously shared photographs they'd found.

In its final stages, my neighbors **Al Papenfus** and **Dick Kennedy** reviewed the text, exposing several bonehead errors. Another neighbor, **Pat Pascale**, designed the book's frontmatter. My son **Rob Vietmeyer** designed the cover and worked to make the pictures clearer on the printed page. My other sons, **Blair Vietmeyer** and **John Vietmeyer** loyally gave encouragement and reviewed the text as it developed. Finally, my wife **Anne Vietmeyer** caught glitches in the text none of the rest of us had seen. Like Margaret Borlaug, Anne was the family rock. She took care of business while, for several years, I was preoccupied with *Borlaug*. Without that support, there'd have been no book.

PICTURE CREDITS

COVER PHOTO: Rockefeller Archive Center

PROLOGUE
18. (Henry Wallace in Mexico) Photo by Carl Mydans/Getty Images
20. (Mud-bound in Mexico) Rockefeller Archive Center, Sleepy Hollow, New York

CHAPTER 1 Heartbreak
22. (map) Rockefeller Archive Center
24. (Norman Borlaug) Rockefeller Archive Center
26. (George Harrar) Rockefeller Archive Center
29. (Gringo Disgrace) The original seems to be lost. This was reproduced from *Campaigns Against Hunger* by E.C. Stakman, Richard Bradfield and Paul C. Mangelsdorf. Harvard University Press, 1967.
30-1. (Mexico City map) *Terry's Mexico.*

CHAPTER 2 Meeting Wheat
40. (Old Look . . . No Glory) University of Arizona Library Special Collections
44-5. (Home-Made Work Place) Rockefeller Archive Center
50. (Beasts of Burden) The original seems to be lost. This was reproduced from *Campaigns Against Hunger* by E.C. Stakman, Richard Bradfield and Paul C. Mangelsdorf. Harvard University Press, 1967
52-3. (Mexico's Breadbasket) Rockefeller Archive Center
64. (Edgar McFadden) College of Agriculture and Biological Sciences, South Dakota State University

CHAPTER 3 A Change of Latitude
70-1. (World's Worst Work Site) Rockefeller Archive Center

CHAPTER 4 Setback
93. (Joe Rupert, Borlaug and Harrar) Rockefeller Archive Center
100. (Breeding Wheat) Rockefeller Archive Center
109. (Richard Spurlock) Rockefeller Archive Center

CHAPTER 5 Breakout
124-5. (Borlaug Grows a Gift) Rockefeller Archive Center

CHAPTER 6 Crossroads
136. (Farmer Field Day) Rockefeller Archive Center
140. (The Family) Richard Gibson
142. (Second Bulk Harvest) Rockefeller Archive Center

PICTURE CREDITS (cont.)

Bracing Books publishes information on promising but novel tools for fixing global problems such as hunger, atmospheric warming, deforestation and tropical diseases. Its publications and website expose to world view innovations capable of rapid deployment.

Many global problems persist because there are no practical "tools" with which to build the foundation for a solution. What is little known—even among specialists—is that means for fashioning such foundations exist among the natural resources native to Africa, Asia and Latin America.

In the main, Bracing Books highlights such promising tropical resources. Built from independent thought, its publications provide inspiration and unconventional insight into ways to attack problems that beset the world. Avoiding popular beliefs, faddish trends, policies and theoretical speculation, these innovative publications highlight natural species (and some manmade materials) that possess the promise to be high-impact hammers for cracking open seemingly insoluble global difficulties.

Moreover, the books are all written in a popular style that combines technical accuracy and professional insight with easy public accessibility.

EXISTING TITLES

In addition to publishing Volume 1 of the Borlaug biography, Bracing Books has secured rights to sell books from the National Academy of Sciences' renowned Board on Science and Technology for International Development. BOSTID's "oldies but goodies" include:

Quality Protein Maize. With its milk-quality protein, this special corn offers a simple, universal, natural means for fortifying millions of malnourished lives every day in every way.

Lost Crops of Africa, Volume 1: Grains. The hungriest continent contains hundreds of native food plants that have yet to get technical support. This volume highlights more than a dozen native cereals that are already in place across Africa and poised to help the hungry lift their lives.

Lost Crops of Africa, Volume 2: Vegetables. This volume highlights 18 native legumes, tubers and leafy edibles packed with vitamins and minerals.

Lost Crops of Africa, Volume 3: Fruits. This volume highlights 24 nutritious native answers for the malnourished continent.

Calliandra. A small tree that soars 20 feet per year, calliandra can be cut annually, providing firewood "forever." It promises not only to reduce rainforest destruction but relieve women's daily wood-gathering burden.

Leucaena. This tree probably absorbs more greenhouse gas than any other. As a legume, it rebuilds soil as it grows and its abundance of furniture-quality timber locks up the absorbed CO_2 for decades.

Microlivestock. This large eye-catching book describes domesticated creatures that are sized for poor-people's space limitations. These can provide subsistence farmers in the tropics with both income and nutrition.

Vetiver. This robust grass forms hedges tight enough to stabilize slopes, preventing soil, water and nutrient losses. Also provides simple ways to corral and/or extract pollutants from contaminated sites while also absorbing and burying greenhouse gas in deeply penetrating roots.

Jojoba. BOSTID efforts got this crop going when it was just a wild desert plant. Now jojoba holds promise as an even bigger contributor to arid areas.

Mangium. This stately tree-legume grows 10 feet a year on the red, acid, largely barren, sites that dominate the tropics. Also helps restore rainforests.

Butterfly Farming. Don't laugh: Tropical butterflies are charmers whose worth is measured by the ounce. Their farm is the forest, so their propagation and preservation adds value to the *standing* trees.

These and other BOSTID books offering answers to global problems are available at modest cost (while supplies last). For details visit BracingBooks.com.

FORTHCOMING TITLES
The following are in advanced stages of completion.

Borlaug. Volume 3. Norm donates his super seeds to hungry nations only to meet with resistance, reluctance, disbelief and even professional sabotage. All this opposition arises in the face of a looming famine projected to be the biggest ever known.

Liquid Life Savers; the New Food Revolution. People forget that baby foods must be more than nutritious . . . they must be liquid. This book shows how to turn local staples into tasty and surprisingly nutritious liquids at low cost.

World's Greatest Dilemma: DDT and Malaria. In the 1940s and 1950s DDT was used to eradicate malaria in scores of nations, including the U.S. This book highlights the amazing long-forgotten results and exposes dozens of reasons why the current fear of DDT just might reflect public hysteria rather than public health.

Forgotten Ways to Fight Global Hunger. Following Borlaug's successes hunger-fighting research centers were established around the world. This book presents 300 tangible research advances that offer a veritable smorgasbord of options for helping slow or stop Global Hunger's return.

ABOUT THE AUTHOR

Norman Borlaug and the author at the Environmental research Laboratory of the University of Arizona in Tucson, Arizona in July 1982. Displayed around them are plant resources Vietmeyer's work had brought to light. These ended up in the Land Pavilion ride at Epcot Center in Disney World. On the right, towers the winged bean, a "supermarket on a stalk" whose edible leaves, tendrils, flowers, pods, seeds and tubers are both prolific and packed with protein.

Noel Vietmeyer earned a PhD in organic chemistry from the University of California. During a long career at the National Academy of Sciences in Washington, D.C. he produced over 30 books describing innovations that can benefit Africa, Asia and Latin America.

Vietmeyer was also a prolific freelance writer, producing some 200 articles for publications such as *National Geographic*, *Reader's Digest*, *Smithsonian*, *Encyclopaedia Britannica*, *World Book*, *International Wildlife* and *Ranger Rick*.

His quarter-century of National Academy of Sciences service was noteworthy for the discovery of tropical crops that were little known to science but that possessed qualities for helping the world's poor nations. It was through this work that Vietmeyer met Norman Borlaug, who graciously agreed to chair several of the review panels the NAS appointed to make the final calls on certain extremely fast-growing trees, nutritious food crops, potentially valuable industrial crops and vegetative environmental supports that stabilize tropical lands.

Off and on over the years, the two traveled together, and Borlaug eventually related roughly 300 personal experiences. They included life-and-death adventures as well as coincidences, escapes from financial disaster, squabbles with those who disagreed with his methods (virtually everyone), and farmers who many times came to the rescue just as his program was about to be axed.

These stories make up the heart and soul of this multivolume biography of the father of the food supply.

IN MEMORIAM

The day before this book went to press Norman Borlaug died. Having spent more than a decade assessing him and his contributions, I sadly append these few last-minute thoughts.

Norman Borlaug's life is amazing mostly for its myriad dimensions:

More than a man of peace, he was a man of the people. His frank, straightforward attitude of comradeship made everyone his friend. His style and personality matched his frame—lean, active, unassuming, unpretentious. People not only responded, they bonded.

Though otherwise a nice guy, he was a fierce, take-no-quarter, Hunger Fighter. His field was action science, not academic science. Among the wheat he was so intense people got hot just watching him work.

He embodied the dictum that a little action beats a lot of argument. In wheat breeding he was a ringmaster who, with professional dispassion, forfeited millions of plants with no second thought. Genes, he knew, are as predictable as forked lightning, and can produce success *or* distress.

He was a master at managing mayhem and had an innate ability to transcend anxiety. Though often treated like a heretic in heaven, he never took offense, never abandoned his convictions, seldom lost composure. When it looked as if the Rockies had crumbled, he went on exploring the mysteries of the wheat world with his normal intensity . . .waiting for just the right gene to surface like a fish in a pool.

He was a rare and special soul who not only accepted years of delay but focused on the present while closely watching the future. He often dubbed himself a quarterback and his great capacity was reading the defense and spotting a way to the goal line.

He had courage and was willing to go out on a limb to do what needed doing, no matter the size of the limb or whether anyone followed. In that regard, he was never afraid to fall and make a fool of himself.

He was not a man of inspiring words, just inspiring wheats. But those spoke volumes.

He was never one to look in life's rear-view mirror; being too busy driving hard into the future for anything so wasteful of time.

The only burden to never afflict him was the burden of extreme wealth. He worked his whole life without personal gain and was happy, nay eager, to let everyone else reap the rewards.

While others dreamed and dithered, he proved his worth through deeds. He chose to *fight* hunger not to write about it. And he chose to fight it full-frontal, full-scale, and in the places that needed food most. Moreover, he was an all-round Hunger Fighter—a source of all the necessary ammunition.

In the age of the specialist, he demonstrated the vital need for generalists. No combination of specialists could accomplish what he did.

His great gift was to share his exuberance and conviction. His spirits were usually as high as the Sonoran Desert thermometer at harvest time. With his associates—many of them disadvantaged youths—he developed an extraordinary *esprit de corps*. They trusted one another, and that provided a key to their success.

He taught us what to do when the diktats of dogma block humanitarian needs. "Fight," he'd often say; "Fight, fight, fight!"

He admired horizon-filling miles of his own wheats but never gloated. He took yields to galactic heights but saw it only as his job and always felt unfulfilled.

His ultimate legacy resulted less from science than from his power to reach farmers and excite them into action. He fed the hungry but also created the right environment for a robust rural private sector. Every Borlaug seed enriched its grower and was its own excitement machine. Millions thereby got a hand up; none a handout.

He showed that a conscientious scientist with no agenda can solve problems that befuddle activists with their special agendas. While others were trapped in partisan views based on the past, he was discovering new pathways and following them straight to the future. He was Peace and Plenty's pathfinder.

When he had to shift the shape of the world's top crop, he embraced the unprecedented challenge. And for decades he and wheat were wrapped in their own private world, swirling in a sort of creative frenzy.

Finally, no one better epitomizes the notion that the 20th century was above all the century of the common man.

Farewell old friend. You came from nowhere. You reached for your stars and caught plenty of stardust. The waving fields of foodstuffs are your legacy. Among the members of the Greatest Generation, you were the greatest!

Noel